Philosophical Adventures in African Higher Education

This seminal volume delves into some of the doctoral research and pedagogical experiences within an African higher education context, making a case for the transformative potential of education and the integration of African indigenous philosophies into global educational practices.

Through a collection of vivid narratives, the book situates philosophy of higher education by embodying the doctoral researcher and their initiation into academic life, revealing how doctoral pursuits in African higher education are not simply academic endeavours but deeply philosophical adventures that challenge, critique, and reimagine the role of education in society. The chapters advocate for a dynamic educational system that, rooted in African philosophies, nurtures democratic citizenship, embraces critical engagement, and fosters social justice. A call to action for researchers, students, and policy makers alike to view doctoral research as a powerful catalyst for change, the book offers fresh perspectives on addressing the continent's unique challenges, contributing to a more just and inclusive world.

Ultimately considering the potential of academic research to shape the future of societies, both within Africa and globally, the book will appeal to researchers, academics, and postgraduate students involved with the philosophy of education, higher education, and citizenship education, as well as these areas in African contexts specifically.

Yusef Waghid is Emeritus Professor of Philosophy of Education, Stellenbosch University, South Africa.

Routledge Research in Higher Education

Identity Construction as a Spatiotemporal Phenomenon within Doctoral Students' Intellectual and Academic Identities
Contradictions, Contestations and Convergences
Rudo F. Hwami

An International Approach to Developing Early Career Researchers
A Pipeline to Robust Education Research
Edited by Stephen Gorard and Nadia Siddiqui

The Development of University Teaching Over Time
Pedagogical Approaches from 1800 to the Present
Tom O'Donoghue

The Layered Landscape of Higher Education
Capturing Curriculum, Diversity and Cultures of Learning in Australia
Edited by Margaret Kumar, Supriya Pattanayak and Nish Belford

Authority, Passion, and Subjected-Centered Teaching
A Christian Pedagogical Philosophy
Christopher J. Richmann

Experiential Learning and Community Partnerships for Sustainable Development
A Foundational Model for Climate Action
Mara Huber, Michael Jabot, and Christina Heath

Philosophical Adventures in African Higher Education
Cultivating Doctoral Encounters within Democratic Citizenship Education
Edited by Yusef Waghid

For more information about this series, please visit: www.routledge.com/Routledge-Research-in-Higher-Education/book-series/RRHE

Philosophical Adventures in African Higher Education
Cultivating Doctoral Encounters within Democratic Citizenship Education

Edited by Yusef Waghid

LONDON AND NEW YORK

First published 2025
by Routledge
4 Park Square, Milton Park, Abingdon, Oxon OX14 4RN

and by Routledge
605 Third Avenue, New York, NY 10158

Routledge is an imprint of the Taylor & Francis Group, an informa business

© 2025 selection and editorial matter, Yusef Waghid; individual chapters, the contributors

The right of Yusef Waghid to be identified as the author of the editorial material, and of the authors for their individual chapters, has been asserted in accordance with sections 77 and 78 of the Copyright, Designs and Patents Act 1988.

All rights reserved. No part of this book may be reprinted or reproduced or utilised in any form or by any electronic, mechanical, or other means, now known or hereafter invented, including photocopying and recording, or in any information storage or retrieval system, without permission in writing from the publishers.

Trademark notice: Product or corporate names may be trademarks or registered trademarks, and are used only for identification and explanation without intent to infringe.

British Library Cataloguing-in-Publication Data
A catalogue record for this book is available from the British Library

Library of Congress Cataloging-in-Publication Data
Names: Waghid, Yusef, editor, author.
Title: Philosophical adventures in African higher education : cultivating doctoral encounters within democratic citizenship education / edited by Yusef Waghid.
Description: New York : Routledge, 2024. | Series: Routledge research in higher education | Includes bibliographical references and index. |
Summary: "This seminal volume delves into some of the doctoral research and pedagogical experiences within an African higher education context, making a case for the transformative potential of education and the integration of African indigenous philosophies into global educational practices. Through a collection of vivid narratives, the book situates philosophy of higher education by embodying the doctoral researcher and their initiation into academic life, revealing how doctoral pursuits in African higher education are not simply academic endeavours but deeply philosophical adventures that challenge, critique, and reimagine the role of education in society. Chapters advocate for a dynamic educational system that, rooted in African philosophies, nurtures democratic citizenship, embraces critical engagement, and fosters social justice. A call to action for researchers, students, and policy makers alike to view doctoral research as a powerful catalyst for change, the book offers fresh perspectives on addressing the continent's unique challenges, contributing to a more just and inclusive world. Ultimately considering the potential of academic research to shape the future of societies, both within Africa and globally, the book will appeal to researchers, academics and postgraduate students involved with the philosophy of education, higher education, and citizenship education, as well as these areas in African contexts specifically"–Provided by publisher.
Identifiers: LCCN 2024028217 (print) | LCCN 2024028218 (ebook) | ISBN 9781032866680 (hardback) | ISBN 9781032869469 (paperback) | ISBN 9781003530091 (ebook)
Subjects: LCSH: Doctoral students–Supervision of–Africa–Philosophy. | Universities and colleges–Africa–Graduate work–Philosophy. | Citizenship–Study and teaching (Graduate)–Africa–Philosophy.
Classification: LCC LB2372.E3 P55 2024 (print) | LCC LB2372.E3 (ebook) | DDC 378.1/55096–dc23/eng/20240618
LC record available at https://lccn.loc.gov/2024028217
LC ebook record available at https://lccn.loc.gov/2024028218

ISBN: 978-1-032-86668-0 (hbk)
ISBN: 978-1-032-86946-9 (pbk)
ISBN: 978-1-003-53009-1 (ebk)

DOI: 10.4324/9781003530091

Typeset in Galliard
by Newgen Publishing UK

Contents

List of editors and contributors   vii
Foreword   xii
Preface   xv

Introduction: On being adventurous   1
YUSEF WAGHID

1 A doctoral supervisor in becoming: Some reflections on being initiated into a doctoral adventure   13
ZAYD WAGHID

2 The use of artificial intelligence to augment student supervision   24
FAIQ WAGHID

3 Dialectical reasoning and communicative rationality as emancipatory forces in African higher education: A reflection on my doctoral encounters   38
LESTER BRIAN SHAWA

4 Democratic citizenship education and its effects on employability: A reflection of my doctoral encounters   51
SITHOBILE PRISCILLA DUBE

5 An analysis of critical thinking skills and its link to democratic citizenship education within the South African chartered accountancy higher educational landscape: A reflection on my doctoral encounter   65
ELTON PULLEN

6	Reflections on a doctoral journey in DCE: Deliberative encounters and the transformational potential JUDITH TERBLANCHE	79
7	Reflections on an academic voyage: Encounters with a democratic citizenship education praxis MONICA ZEMBERE	95
8	Democratic citizenship pedagogy as recognition of the student's situatedness in doctoral supervision CHIKUMBUTSO HERBERT MANTHALU	104
9	Reflections on doctoral work in philosophy of education: Narratives in becoming JUDITH TERBLANCHE, ELTON PULLEN AND YUSEF WAGHID	121
10	Beyond borders: Igniting global citizenship education in doctoral studies in Jordan NAIMA AL-HUSBAN AND HAMMADALLAH AHMAD AL-HUSBAN	138
11	An interpretive analysis of Namibian education policy and its link to citizenship education: A reflection on my doctoral encounters TADEUS SHIKUKUMWA	148
Coda	The ethical university: From service delivery to development of critical consciousness EMILIANO BOSIO	163

Index *181*

Editors and contributors

Hammadallah Ahmad Al-husban holds a PhD in Business Administration from the World Islamic Sciences and Education University. He is fluent in English and Arabic. He has experience in empowering human resources in companies, with a career spanning from 1998 to 2017. Al-husban served as a senior administrative enforcement official within the Public Security Directorate in Jordan, gaining extensive human resources management experience. Al-husban is interested in conducting research in dynamic capabilities, strategic planning, technological vigilance, organisational ambidexterity, and factors influencing job satisfaction.

Naima Al-husban (PhD in EFL Curriculum) is Associate Professor at Arab Open University-Jordan. Her academic pursuits primarily focus on international projects in education, particularly those addressing the needs of female refugees and the empowerment of English-as-a-foreign language (EFL) teachers working with refugee populations. She has played a pivotal role in overseeing the implementation of plans for ten projects within the HOPES initiative, funded by the EU. Additionally, she assumed the position of coordinator for a project sponsored by the British Council, dedicated to teaching English to youth refugees. She also participated in RAISD project funded by the EU and won the 1st prize of research for change competition. Her research interests extend to diverse topics such as EFL for vulnerable groups with psychosocial disorder, GCE, and education in emergency.

Emiliano Bosio is an educator, author, and public intellectual. Currently, he is a researcher at Toyo University in Japan. He is the editor of *Conversations on Global Citizenship Education* (Routledge, 2021) and editor of *Global Citizenship Education in the Global South* with Yusef Waghid (Brill, 2022). His most recent publications include *Revolutionary Critical Pedagogy and Critical Global Citizenship Education* with Peter McLaren (2022), *Ethical Global Citizenship Education* with Hans Schattle (2021), *Critical Pedagogy* and *Global Citizenship Education* with Henry Giroux (2021), and *Global Citizenship Education at the Crossroads* with Carlos Alberto Torres (2020).

Sithobile Priscilla Dube is a qualified and experienced teacher/lecturer, administrator, and post-doctoral researcher revisiting the management of the postgraduate supervision processes as a post-doctoral researcher, Department of Education Leadership and Management, University of Johannesburg, South Africa. She is a Stellenbosch University, South Africa, PhD graduate in the Department of Education Policy Studies (December 2019) under Yusef Waghid's leadership with her thesis titled "Examining relations between education policy and higher education students' access to industry in Zimbabwe". She has worked at the National University of Science and Technology (NUST), Zimbabwe (April 2007–January 2022) as a senior administrator in various departments and became a lecturer in the Department of Psychiatry and Social Behavioural Sciences, Faculty of Medicine, since February 2022. She is also engaged in continuous research on a Staff/Lecturer Exchange Visitor engagement with Uppsala University, Sweden, from 2022 to date. Her great passion in DCE has seen her attend and participate in international conferences in education and having papers published, including an article titled "Decoloniality and educational change: Cultivating a living philosophy to overcome decoloniality and violence in African universities", co-authored with Yusef Waghid.

Chikumbutso Herbert Manthalu is Associate Professor in the Department of Higher Education and Professional Development, School of Education, University of Malawi. His research areas include higher education in Africa, education for democratic and global citizenship, global justice and education, and African philosophy and education. He is a co-author of the book, *Cosmopolitan Education and Inclusion: Human Engagement and the Self* (Palgrave Macmillan, 2020) and a co-editor of two books: *Education, Communication and Democracy in Africa: A Democratic Pedagogy for the Future* (Routledge, 2022) and *Education for Decoloniality and Decolonisation in Africa* (Palgrave, 2019).

Elton Pullen is a chartered accountant and Senior Lecturer in Management Accounting & Financial Management at the University of the Western Cape in South Africa. His publications include a chapter titled "Equipping aspiring chartered accountants as responsible leaders" in a co-authored book titled *Chronicles on African Philosophy of Higher Education* (Brill, 2023) with Yusef Waghid as editor. He has also published a co-authored article titled "Towards global citizenship education: Benefits and challenges for the South African higher education accounting system" with Yusef Waghid (*Progressio*, 2023).

Lester Brian Shawa is Associate Professor of Higher Education Studies at the University of KwaZulu-Natal in South Africa. Drawing on Philosophy of Education and researching on Higher Education, he focuses on policy praxis (policy, governance, and management), quality discourses, pedagogy, curricula, and international development. His publications include a co-authored book, *Towards an Ubuntu University: African Higher Education Reimagined* (Palgrave Macmillan, 2023) with Yusef Waghid, Judith Terblanche, Joseph Hungwe, Thokozani Mathebula, Faiq Waghid, and Zayd Waghid.

Tadeus Shikukumwa is Distance Education Coordinator for Tertiary Programmes at the Namibian College of Open Learning in Namibia. He lectures part-time at several universities in Namibia and Zimbabwe. His doctoral degree focuses on education policy. He has interests in citizenship education, management, and leadership. This is his first publication.

Judith Terblanche is a chartered accountant (CA) (SA) and is the Head: BCom Development at Milpark Education in South Africa. She sits on the Independent Regulatory Board of Auditors's Education and Transformation Committee and previously worked at Stellenbosch University and the University of the Western Cape as an associate professor with a focus on auditing. She co-authored *Towards an Ubuntu University: African Higher Education Reimagined* with Joseph Hungwe, Lester Brian Shawa, Judith Terblanche, Thokozani Mathebula, Zayd Waghid, and Faiq Waghid (Palgrave Macmillan, 2023).

Faiq Waghid (PhD) serves as Head of the Department for Academic Staff Development at the Fundani Centre for Higher Education Development, Cape Peninsula University of Technology (CPUT). In this role, Waghid has been instrumental in leading initiatives aimed at enhancing the professional growth of academic staff, with a vision to foster a culture of relentless excellence and innovation at CPUT. This positions the institution as a leader in the realm of higher education. Waghid's research is deeply rooted in participatory action research, advocating for collaborative efforts that enhance teaching and learning experiences. Amid the changing dynamics of education, Waghid has explored the transformative impact of educational technology, particularly in challenging times. A notable area of focus has been the exploration of artificial intelligence (AI) in education, recognizing the significant shift AI has introduced in teaching and learning processes. Waghid coordinated the development of CPUT's AI guideline, a strategic framework addressing the challenges posed by AI and examining its capacity to overhaul traditional teaching methodologies and provide tailored learning experiences.

Yusef Waghid is Emeritus Professor of Philosophy of Education at Stellenbosch University in South Africa. He is an executive member of the Council on Higher Education and chief editor of both *Citizenship Teaching and Learning* and the *South African Journal of Higher Education*. He has authored *On Wonder, Wander, and Whisper in Higher Education: Philosophical, Educational and Moral Openings in Doctoral Pursuits* (Routledge, 2023, under consideration) and co-authored *Towards an Ubuntu University: African Higher Education Reimagined* with Joseph Hungwe, Lester Brian Shawa, Judith Terblanche, Thokozani Mathebula, Zayd Waghid, and Faiq Waghid (Palgrave Macmillan, 2023).

Zayd Waghid is Associate Professor in the Faculty of Education at the Cape Peninsula University of Technology in South Africa. He is the co-author of five books: *Educational Technology and Pedagogic Encounters: Democratic Education in Potentiality*; *Rupturing an African Philosophy of Teaching and Learning: Ubuntu Justice and Education*; *Cosmopolitan Education and Inclusion: The Self and Others in Deliberation*; *Conversations on Higher Teaching and Learning: A Renewed Focus on Critical Praxis*; and *Towards an Ubuntu University: African Higher Education Reimagined*. He is a South African National Research Foundation-rated researcher and a recipient of the CHE-Heltasa National Teaching Excellence Award (Commendation) in 2019. In 2023, he received the prestigious Fulbright Visiting Scholarship and served as the Acting Director and Interim SARChI Chair in the Center for International Teacher Education.

Monica Zembere (PhD) is Senior Lecturer in the Faculty of Social Sciences and Humanities at Bindura University of Science Education in Zimbabwe. She holds a Doctor of Philosophy in Education Policy from Stellenbosch University, South Africa. Her master's degree from the University of Zimbabwe is in Curriculum and Arts majoring in History. At master's level, she teaches the following courses: Education, Philosophy, and International Relations. She has written and presented papers at international conferences centring on democracy, human rights, and constitutionalism in Zimbabwe. In 2019, Monica was attached to Wits University for 8 months as a researcher on sabbatical leave. She has 16 journal publications and 4 book chapters to her credit. She has presented papers at both local and international conferences. She had the opportunity to present papers in Nairobi, Kenya, in 2012; Johannesburg, South Africa, in 2015, 2018; Seville, Spain in 2016; and Botswana in 2018. Her areas of research interests include democratic citizenship education, teacher education, decoloniality, and social issues emanating from policy and conflicts. Her recent articles published in refereed high-impact journals include "The potentiality of cultivating a culture of mutuality in multicultural society: A transformative pedagogical encounter with the other" and "Gendered leadership in Zimbabwe's institutions of higher learning: A call for decolonization of equality and justice".

Foreword

Philosophical Adventures in African Higher Education: Cultivating Doctoral Encounters within Democratic Citizenship Education valuably combines African sensibilities of global relevance with a compelling philosophical outlook on higher education and democratic pedagogy. Throughout this new book, doctoral encounters are couched in the spirit of democratic citizenship education and are expected to be adventurous. In other words, doctoral theses are not only academic exercises but also, or more, *adventurous encounters*. That the adjective "adventurous" premodifies the encounter has a special significance, if we consider what is entailed by "adventure". Not just any doctoral encounter will do, if our aspirations extend beyond mere specialization, outcomes, and technicist research proliferation. The encounter must be adventurous, which means, as is emphasized in the book, that it must be open-ended and thought-enlarging. I would add that inherent in the notion of adventure is one's being prepared to endure hardships, the risks of chance and finitude, and the adversities of the unexpected in one's course to a set destination. In this sense, the choice (and use) of the metaphors of "adventure", "journey", and "navigation" throughout the book is most felicitous and pertinent, given the complexities and challenges of a worthy doctoral endeavour. Indeed, the chapters in this engaging book advance, each in its own unique and original way, a more heightened consciousness of what doctoral research as an adventurous journey requires.

To undertake the whole operation of carrying out doctoral research, one must be prepared through a family of virtues and values and, in a productive vicious circle, committed to furthering these virtues and values through the research itself. Democratic citizenship education is presented in the book as one such virtue and value, intrinsic to an African philosophy of higher education. Furthermore, re-imagining, disruption, transformation, democracy, mentorship, dialogue, and iterations are some of the key normative concepts that guide the structure of the book and have great philosophical and practical import as well as international significance and influence. Through such notions and their demarcation of what is worthwhile, the book transcends philosophical abstraction. It situates philosophy by embodying the doctoral researcher and their initiation into academic life as a self shaped by the course of their studies and simultaneously shaping the political and scholarly culture through their active loyalty to democracy and transformation.

Faithful to this adventurous spirit and the virtuous, critical, and painstaking engagement that it requires, the book registers doctoral narratives of self-exploration and transformative intervention in the status quo of the African continent and beyond it. As the afterword to this book indicates, the journey is not easy, given that, in the global context, the neoliberal paradigm prevails, gets transferred to various localities around the world, and commodifies education worldwide. In this neoliberal context, it is not unusual to encounter reifying studies of doctoral research and higher education. PHDs then are seen merely as routes towards success, access to academic careers, and social mobility. Against this backdrop, the book powerfully contributes a more experientially oriented perspective with practical intent and democratic, transformative aspirations. It goes beyond "technical" or "managerial", so to speak, engagements with doctoral research, those which see in such research little more than a profitable accomplishment of scientific work of no political and existential relevance and implications.

In its effort to keep away neoliberal logics and logistics, the book does not, however, downplay or ignore that to have social effects and make a lasting change, a new scholarly research presupposes the researcher's employability. Commendably, *Philosophical Adventures* is a book that undertakes the task of exploring how the gap between academic achievement and professional success could be bridged or, at least, reduced. Also important for the book's intervention in actual realities is that it acknowledges that the turn of philosophical ideas into transformative givens requires the influential role of the private business sector concerning social redress mechanisms, such as poverty alleviation, through job creation. Because the authors of the book's chapters bring along their own sensibilities and diverse perspectives, a wide variety of such topics and challenges are tackled. Thus, tensions between visions that aspire to act as catalysts for a democratic world and doctoral programs that adopt the prevalent neoliberal educational priorities are not at all neglected. Likewise, due attention is given to how anti-democratic habits and problematic professional practices in specific African localities, and globally, raise obstacles to philosophically imagined futures and invite urgent democratic problem-solving.

The doctoral thesis as a fulfilling experience and a major scholarly accomplishment comes inter alia from appropriate dynamics of the supervisor-supervisee relationship through active dialogue and intellectually rewarding exchanges of ideas. In many ways and through various paths, the authors contribute most helpful insights into how supervision could and should be enhanced through enabling learning environments. They promote a symmetrical relationality that disrupts power hierarchies, facilitates growth, and promotes reciprocal learning. Admirable editing work (along with an illuminating introduction) has ensured the striking coherence of the project and the cohesion of individual contributions that reflect varying and heterogeneous perspectives in a way that affirms unity in diversity. The smooth and elegant flow of this edited book's main ideas reveals, piece by piece, the vision of doctoral students as reflective and active participants in their societies who develop into African intellectuals able to energize and revitalize the cultural heritage of their localities. The book treats doctoral research as a multiplicity of paths: leading back to roots (African philosophy such as *Ubuntu*); meandering to yet little explored prospects for a more democratic future; reaching new possibilities that novel technologies (e.g., generative and paraphrasing AI) or new directions (e.g., post-colonial frameworks that investigate Africa's unique experiences and prospects) open for more desirable futures; and directing towards existentially and ethico-politically rich commitments to disrupting the unjust and gloomy realities of the world of today. Thus, although the book sets out from, and dedicates much of its effort to, the African context, its global significance is an antidote to the neoliberal spirit and its corrosive force in the world of today.

Marianna Papastephanou, University of Cyprus

Preface

A decade after having published *Dancing with Doctoral Encounters: Democratic Education in Motion* (Waghid 2015), this seminal work emerges as a sequel to the latter publication for three reasons: Firstly, I consider this work as an extension of my earlier thoughts on doctoral supervision; secondly, it accentuates the importance of deliberative pedagogical encounters in sustaining credible doctoral work; and thirdly, it enhances a notion of democratic citizenship education in Africa and fosters a culture of critique and disruption.

I extended an invitation to several scholars whom I have either promoted and supported throughout their studies or developed an academic relationship with based on our common epistemological concerns and interests. By implication, their contributions mostly connected with what it means to cultivate an African philosophy of higher education and the concomitant transformative potential of such a philosophy of education. In the main, the contributions of my academic friends mostly revolve around the possibility of a philosophy of higher education to respond to social problems and, more interestingly, to advance critique, deliberative engagement, and societal transformation and/or justice.

My contention is that doctoral education ought to be responsive to Africa's societal predicaments. Consequently, we offer a compelling argument for an African philosophy of higher education that is adventurous, critical, and deliberative, aiming to cultivate citizens who are both reflective and active participants in their communities. Both contributors and I hold the view that any philosophy of higher education comprises of meanings that can stimulate change, produce individuals who can initiate transformative change in their societies, and themselves develop the capabilities to advance local-global intellectual interests. The diversity of the contributions most notably, from South Africa, Malawi, Zimbabwe, and Namibia, suggests a southern African response to the discourse of doctoral education. In addition, the responses of scholars from Jordan and Japan provide a much-needed philosophical impetus for the understandings of doctoral education that emerged from this study. Yet, all the contributions conceptually connected with what it means to advance a philosophy of higher education in Africa. Why is it so important to advance the idea of an African philosophy of higher education?

First, African societies have undergone significant social, political, and economic changes over several decades, and the once revered African teachings through sagacity and oral traditions have been challenged by colonial imperialist thought that left the continent in intellectual disarray. Scholars like Kwasi Wiredu, Paulin Hountondji, and Henry Odera Oruka recognised the intellectual trauma faced by Africans and argued for a revitalized philosophy that was not just academic but also practical in its response to the continent's socio-political and economic challenges. Thus, through the notion of an African philosophy of higher education they advocated for conceptual and pragmatic change in responding to Africa's intellectual and social dilemmas. Their seminal works can be seen as constituting the groundwork for what has evolved into a legitimate African philosophy of higher education. That is, their work is philosophical in the sense that thought and practice respond to problems on the continent; and the educational impetus of their work is constituted in the reimagination of human encounters in practices and institutions.

Second, an African philosophy of higher education is constituted by notions such as communalism or human interdependence, respect for all humans, and dignified action. These constitutive actions of an African philosophy of higher education intertwine with a notion of *ubuntu*, thus rendering such a philosophy action oriented. In African societies, cultivating communalism is central to human living, and if an African philosophy of higher education advances such action, then using such a philosophy seems humanely and morally plausible. Likewise, to pursue academic inquiry using communal knowledge is a recognition that indigenous forms of knowledge are valorized. And to bring such knowledge in harmony with universal understandings seems justifiably so to be the task of an African philosophy of higher education.

Third, to pursue doctoral studies in the context of an African philosophy of higher education invariably makes students attentive to practical problem-solving orientation of such a philosophy. And in doing so, such a philosophy becomes a site for practical and ethical considerations where both local and global knowledge traditions are equally considered to address Africa's dilemmas. Such a philosophy in turn would encourage students to engage in questioning, critique, and reflectiveness as they endeavour to respond to Africa's realities.

So, to fully realise the potential of African philosophy of higher education in doctoral supervision, academic institutions need to embrace a more communal, problem-solving, and ethically viable notion of African philosophy of higher education – the thrust of the arguments in this book. In this way, doctoral studies would become more engaging and creative. The narratives in this book speak to such a tenable notion of philosophy of higher education which enhances its credibility as a genuine African discourse.

Yusef Waghid
Stellenbosch University

Reference

Waghid, Y. 2015. *Dancing with Doctoral Encounters: Democratic Education in Motion.* Stellenbosch: SUN PReSS.

Introduction
On being adventurous

Yusef Waghid

Setting the scene

Philosophical Adventures in African Higher Education: Doctoral Encounters within Democratic Citizenship Education is a seminal book that delves into the doctoral research and pedagogical experiences within an African higher education (HE) context. It underscores the transformative potential of African philosophical underpinnings in doctoral education, advocating for a paradigm deeply entrenched in African thought and practice.

We – contributors and I – reflect on eleven doctoral encounters in (African) HE. We specifically focus on three aspects of such encounters: firstly, why the encounters can be referred to as philosophical adventures; secondly, why the encounters enhance notions of democratic citizenship education (DCE); and thirdly, why these encounters can be conceptually connected to an advocacy for critique and disruption. The following authors were invited to contribute to this volume: Zayd Waghid (Chapter 1); Faiq Waghid (Chapter 2); Lester Brian Shawa (Chapter 3); Sithobile Priscilla Dube (Chapter 4); Elton Pullen (Chapter 5); Judith Terblanche (Chapter 6); Monica Zembere (Chapter 7); Chikumbutso Herbert Manthalu (Chapter 8); Judith, Terblanche, Elton Pullen, and Yusef Waghid (Chapter 9); Naima Al-husban and Hammadallah Ahmad Al-husban (Chapter 10); Tadeus Shikukumwa (Chapter 11); and Afterword (Emiliano Bosio). All these authors, including myself, have engaged with work in and about DCE, and most of our work has been influenced heavily by an African philosophy of HE. The afore-mentioned forms of education are conceptually connected based on a rationale that seems to underscore both. That is, both forms of education are constituted by a problem-solving rationale and its ramifications for HE in Africa. Put differently, both democratic citizenship (higher) education and an African philosophy of HE are concerned with the resolution of problems that have implications for HE on the African continent. As my colleagues and I venture through our contributions, we therefore identify the problem-solving capacities of such forms of education and how African HE – mostly higher teaching and learning – should be affected.

DOI: 10.4324/9781003530091-1

Towards an adventurous African philosophy of higher education

To begin with, we consider our own work in and about an African philosophy of HE as an adventure. We use the notion of an adventure to depict that intellectual experience that allows one to articulate one's thoughts based on one's encounters with knowledge and interests guided by whatever rationale. In one's venture, one can conjure up thoughts that influence the ways one conceives HE in Africa, and in turn, how one's thoughts are equally influenced by the encounters one had. Although one does not always know where such encounters will take one, one remains conscious that adventures would create opportunities for the new and unimaginable – that is, what one has not thought of previously. Although one is engaged with notions of DCE, African HE, and a philosophy of HE, one is not always aware where this journey will end, whether there is any possibility that such a journey could or should be concluded. Consequently, because the interest is not in achieving finality, the point about articulating one's thoughts is a matter of embarking on an adventure where the possibility always exists that one might come up with something not predicted or thought about previously. What follows is a succinct analysis of my contribution to the theme of this book and how the contributions of colleagues could be conceived as they ventured on this epistemological pathway.

Since having been initiated into a philosophy of HE, I always grappled with the idea of why it – i.e. a philosophy of HE – had been distinctly African. The distinctly African orientation of my work is not only related to a spatio-physical locality but also to the view that problems in Africa can be conceptually articulated with the aim to resolve problems in and about African HE. My biggest concern has therefore always been the military dictatorships that seem to crop up time and again on the continent. At the time of writing (February 2024), two more countries – Niger and Gabon – had experienced military coups; thus, corroborating the claim that political life on the African continent seems to be constrained by violent seizures of power from legitimately elected governments. When practicing an African philosophy of HE, one should be concerned with an analysis of why the problem of militarism seems to undermine any legitimate aspiration for democratic governance. My initial thought is that dictatorships subvert any form of critical and dissonant voice. When this happens, HE becomes vulnerable to exclusion and domination. The adverse effect is that HE discourse, such as teaching–learning, would become remiss of deliberative iteration because the production of such a citizenry is no longer seen as necessary for the cultivation of plausible human experience. Citizens, as expected, are supposed to adhere to dictatorial political rule where nothing should be questioned and scrutinised. If this is what is expected from a citizenry, what is the point of cultivating critical discourses that accentuate the importance of critique and dissonance? In the main, dogmatic, exclusionary, and intentionally subverted views make an African philosophy of HE a genuinely transformative venture.

From the above follows that an African philosophy of HE ought to become an intellectual adventure because such a discourse would make it possible for teachers and students to question that which constrains human action. Questioning subversive actions that are often associated with dogmatic and exclusionary positioning is the first step when taking issue with that which brings human action into disrepute. An African philosophy of HE obliges teachers and students to question unbridled and oppressive human action where dissent becomes an enabling condition for democratic change. Moreover, the prejudice of an African philosophy of HE towards the cultivation of DCE is precisely because such a discourse foregrounds what Africans need to do to ensure genuine change. It is through DCE that teachers and students learn to act iteratively, thus subverting those positions in society that cripple any legitimate attempt to democratise society. Learning to articulate oneself, to listen to contending and diverse views, and to recognise one's right to talk back to such views are actions that could ensure the manifestation of plausible African thought and practice. Next, we examine the view that an African philosophy of HE could provoke encounters that could be conceived of as adventurous.

On the cultivation of adventurous doctoral encounters

African philosophy of HE summons people (i.e. students and teachers) to think for themselves without always having to be told what to do. The very idea of an African philosophy of HE is associated with what inspires humans to think independently and to come up with understandings not previously considered. In this way, doctoral work can be said to be associated with the notion of an encounter – that is, human action related to what people do together. When people act collectively with a seriousness of mind, willing to alter that with which they are confronted, they can be said to be adventurous beings. Their adventure lies in the pursuit of encounters where they cannot predict in advance what the outcomes would be. In this way, doing a doctorate does not mean that one knows in a predetermined way what the result of one's inquiry would reveal. It is because of being adventurous that one is prepared to remain reflexively open to what is still to come. This seems to be the epitome of doctoral work that inspires one to think differently and to reimagine things anew – a matter of pursuing an adventure. When I asked contributors to this book to reflect on their doctoral encounters, I wanted them to foreground whatever thoughts they could come up with in the pursuit of their encounters. This meant that they had to relook their own engagement with African thought and practice, and how they became what they are today. They would thus be able to track their own adventures as they grappled with or not the notion of an African philosophy of HE.

Enhancing democratic citizenship education through doctoral work in African philosophy of higher education

Throughout our adventures into the realm of an African philosophy of HE, we began to assume a repositioning of our thoughts related to notions of DCE. Salient features of the adventures espoused in this book relate to conceptual shifts in our understandings of DCE: firstly, the concept is portrayed as a virtue of an African philosophy of HE, that is, one cannot think of such a philosophy without considering it vis-à-vis what DCE entails. We therefore thought about an African philosophy of HE as a form of autonomous action whereby humans (in this case, us) exert our will to make sense of what we think and that upon which we act. Similarly, for us, an African philosophy of HE ought to have an iterative function in the sense that one engages repeatedly with texts and contexts to ascertain why and how our analyses had been deepened when new thoughts were on offer. One is specifically reminded of the iterative work of linking and delinking concepts, and how these concepts influence the pedagogy of higher teaching–learning we espoused in our work.

In Chapter 1, Zayd Waghid gives an account of doctoral supervision, guided by notions of wonder, wander, and whisper. For him, these principles signify transitioning from conventional supervisory roles to a more nurturing, empathetic, and collaborative approach. Based on his experiences and deep introspection, Waghid expresses a growing recognition of the essential role of a strong foundation of ethical responsibility within the supervisory relationship. He argues for disrupting prevailing power hierarchies within educational settings and proposes cultivating a symmetrical supervisor–student relationship that fosters reciprocal learning and progress. This approach focuses on engaging with students' points of view and on facilitating empathetic and attentive interactions. The unfolding narrative reflects a dedication to nurturing authentic and lasting relationships that transcend beyond conventional supervision. It emphasises promoting personal and professional development in students, particularly in their post-doctoral contexts. His chapter serves as a reflection of his development and as an important contribution to the continuing debate around progressive doctoral supervision. It provides valuable perspectives that are particularly beneficial for supervisors who are new to the supervisory role. The argument posits that adopting these principles initiates a shift in the supervisory function, fostering the development of post-graduate students into expanded iterations of themselves and promoting favourable and mutually beneficial relationships within academia.

In Chapter 2, Faiq Waghid explores the integrative role of artificial intelligence (AI), particularly generative and paraphrasing AI, in enhancing student supervision. The primary focus of this research centres on the facilitation of active conversations and discussions among students and supervisors utilising technological tools, such as ChatGPT and QuillBot. The chapter discusses the synergistic role of AI in student supervision enhancements, focusing particularly on generative and paraphrasing AI technologies, such as ChatGPT and QuillBot. It posits these tools as instrumental in fostering active dialogues and discussions between students and supervisors, aligning with Benhabib's notion of 'intercultural dialogue' and Vygotsky's theory on the social dimension of learning. Generative AI, exemplified by ChatGPT, is highlighted for its ability to simulate human-like responses, facilitating in-depth interactions that could enrich the supervisory relationship. In academic writing, paraphrasing tools, such as QuillBot, are underscored for their capability to improve the quality of scholarly work, aiding students in overcoming challenges related to language proficiency and ensuring academic integrity. The chapter underscores the transformative potential of these AI tools in enhancing communication, critical thinking (CT), and mutual understanding within the educational context. It argues that AI technology not only aligns with the goals of DCE by customising teaching strategies and fostering a collaborative, inclusive environment but also contributes significantly to the development of democratic citizens. The integration of generative and paraphrasing AI is portrayed as a progressive step in education, offering a dynamic and engaging learning experience necessary for fostering democratic participation and enhancing the diversity of the educational ecosystem.

In Chapter 3, Lester Brian Shawa reflects on his doctoral adventure and shows how it was influenced by democratic citizenship (higher) education and an African philosophy of HE. Two philosophical ideas informed his adventure: dialectical reasoning and communicative rationality, which he suggests are necessary for emancipatory doctoral education. He reflects on his doctoral journey, focusing on how his exploration of democratic citizenship in HE and an African philosophy has illuminated the challenges and solutions pertinent to HE on the African continent, particularly in Malawi. His narrative delves into how these philosophical perspectives helped uncover anti-democratic practices in both international and local HE settings in Malawi, and the way this influenced his approach to resolving such issues. The outcome of these encounters with knowledge is shown to extend beyond academic inquiry, shaping his professional practices in post-graduate teaching, learning, supervision, HE research, community engagement, and governance.

In Chapter 4, Sithobile Priscilla Dube gives a presentation of her doctoral encounters with the issue of democracy. She pursued the topic to determine whether there existed democracy in university programmes that produce graduates who could be absorbed into the marketplace. The focus was on education, training, and development to establish whether the curriculum was suitable to produce employable graduates. The primary focus of this chapter is on discussing the effects of DCE on employability. Dube delves into the pressing issues of graduate employability and underemployment in Zimbabwe, highlighting the increasing concern among HE institutions, government, and industry. The gap between university graduation and successful integration into the workforce is explored as a significant challenge that pressurises not only universities to deliver employable graduates but also affects economic sustainability and the abilities of employers in Zimbabwe to navigate the complex transition of graduates into the job market. The focus of Dube's doctoral research was to investigate the presence of democratic principles within university programmes, aiming to assess whether these programmes prepare graduates adequately for employment. This inquiry into democracy in education sought to evaluate whether the curricular content in universities is suitably designed to produce employable graduates, thereby potentially reducing the gap between academic achievement and professional success.

In Chapter 5, Elton Pullen shares insights from his doctoral research on the integration of DCE and CT into South African (SA) university accounting programmes accredited by the South African Institute of Chartered Accountants (SAICA). The research employed a conceptual-deconstructive analytical approach to evaluate the progress made by SAICA-accredited universities in advancing CT and DCE competencies. The core of the investigation revealed a significant tension between the need for fostering CT and DCE skills and the prevalent technical-focused pedagogical approaches adopted by these accounting programmes. This dichotomy underscores a broader educational challenge: how to reconcile the demand for professional technical skills with the imperative for broader educational outcomes, such as CT and democratic engagement. To address this inherent conflict, Pullen proposes exploring alternative strategies that could potentially bridge the gap between technical proficiency and the development of critical, democratic competencies within the chartered accountancy education.

In Chapter 6, Judith Terblanche delves into her doctoral journey, culminating in a PhD in philosophy of education with a focus on democratic citizenship, through the lens of the chartered accountancy educational landscape in South Africa. This exploration recognises the significant influence of the private business sector, particularly chartered accountants (CAs), on social redress mechanisms, such as poverty alleviation, through job creation. The narrative underscores the dual role of business practices as a perpetuator of inequality on the one hand, or as a force for dismantling unjust systems on the other. Terblanche's personal transformation is highlighted, emphasising the profound influence of the supervisory relationship during her doctoral studies. This relationship prompted deep reflections on the essence and potential of DCE, not just within the academic sphere but also extending into the realm of business leadership. The chapter suggests that the principles of DCE could profoundly influence business leaders, advocating for coaching practices that might accelerate positive social change in the challenging social context in South Africa. Through this introspective account, Terblanche sheds light on the potential for educational pursuits in philosophy and democratic citizenship to foster significant personal growth and professional development. This growth is not confined to academic achievements but extends to envisaging a role for business leaders as agents of societal change, driven by the values and principles embedded in DCE. The narrative positions this transformative journey as a catalyst for broader societal effect, especially in addressing pressing social inequalities in South Africa.

In Chapter 7, Monica Zembere embarks on a reflective exploration of her PhD research journey, from the inception of a researchable topic to the submission of her final thesis. Central to this reflection is Zembere's interaction with her promoter and the incorporation of new philosophical frameworks, particularly emphasising the influence of their dialogical encounters and the development of a friendship with Prof. Waghid, viewed through the prism of DCE. Zembere details the employment of a literature review and reflexivity as key research methods, highlighting the importance of reflexivity in qualitative research. This approach is emphasised as crucial for navigating discussions on subjectivity, objectivity, and the generation of social science knowledge. Through reflexive analysis, she was able to ensure the integrity and trustworthiness of the data, situating herself within the research and acknowledging her perceptions and biases. This reflective journey points out the critical role of the supervisor–student relationship in the successful completion of a PhD within a specified time frame. By analysing this relationship and its influence on the research process, Zembere acknowledges the profound influence of mentorship and collaboration on academic development and the realisation of research goals.

In Chapter 8, Chikumbutso Herbert Manthalu advances the argument that making doctoral supervision encounters democratic should include having the university, through the supervisor as its agent, recognise the student's subjective situatedness as being key in the study process. Making the doctoral supervision democratic thus entails recognising the situationality of the student and the bearing this situationality has on conceptualisation of the research problem, and inquiry tools such as the theoretical lenses to be employed in understanding the phenomena, namely undemocratic human experiences. A mode of supervision that demands that a student's non-mainstream lived experiences conform to the assumptions of dominant theories and epistemologies is thus undemocratic. It is further argued that social theories have foundational assumptions that are rooted in the lived experiences of the developers of such social theories. The doctoral student's lived experiences, which are considered incompatible with the assumptions of the dominant theories, should therefore not be forced to conform to the dominant theories. Rather, where necessary, supervision should be so open-minded that it will demand a re-imagination of methods and dominant theories required. For this to happen and drawing from Manthalu's doctoral journey, the chapter argues that the supervisor should embrace democratic attitudes that are not limited by a surreptitious absolutism of social theories.

In Chapter 9, Judith Terblanche, Elton Pullen, and Yusef Waghid discuss the transition of chartered accountancy educators in South Africa into academia, challenging the prevailing assumption that professional success as a CA equips one for educational roles within accounting. This assumption, deeply rooted in the academic and professional pathways that emphasise passing the SAICA Initial Test of Competence (ITC), risks perpetuating a narrowly focused technical pedagogy that might not align with contemporary educational goals, such as those outlined in the SAICA CA2025 competency framework. This framework seeks to reimagine the role of CAs by integrating citizenship competencies, indicating a shift towards broader educational aims. Drawing on Britzman's (1986) notion that educators' "implicit institutional biographies" shape their teaching perspectives, and Baszile's (2017) argument on the co-productive nature of self and curriculum, the chapter advocates for the use of *currere* as a transformative practice. *Currere*, understood as a form of self-praxis, enables educators to engage critically with their educational experiences and assumptions, thereby opening possibilities to reshape accountancy education in line with the objectives of CA2025. This involves not just a passive reception of the curriculum but rather an active engagement that allows for resistance, rearrangement, or reinterpretation of the curriculum.

In Chapter 10, Naima Al-husban and Hammadallah Ahmad Al-husban provide a deep retrospective analysis of the PhD journey, highlighting transformative experiences and collaborations, particularly with international scholar, Yusef Waghid. This chapter challenges traditional views of academic research as a purely mechanistic endeavour aimed at achieving degrees or advancing careers. Instead, it presents research as a deeply humanistic pursuit, with the potential to contribute significantly to community values, learner development, and the nurturing of human flourishing. Al-husban and Al-husban aim to illuminate the contemporary landscape of doctoral studies in Jordan through both personal and collective experiences. They address challenges encountered by doctoral students and supervisors, advocating for global citizenship education (GCE) as a catalyst for transforming research paradigms. This approach suggests moving beyond traditional research frameworks to embrace a humanistic perspective that instils lasting values and fosters the development of individuals who can act as agents of positive change. By integrating GCE into doctoral research, the chapter posits that research can transcend academic and geographical boundaries, fostering a global community of scholars committed to ethical, powerful, and effective study. This vision for doctoral studies emphasises the importance of nurturing a global perspective among researchers, one that values diversity, promotes mutual understanding, and encourages a commitment to addressing global challenges collaboratively.

In Chapter 11, Tadeus Shikukumwa presents his doctoral adventure and the influence of DCE with a special focus on Namibian education policy. His journey comprised an interpretive study concerning Namibian education policy and its link to citizenship education. His primary intention on this doctoral journey was to present his discovery and understanding of the role of the new Namibian education policy, the National Curriculum for Basic Education 2015, in the development of DCE. Furthermore, in this chapter, he reflects on strategies that are in place to ensure that learners in Namibia have access to democratic education. Moreover, he intends to reveal how the new Namibian education policy (i.e. the National Curriculum for Basic Education, 2015) contributes to the advancement of DCE. In addition, he aims to discuss whether the new education policy would be effective in enhancing educational transformation in Namibia.

In the Afterword, Emiliano Bosio delves into the transformative role of universities – the main provider of doctoral education – under the influence of neo-liberalism, as articulated through the lens of various works by Bosio and collaborators, among others. The discourse challenges the prevailing neoliberal paradigm that has commodified education, emphasising the responsibility of the university to cultivate critical knowledge and values, such as human dignity, cultural diversity, and democracy. Drawing on the theoretical foundations laid by scholars, such as Mignolo, Slaughter, Leslie, and Freire, he (Bosio) proposes the concept of an 'ethical university' as a vehicle for developing critical consciousness and a global ethic inspired by critical pedagogy. The ethical university, as envisioned, transcends the focus of the neoliberal model on commercialisation and commodification, aiming instead to foster an inclusive, reflective, and socially responsible academic environment. This model prioritises the development of learners – not just as future employees for the global job market but also as conscientious citizens capable of critical thought and social transformation. The 'ethical university' is conceptualised as a space of conscientisation, facilitating deep understanding of the world, exposure to social and political contradictions, and the nurturing of identity through intergenerational knowledge and value transmission. Bosio argues for a pedagogical shift towards an ethically engaged form of education that acknowledges the role of the university in addressing contemporary societal challenges, including social justice, ecological sustainability, and decolonialism. By advocating for a value-based pedagogy or a pedagogy of hope, the ethical university aims to inspire social change, critical awareness, and the empowerment of humanity towards the common good. This approach is grounded in the critical theories of Freire, Bohman, McLaren, McLean, Mignolo, and Walsh, emphasising the importance of critical self-analysis, deep reflection, and wise action in the pursuit of a sustainable and just society. It is such an understanding of the ethical university that could play a significant role in the pursuit of credible doctoral education in Africa.

The quest for critique and deconstruction

Finally, our doctoral adventures in an African philosophy of HE have attempted to advance notions of critique and deconstruction. We were always inspired to embark on our adventures within a liberatory framework of critical pedagogy. When pedagogy is meant to emancipate thought and practice, then such pedagogy seems to enhance the exercise of critique. Gert Biesta (2009) offers two accounts of critique: critical dogmatism and transcendental critique. Firstly, to have some understanding of what it means to be critical, one ought to think of critique as critical dogmatism whereby educational theory and practice are evaluated in terms of its emancipatory potential (Biesta, 2009:84). When doctoral adventures can advance the emancipation of human practices, then such adventures would be considered critically dogmatic, as "it gives an evaluation of a specific state of affairs" (Biesta, 2009:84). Our doctoral work can be said to be critically dogmatic because our arguments are meant to subvert parochialism and freedom of thought. Moreover, transcendental critique involves "a specific form of internal critique … in order to reveal whether such a position or argument is rational or not" (Biesta, 2009:88). When doctoral work in

African philosophy of HE is subjected to an internal critique based on rational justifications, then such adventures can produce more justifiable actions in responding to pedagogical predicaments. In this way, doctoral adventures can be considered an act of critique, that is, for its enhanced rational justification and reconsideration of emancipation in the pursuit of critical pedagogical interests.

Do our doctoral adventures connect with deconstruction? Following Jacques Derrida (1991:273), deconstruction considers a crisis of judgement or discernment as one of its essential themes. When humans proffer unjustifiable claims, it is therefore considered a crisis that requires deconstruction. In response, Biesta (2009:90) posits, "deconstruction is first and foremost an affirmation of what is excluded and forgotten – an affirmation, in short, of what is other". What follows is that, when doctoral adventurers search for reasons that perhaps cannot be thought of, in other words "an affirmation of an otherness that is always to come" (Derrida, 1992:27), then they embark on deconstruction. Biesta (2009:91) therefore avers, "deconstruction is an openness towards the unforeseeable incoming". The point about considering doctoral work in an African philosophy of HE in the contexts of critique and deconstruction is to suggest that such adventures aim to advance philosophy of HE as a preparation "for the incalculable" (Biesta, 2009:35). Our doctoral work has consequently always been ready to deal with the unexpected and the incalculable.

Conclusion

One of our intellectual mentors, Jacques Derrida (2004:152), proffers, "truth has to be spoken without controls and without concern for utility". When doctoral adventures are therefore pursued with 'truth', more specifically, professional rigour, competence, and responsibility (Derrida, 2004:150), such adventures would be responsible. Firstly, an African philosophy of HE couched as a responsibility happens when teachers and students provoke one another to think reflectively and with a sense of renewal, that is, to be thoughtful about what is still to come – a matter of instigating an alterity in a deconstructive way. Secondly, enacting responsibility associated with doctoral adventures brings into play the notion of suspicion. To be suspicious means to raise doubts about the possible advances and regresses of doctoral adventures. Thirdly, when doctoral adventures manifest responsibly, participants are not only prepared to postulate with the intent to alter undesired situations – whether in a faculty or a community – but also endeavour to play one risk off against another (Derrida, 2004). Throughout our doctoral adventures, we therefore acted with autonomy and deep reflection, authenticity and suspicion, and a determination to play off risks against each other. Only then could the possibility for change be enhanced towards "the risk of the future" (Derrida, 2004:150).

Finally, this book presents a distinctive approach to doctoral research and supervision, emphasising experiential learning and practical application within the context of African HE. Its strength lies in offering a nuanced perspective that challenges the conventional view of PhDs as mere stepping stones to academic careers and social mobility. Instead, it portrays doctoral research as a multifaceted journey that not only roots scholars in African philosophical traditions like *Ubuntu* but also propels them towards exploring democratic futures and making ethico-political commitments to transform unjust global realities. The book emphasises the importance of grounding doctoral research in African philosophical traditions, particularly *Ubuntu*, which stresses community, interconnectedness, and mutual care. This approach positions doctoral research as a process of returning to one's roots, where scholars engage deeply with the values and principles that define African societies. By embedding these philosophical underpinnings in doctoral supervision, the book advocates for a research paradigm that is not only intellectually rigorous but also culturally and ethically resonant with African realities.

The contributions in the book highlight the role of doctoral research in envisioning and shaping democratic futures. Through a critical and reflective engagement with the African HE landscape, scholars are encouraged to question established norms and envision new educational paradigms that promote democracy, equity, and inclusivity. This forward-looking perspective is crucial for cultivating scholars who are not only adept at navigating the present complexities of the academic and societal landscape but are also capable of contributing to the emergence of a more democratic and just future.

Likewise, the book underscores the importance of doctoral research as a platform for making ethico-political commitments to address the challenges of the contemporary world. By engaging with the pressing issues of our times, such as social injustice, inequality, and environmental degradation, doctoral research is positioned as a transformative intervention that transcends academic boundaries and contributes to societal change. This approach fosters a sense of responsibility among scholars to use their research as a tool for advocacy and action in the pursuit of a more equitable and sustainable world.

In the main, doctoral research, as depicted in the book, is an adventurous journey of self-exploration, where scholars embark on a path of personal and intellectual growth. This journey is not only about acquiring new knowledge but also about challenging one's own beliefs and assumptions, leading to a transformative experience that shapes one's identity as a scholar and as a global citizen. The book presents doctoral supervision as a collaborative process that supports this journey, fostering an environment where scholars can thrive and realise their full potential. *Philosophical Adventures in African Higher Education* contributes significantly to the discourse on doctoral research in Africa by offering a comprehensive, experientially oriented perspective that aligns with the continent's philosophical, democratic, and ethical imperatives. Its emphasis on doctoral research as a journey of rooting, exploring, and committing to transformative change elevates the discussion beyond conventional academic pursuits to a broader contemplation of the scholar's role in society. This approach not only enriches the doctoral experience but also positions African HE as a pivotal force for societal transformation.

In summary, the book reflects on eleven doctoral encounters in HE, focusing on the philosophical adventures, enhancement of DCE, and advocacy for critique and disruption. Here's how it addresses these three aspects: Firstly, the term "philosophical adventures" denotes the intellectual journey undertaken during the doctoral process, characterised by exploration, questioning, and the quest for deeper understanding. The book portrays these encounters as adventures because they involve navigating complex ideas, challenging existing knowledge paradigms, and venturing into unexplored territories of thought. Each doctoral journey is unique, pushing boundaries of conventional wisdom and contributing to the evolution of African philosophical thought. The encounters are not just academic exercises; they are transformative experiences that encourage scholars to engage with, and contribute to, the rich tapestry of African intellectual traditions. Secondly, DCE is central to the doctoral encounters described in the book. These experiences are seen as platforms for fostering democratic values, CT, and civic engagement among scholars. The doctoral journeys contribute to DCE by equipping scholars with the tools to question and analyse societal issues, thus preparing them to play active roles in their communities and contribute to the democratic processes within African societies. Through these encounters, the scholars learn to appreciate the interconnectedness of individuals within communities, emphasising collective well-being, moral obligations, and the pursuit of justice and equity, which are crucial elements of democratic citizenship. Thirdly, the book connects these doctoral encounters with the need for critique and disruption in the HE system. It posits that African HE should not only impart knowledge but also encourage a culture of questioning and challenging the status quo. These encounters serve as catalysts for change, urging scholars to critique entrenched systems and disrupt complacent academic and societal norms. This process is essential for creating an academic environment that is reflective, critical, and dynamic. The narratives within the book corroborate how doctoral education can serve the interests of intellectual (critique and dissonance) and social (democratic) transformation.

References

Biesta, G. 2009. From critique to deconstruction: Derrida as a critical philosopher, pp. 81–96. In M.A. Peters & G. Biesta (Eds.), *Derrida, deconstruction, and the politics of pedagogy.* New York: Peter Lang.

Derrida, J. 1991. Letter to a Japanese friend, pp. 270–276. In P. Kamuf (Ed.), *A Derrida reader between the blinds.* New York: Columbia University Press.

Derrida, J. 1992. *The other heading: Reflections on today's Europe.* Bloomington, IN: Indiana University Press.

Derrida, J. 2004. *Eyes of the university: Right to philosophy 2.* In J. Plug and others (Trans.). Stanford, CA: Stanford University Press.

1 A doctoral supervisor in becoming
Some reflections on being initiated into a doctoral adventure

Zayd Waghid

Introduction

Embarking on the journey towards a doctoral degree is a truly fulfilling pursuit, encompassing rigorous research, scholarly discussions with one's supervisors and experts in the field, writing up the thesis and, ultimately, engaging in the doctoral oral examination or viva voce. This endeavour holds significant professional and personal rewards, particularly in terms of academic career prospects and advancements. The doctoral journey, with its comprehensive and formal process, is augmented by the doctoral adventure, which brings forth an array of perspectives. These perspectives encapsulate the scholarly excitement of pedagogical, methodological, and professional discoveries, along with unforeseen challenges and personal transformations.

Undertaking a PhD at a university in South Africa several years ago while fulfilling my responsibilities as a secondary school teacher in Cape Town demanded considerable time and dedication. Balancing these demanding roles meant addressing eager learners' inquiries about their assessments while simultaneously immersing myself in scholarly reading and writing, all while managing administrative duties and meetings. Attempting to manage this balance was challenging, as it often entailed reconciling my commitments to both my career advancement and my professional duties. Compromises had to be made at certain points. Nonetheless, this self-discovery journey within the doctoral experience and adventure played a vital role in shaping me as a novice doctoral supervisor.

The idea of an African adventure, as described by John Murungi (2023), resonates with me, as it captures the essence of doctoral supervision as an explorative journey into uncharted territories. For most novice supervisors, the novelty stems from the fact that they have not embarked on such an adventure before. This makes their initiation into this realm unpredictable, as they are unaware of where the journey will lead, for both them and their students.

In this chapter, I delve into the concepts of risk-taking through trust; resilience through thoughtful, comprehensive, and energetic responses; and an ethics of care. Specifically, I draw inspiration from the ideas of Giddens

DOI: 10.4324/9781003530091-2

(1990) as well as Reivich and Shatte (2002). I also incorporate Nodding's (2010) seminal thoughts on the four components of moral education (i.e. modelling, dialogue, practice, and confirmation), relating them to the context of doctoral supervision. Furthermore, I discuss the elements of wonder, wander, and whisper, providing insights for the potential growth of supervision. To protect anonymity, pseudonyms are utilised throughout this chapter.

Journeying through the art and science of post-graduate supervision: Navigating expectations and outcomes

In 2015, during my initial year of higher education at my current institution, I had the privilege of attending a workshop on the science and art of post-graduate supervision. This workshop catered to both novice supervisors, who had yet to guide master's and doctoral students to completion, and experienced supervisors seeking to unlearn old supervisory practices and relearn new supervisory practices. The name of the workshop piqued, my interest, as it probed into the scientific and logical aspects of post-graduate supervision. The workshop involved learning how to provide appropriate guidance to post-graduate students in selecting suitable topics, designing research, employing methodologies, conducting literature reviews, and honing scholarly writing skills. The scientific dimension further entailed sharing disciplinary knowledge, research skills, and CT capabilities to support students in their scholarly writing endeavours.

The workshop also embraced the artistic side of supervision. It emphasised the creative aspects concerning non-traditional, imaginative, and engaging ways of supervision and the importance of fostering relationships with students. This involved establishing a strong rapport and cultivating an environment grounded in trust, transparency, and cohesion. I distinctly remember a session during which the facilitator encouraged participants to explore the use of Wikipedia as an internet source to assist students in discovering relevant resources for their research. Initially, I harboured doubts and scepticism about relying on such an unreliable internet source and exposing my students to such an unconventional approach. As the facilitator engaged in innovative ways of encouraging students to explore different research avenues, it however became apparent that unconventional methods were pivotal in the art of post-graduate supervision.

The initial focus of the workshop was to familiarise us with the level descriptors for master's and doctoral students according to the South African Qualifications Framework (SAQA, 2012). These descriptors highlight the contrasting expectations for students at each level. For instance, while master's students are still in the process of exploring research topics and gaining familiarity, doctoral students are expected to have already formulated a title, identified a problem, and developed a primary research question. This differentiation in student roles and responsibilities underscored the importance of establishing alignment between supervisors and students, emphasising the significance of an informal memorandum of agreement (MoA).

When I first attempted to assess a particular student using the informal MoA to determine suitability, I initially harboured scepticism about working with the student. Considering that I was a novice supervisor and finding post-graduate students was initially challenging; however, I took the risk and accepted the student for co-supervision with my experienced colleague, who had successfully supervised several master's students to completion.

Initially, our meetings were lengthy, but I gradually acquired certain supervisory skills by observing my colleague's interactions with the student and subsequently adopted some of the approaches with my students. I ended up co-supervising multiple master's students alongside certain colleagues. While the knowledge gained from the supervisory workshop was beneficial, it posed challenges when introducing it in practice due to the differing supervisory approaches among my colleagues and their interactions with our students. These experiences, although valuable learning opportunities for me, did not yield the desired outcomes, as several students ultimately dropped out of the programme due to conflicting personal commitments or promotional career advancements. Moreover, during that time, I was also supervising several Bachelor of Education (B.Ed.) Honours students and overseeing their research projects. It was quite surprising to me that the progress of many of my students did not align with my initial expectations.

Balancing risk-taking, trust, and empathy in guiding resilient students towards academic success: The cases of Thabo, Anathi, and Andrew

In their book *The Resilience Factor: 7 Keys to Finding Your Inner Strength and Overcoming Life's Hurdles*, Reivich and Shatte (2002:11) assert that resilient individuals have found a system – a veritable system – for rallying themselves and confronting challenges "thoughtfully, thoroughly, and energetically". My understanding of this approach is that these individuals do not merely react impulsively or hastily to challenges. Rather, they approach challenges with consideration and care (i.e. thoughtfully), thoroughly addressing every aspect of the challenge, and doing so with enthusiasm and determination (i.e. energetically).

Initially, the task of supervision was a frustrating experience, as two years had passed since my initial supervision encounter with a master's student without me successfully supervising a single student to completion, despite having worked with three master's students. A significant breakthrough however occurred during a particular meeting in 2018. A former honours research project student approached me with a request to serve as his supervisor for his post-graduate studies. Although I had not yet supervised a student to completion, according to faculty policy, I was only allowed to co-supervise with a more experienced colleague.

At the commencement of our meeting, an unfortunate incident occurred when the student interrupted me while I was engaged in a conversation with a colleague, pertaining to matters related to research. This interruption caught me off guard, and without delay, I directed the student to my office. Initially, I was displeased with the student's actions and made it known, although in retrospect, I realise that my approach was incorrect. Despite the unfavourable start to our meeting, it ended amicably and proved to be fruitful.

To begin with, a student – whom I refer to as Thabo in this chapter – had already formulated an idea for a study and displayed confidence in his proposed research. Thabo's enthusiasm for his studies was evident, but what truly set him apart, was his unwavering resilience in the months that followed. I often advise my students to have a tenacious spirit, and to take my comments as an opportunity for growth. While some may perceive this as undermining their writing, Thabo embraced my feedback to enhance his work, showing resilience. This resilience distinguished Thabo from others who initially exhibited great potential and enthusiasm but eventually withdrew from the M.Ed. course due to personal commitments.

During the initial stages, my co-supervisor and I frequently convened to discuss Thabo's progress. A good rapport with my co-supervisor gave me the opportunity to take a prominent role in the supervision process, allowing me to apply what I initially learned in the post-graduate supervision workshop. Due to English not being Thabo's first language, I frequently offered suggestions for improving his writing, which he graciously accepted. Upon reflecting on my initial approach, I however realised that the power dynamics between Thabo and myself could have resulted in a strained supervisor–student relationship had it not been for his robust character. Thabo demonstrated to me the importance of humility in my supervisory practices. Attempting to maintain a balance between firmness and allowing students to forge their own paths is undoubtedly a challenging endeavour. This is precisely why embracing risk-taking is integral to the supervisory process.

Giddens (1990:35) postulates an interconnectedness between risk and trust, where trust assumes the crucial role of mitigating or diminishing the perils inherent in various endeavours. Giddens suggests that, when one trusts an individual or system, one is likely to accept the risks accompanying the encounter. This is what Giddens (1990:35) further maintains when he submits that skill and chance act as factors that constrain risk; yet, in most cases, risk is deliberately assessed and calculated. In this regard, one would typically consider the potential dangers and weigh them against potential benefits before acting. Giddens (1990:35) eloquently states:

> In all trust settings, acceptable risk falls under the heading of "weak inductive knowledge", and there is virtually always a balance between trust and the calculation of risk in this sense. What is seen as "acceptable" risk – the minimising of danger – varies in different contexts, but is usually central in sustaining trust.

Giddens (1990) implies that the acceptance of risk is often based on one's experiences; however, such acceptance is not absolute or universally acceptable. Risk-taking within the framework of my supervision played a vital role in fostering an environment characterised by trust, mutual respect, and collaboration, enabling the voices of my post-graduate students to be heard. The profound influence of this transformative approach to learning and teaching – as opposed to the conventional teaching–learning paradigm – gradually unfolded as I embraced the concept of risk-taking in my supervisory role. This entailed a conscious shift from an unintentional position of power towards an active involvement of my students, exemplified by the student in a collaborative learning process aimed at cultivating student autonomy and co-constructing knowledge.

While risk-taking played a vital role in the supervision process, I frequently found myself needing to adopt the perspective of my students who – like me in the past – embarked on post-graduate studies while attempting to balance work commitments. Several of my students came from historically disadvantaged communities. In this regard, managing work, family responsibilities, and post-graduate studies meant that they had to take on significant financial and personal risks. Two students in particular – Anathi and Andrew – often felt frustrated with my supervision approach, mainly because of my initial harsh comments concerning their work. I would often request them to rework several of their chapters, which frustrated them in many instances. I realised that their time spent was associated with financial risk, and while they mostly agreed to complete their chapters within a specified time frame, this was not always possible. While it was time-consuming for them, my intention was always to start the supervision process from a student-led approach. I realised at the time that I needed to follow a different supervision style, which had to be a balanced approach that would develop in Anathi a great degree of autonomy while still playing a more directive role in certain instances during supervision where her thoughts might not have been formulated accurately.

Initially, I hesitated to adopt such an approach because there was an expectation that post-graduate students should already possess the necessary research skills and writing abilities to work independently. Along with several other students, neither Anathi nor Andrew was however familiar with academic writing at master's level. Consequently, many of them faced challenges in this area. Andrew struggled with choosing an appropriate title, and throughout the supervision process, he preferred to work collaboratively with Anathi and his co-supervisor. I often reminded Anathi and my other students that academic writing is a journey. Although my comments might have seemed strict, my intention was always to encourage them to think critically about their work, knowing that revisions would be necessary before final approval of a chapter.

Immersing myself in their context and experiences allowed me to cultivate a heightened sense of empathy. Through this empathetic lens, I gradually became aware of the challenges many of them faced, which at times made me uneasy, particularly when considering the dynamics of unequal power. What became increasingly apparent, however, was the importance of establishing an emotional connection with my students, a fundamental aspect that the supervision workshop sought to emphasise throughout our sessions. While I initially believed that guiding students through the sharing of knowledge was of paramount importance, I came to realise that establishing a strong social presence with my students was even more crucial. Risk-taking and empathy plays a crucial role in the supervision process. Understanding the unique challenges my students faced allowed me to adopt a balanced approach, guiding them towards academic success while acknowledging the journey of academic writing.

Balancing trust, power, and collaboration in guiding a doctoral student towards coherent arguments: The case of Betty

In 2019, while delivering a research presentation at a seminar in the faculty, I could not anticipate that it would mark the beginning of my inaugural encounter with a doctoral student. After the event, the Head of Research in the faculty approached me, expressing a keen interest in my potential involvement as a supervisor for a student whom I shall call 'Betty'. Betty found herself bereft of guidance due to the retirement of her previous supervisors. Despite my lack of experience in supervising students, I embraced the opportunity and accepted the responsibility.

My initial encounter with Betty occurred during a student conference and, although it was brief, we had a chance to meet in a face-to-face setting, since most of our communication happened telephonically and through emails. In my first reading of her work, Betty's work reflected an abstract nature, often entailing a myriad of theories and ideologies without the requisite contextualisation. Although her writing exhibited commendable skill, she grappled with the coherent articulation of her thoughts. Consequently, when the moment arrived for her to present her proposal to the faculty research committee, she encountered considerable difficulties. The idea behind the proposal defence as part of the doctoral journey is significant, as it affords the student an opportunity to convey his or her proposed research convincingly to a panel comprising esteemed faculty members. Moreover, it serves as a conduit for the student to receive invaluable critical feedback aimed at refining his or her research proposal. Initially, she faced challenges in her responses during the proposal defence. Moreover, she struggled to present her thoughts logically, leaving the panel members unable to grasp her ideas easily. This situation left me unsettled, as I could not assist her during the proposal defence. After her presentation, conflicting thoughts arose, making me question whether I had adequately prepared her for the proposal defence. In contrast to the preference of some supervisors who require their students to present their research beforehand, I trusted Betty to take ownership of her work. My philosophy has always been to empower students to think for themselves and to work independently, even if the outcome might not always be favourable. To me, the learning experience holds greater significance than the actual result.

This thus presented me with the considerable task of assisting Betty in reformulating her work and assisting her in the construction of a cohesive and pragmatic argument, an essential facet of doctoral studies. Eventually, Betty's proposal obtained approval, albeit subject to the conditions stipulated by the Chair at the time. In the months that followed, she worked progressively and independently, seldom asking me questions pertaining to her research. Most of our conversations were via email while there were times during the year where we had online meetings to evaluate her progress. While I encouraged Betty to think laterally –and she was, of course, inclined to do so considering that she was a registered doctoral student – it often led me to attempt to understand how the research was unfolding. It was not an easy task at first. I often felt that I needed to keep up with her thoughts. Reading up on her ideas concerning arts-based theories, albeit abstract, was however significant for my own development.

During her studies, her research methodology underwent changes. Despite previous experiences with students that led to tension when attempting to guide them, I deemed it necessary to take the risk and trust Betty. Building a good rapport with her took time, while she was eager to complete her studies. In the first few months, I took on the role of supervisor, successfully guiding her through the proposal stage. After three years, however, she was anxious about completing her studies within the next two years. I empathised with her frustration of wanting to finish despite not having completed the required chapters. It was not a simple matter, and I often questioned whether I was the right supervisor for her. Realising the importance of earning her trust, I focused on establishing a comfortable and collaborative learning environment. She would even query my questions, which, although initially frustrating for me, I understood as necessary to build trust. While I had preconceived notions about how her study had to be reshaped, I learned to surrender some power, allowing her greater autonomy and trusting the collaborative process. Although there were initial gaps in her knowledge, both a language editor – to whom I was grateful – and myself assisted her in refining her abstract thoughts into more coherent arguments.

Navigating an ethics of care in doctoral supervision through modelling, dialogue, practice, and confirmation

Noddings (2010) approached the concept of empathy cautiously, particularly in terms of the interplay of power, where individuals immerse themselves in the experiences of others to comprehend such experiences. This tendency to project oneself in the context of the 'other' is in contrast with the notion of receptivity, which emphasises the perspective of the 'other'. According to Noddings (2010), genuine dialogue involves two essential elements: empathic accuracy, which entails accurately grasping the emotions of the other; and a sympathetic response, where one emotionally connects and 'feels with' the other. While Noddings (2010) acknowledges the importance of empathy in specific situations, the absence of sympathy negatively affects the notion of care. In other words, empathising by projecting oneself into the other person's context might be possible, but without a sympathetic response, the sincerity of the empathy becomes questionable.

According to Noddings (2002, 2005, 2010), an ethics of care significantly influences moral education, leading to an exploration of four core concepts: modelling, dialogue, practice, and confirmation. *Modelling* plays a crucial role in moral education, where individuals exemplify caring behaviour by genuinely demonstrating care (Noddings, 2010). It is important to note that the intention is not to care to be a role model but rather to naturally become a 'model of care' through genuine caring actions (Noddings, 2010). The second aspect is *dialogue*, in which both parties actively communicate and listen within a caring relationship, strongly emphasising understanding the other person (Noddings, 2010). Even if dialogue fails to produce a mutually acceptable solution, it should always preserve a compassionate bond (Noddings, 2010).

The third element is *practice*, which cultivates empathy and sympathy. Educators play a crucial role in providing students with opportunities to practise and develop empathy (Noddings, 2010). Educators must however be cautious to ensure that these engagements reflect authentic care (Noddings, 2010), as rewarding specific behaviours may obscure a student's genuine desire to care. To demonstrate care, students must consciously or implicitly comprehend the notion of being cared for. This understanding is essential for the development of genuine care within them. The fourth element is *confirmation*. According to this element, educators guide students through their ethical dilemmas by engaging in dialogue, helping them realise the implications of their actions reflectively (Noddings, 2010). This process aims to lead students towards becoming a better version of themselves, tapping into their potential for positive growth. Noddings (2010) emphasises that confirmation should not be treated as a mere recipe or technique. Instead, it requires educators to possess prior knowledge and experience of their students and being able to identify the most appropriate and realistic motives for growth. The aim of confirmation in such an instance is to bring out the better self that already exists within the student, albeit in a potential or unexpressed form (Noddings, 2010).

Reflecting on my journey with Betty, I recognise that my supervision approach in relation to an ethics of care (Noddings, 2010) was necessary to understand the supervision journey itself, which was a significant learning encounter – littered with challenges and my own shortcomings.

First, in terms of the element of *modelling* – considering that I was new to doctoral supervision and strived to be a 'model of care' – the instances where I questioned my capacity to supervise Betty together with the pressure of establishing myself as a model for her was a significant risk. Despite my attempts, I often wondered whether I was genuinely demonstrating care or whether I was merely going through the motions, by trying to navigate this uncharted territory. I learned however to manage this pressure, focusing on being sincere and authentic in my actions rather than trying to fit a particular mould. I tried to exemplify genuine care in my interactions with Betty, hoping that these actions would naturally position me as a 'model of care' rather than forcing myself into the role.

Second, concerning the *element* dialogue, while Noddings (2010) emphasises the significance of understanding and respecting the 'other's' perspective, the moments in which I struggled to comprehend Betty's abstract ideas fully through my own misconception and lack of understanding, on my part, was in retrospect a barrier towards guiding her effectively through the process. Instead of letting this hamper our progress, I took it as an opportunity to deepen my own understanding. I spent extra time reading and researching the concepts Betty presented, gradually building an improved understanding of her ideas and the way to guide her in articulating them coherently.

Third, concerning the element of *practising care*, while I sought to provide Betty with the spaces necessary to develop empathy and independent thinking, I also grappled with the fear of her finding herself in a position where her arguments could not be defended well in her thesis. Attempting to find a balance between enabling her autonomy and ensuring that her research was shifted in the right direction was far more challenging than I had anticipated. I learned to trust the process, continually reminding myself that nurturing empathy from my experiences with my previous students was a crucial part of their journey. I provided guidance where necessary but also gave her room to explore, make mistakes, and learn from them.

In relation to *confirmation*, this was perhaps the most challenging element since I was expected to guide Betty towards becoming the best version of herself. Trusting in Betty's abilities and the collaborative process was a task that took a considerable amount of time and effort. I learned however to trust in Betty's abilities and in our collaborative process. I further understood that my role was not to mould Betty into a specific type of researcher but to help her realise and confirm her potential.

Although the adoption of Noddings' (2010) ethics of care was by far no easy task – and it indeed posed significant challenges – I used these hurdles as stepping stones. Each challenge offered me an opportunity for growth, helping me to become a better mentor. I learned to empathise more than before, to trust in my student's abilities, and to understand that authentic care was about fostering a sense of autonomy and independence. Despite the uncertainty, I believe this journey towards shaping me into a better supervisor was ultimately necessary. It helped me to foster a positive, collaborative relationship with several of my students, such as Betty. While the learning was in progress, these experiences equipped me to navigate future hurdles better.

Wonder, wander, and whisper: Reflective elements for progressive doctoral supervision

As I critically contemplate my interactions with my post-graduate students, I am increasingly aware of the profound influence of the elements of wonder, wander, and whisper. These elements align with the instances described previously in our work (Waghid & Waghid, 2019), namely instances of university students experiencing discomfort when prompted to think about and reflect critically on their work. These elements are necessary towards shaping one's approach to doctoral supervision in transformative ways.

While I have always been genuinely interested in and fascinated by my students' work, their distinct ideas, and their capacities, I now find myself pondering how their research can flourish in their post-doctoral contexts. Embracing the role of mentor, I strive to maintain a curiosity in their work, going beyond mere supervision. This is a lifelong journey of supervision that extends beyond critically reviewing their dissertations and theses, focusing on cultivating meaningful relationships to help them evolve as accomplished researchers in post-doctoral settings.

I further acknowledge that understanding my students' perspectives can sometimes be challenging, especially when dealing with their perhaps abstract ideas. In such instances, the act of wandering and navigating through unfamiliar territories becomes essential for a mutual exchange that fosters personal growth and development for both my students and myself. Venturing into their thoughts and embracing cognitive exploration nurture a significant sense of empathy and sympathy, as I come to appreciate the richness of their ideas amidst their diverse personal circumstances. Practising and modelling empathy is vital for finding synergies between these elements of an ethics of care and providing guidance to students while creating spaces for their autonomous thought. This practice of wandering is crucial in supporting one's students fully at times when they most need guidance and affirmation.

The concept of whispering symbolises the humility required in post-graduate supervision. Acknowledging that there is much to learn from one's students dismantles any unequal power dynamics that might exist between a supervisor and his or her student. By approaching their work with care, respect, and understanding, the notion of whispering fosters equitable dialogue that is conducted through respectful and attentive conversations. Demonstrating such care necessitates an authentic approach to help shape one's students into better versions of themselves.

As one continues on the supervisory journey, one needs to recognise the profound significance of wonder, wander, and whisper. These principles will continue to become invaluable to one's growth as a supervisor. Embracing uncertainty and discomfort, developing deeper empathy, trusting one's students' abilities, and cultivating authentic care are essential in shaping one into becoming a better supervisor and fostering positive, collaborative relationships with one's students.

Summary

In this chapter, I embarked on a journey to illustrate an all-encompassing approach to doctoral supervision, infused with an ethics of care and guided by the principles of wonder, wander, and whisper. Through introspective narration, I delved into the intricacies of this voyage, which entails both challenges and rewards while nurturing empathy, compassion, and autonomy among students. Alongside overseeing dissertations and theses, this expedition necessitates the cultivation of meaningful relationships, fostering post-doctoral success in students. Amidst the complexities of demonstrating care through modelling, dialogue, practice, and confirmation in doctoral supervision, I argue that these challenges are opportunities for growth and advancement in the supervisory role. My critical reflections evince a mind-set necessary for embracing humility and equitable dialogue, effectively dismantling any potential power imbalances between supervisors and their students. These principles offer valuable insights for novice supervisors and significantly contribute to the ongoing discourse on transformative doctoral supervision.

References

Giddens, A. 1990. *The consequences of modernity*. Cambridge: Polity Press.
Murungi, J. 2023. *African philosophical adventures*. Lanham, MD: Lexington Books.
Noddings, N. 2002. *Educating moral people*. New York: Teachers College Press.
Noddings, N. 2005. *The challenge to care in schools*. Second edition. New York: Teachers College Press.
Noddings, N. 2010. Moral education and caring. *Theory and Research in Education*, 8(2):145–151.
Reivich, K. & Shatte, A. 2002. *The resilience factor: 7 keys to finding your inner strength and overcoming life's hurdles*. New York: Broadway Books.
SAQA (South African Qualifications Authority). 2012. *Level descriptors for the South African National Qualifications Framework*. Pretoria: SAQA.
Waghid, Y. 2024. *Philosophical, educational and moral openings in doctoral pursuits and supervision: Promoting the values of wonder, wander, and whisper in African higher education*. London: Routledge.
Waghid, F. & Waghid, Z. 2019. Educational technology, pedagogy and caring. In Y. Waghid (ed.). *Towards a philosophy of caring in higher education: Pedagogy and nuances of care*. New York: Palgrave Macmillan, 159–171.

2 The use of artificial intelligence to augment student supervision

Faiq Waghid

Introduction

According to Benhabib (2002), democratic citizenship education (DCE) encompasses three interconnected elements: collective identity, membership privileges, and social rights and benefits. To educate individuals effectively as democratic citizens, it is imperative to consider their linguistic, cultural, ethnic, and religious affinities (Benhabib, 2002). Finding a civic space to share similarities is based on the premise that people have to learn to live with others' otherness, which may be very threatening to their own otherness (Benhabib, 2002). By creating a civil space, what Benhabib (2002) calls intercultural dialogue, where people can enact what they have in common and make public their competing narratives and significations, people may be able to coexist. Consequently, they would create a community of discourse and interdependence (shared commonality) and disagreement (dissensus) without demeaning others' lifeworlds. To put it another way, when people are having a conversation based on interdependence and disagreement, they engage in an educational process with a shared identity. The process of fostering democratic citizenship entails the establishment of civil environments in which individuals can acquire the skills to acknowledge shared values, and where they can exhibit respect for diverse perspectives. This claim highlights the significance of active involvement, a sense of belonging, and active engagement in discussions as fundamental components of DCE (Benhabib, 2002). Such active engagement is not only crucial in the realm of citizenship but also in the broader context of education and learning.

Building on this idea, the social aspect of learning, as identified by Vygotsky in his studies of children learning in school, underscores the importance of discussion. It is frequently cited as the origin of the notion that discussion plays a vital role in learning, not only at all levels of education but also in the broader context of social interactions (Laurillard, 2013).
Vygotsky (1978: 140) states:

> Communication produces the need for checking : 140and confirming thoughts, a process that is characteristic of adult thought ... learning

awakens a variety of internal developmental processes that are able to operate only when a child is interacting with people in his environment and in cooperation with his peers. Once these processes are internalised, they become part of the child's independent developmental achievement.

Combining the findings of several investigations, Laurillard (2013) proposes that effective peer discussion include the following:

- adopting a particular stance regarding a theory or hypothesis;
- offering examples and justifications for their claim or perspective;
- considering, addressing, or refuting alternative arguments;
- sharing and evaluating ideas;
- reflecting on one's perspective with respect to others;
- working toward an agreed-upon result, negotiating meaning, or deciding together; and
- implementing what we have learned to use.

Although the reference is to peer discussion, the above may also be considered relevant regarding supervisor and student engagements. The discussions between supervisors and students may be meaningful in many ways. Through discussions, students may, for instance, share their hypotheses and ideas for their research. Discussions may assist students in refining ideas, directing them to appropriate literature. Then, a discussion of ideas and a more elaborated conceptual understanding may be realised (Laurillard, 2013). Based on these discussions, students are often challenged to think beyond their initial understanding of a research topic, thus encouraging vigorous research (Laurillard, 2013). Inherently, students may come across numerous challenges and obstacles while engaged in research. In this case, discussions between supervisors and students can be used as opportunities for problem-solving as supervisors creatively explore solutions. Furthermore, when students submit their work to supervisors, the potential exists for the mutual exchange of feedback. In this way, learning is bidirectional (OpenAI, 2023).

In this chapter, we discuss the potential of artificial intelligence (AI) to enhance active engagements, encompassing discussion between supervisors and students throughout the supervision process. In this way, there exists the potential for DCE to be realised.

Current uses of artificial intelligence

Educational Technology (EdTech) is described as the combined use of hardware, software, theory, and practice (Sharples, 2023). As hardware and software are continually evolving and being developed, EdTech exists in a continuum. Not since the advent of the internet has there been a digital technology as disruptive as AI (Sharples, 2023). We have seen AI gradually affecting everyday activities, such as online shopping, where suggestions of items in which we may be interested appear on our feeds. Already, AI has been used in higher education through predictive analytics models, predicting whether students are potentially at risk of completing courses with varying degrees of success (Sharples, 2023). These uses of AI, however, pale compared to the development of generative AI.

Generative AI refers to language models that are trained with a considerable quantity of different text data to comprehend and create content that resembles human writing. They can engage in conversational tasks, respond to questions and statements, and provide coherent responses. Generative AI models are knowledgeable in science, technology, literature, history, and more (Sharples, 2023). Training of generative AI incorporates exposure to books, websites, and other knowledge sources. The generative AI model tries to generate contextually relevant responses by looking at patterns and relationships within the knowledge sources. It may, however, produce factually incorrect information, referred to as 'hallucinations', although recent iterations of generative AI have a reasonable accuracy rate in their responses (Sharples, 2023).

In addition to generative AI, a different subset of AI technologies referred to as paraphrasing AI technologies may also contribute to supporting student supervision (Sharples, 2023). When it comes to academic writing, a writer has to be able to pick an organised language and should know how to paraphrase and utilise words properly (Nur Fitria, 2021). According to Murray (2012), when we take the work of another writer and rewrite it in our own words, we need to review it twice to ensure that our interpretation of the idea(s) of such a writer is accurate. The conventions of syntax and vocabulary, as well as the ability to grasp accurate diction, are then required to define the structure of paragraphs (Nur Fitria, 2021). Additionally, the expression of concepts developed for the author's imagination and invention must be included in the composition of a paragraph (Nur Fitria, 2021).

According to Nur Fitria (2021), academic writing needs much practice. An essential aspect of academic writing is paraphrasing existing research into a writer's own words and referencing the original author. Paraphrasing involves writing in one's own words something that conveys the original meaning of a passage from a book or other study source (Nur Fitria, 2021). According to Fandl and Smith (2014), paraphrasing is an attempt to rephrase ideas conveyed by another person in an alternative manner. It is not in the scope of a supervisor to give students constructive feedback on their academic writing abilities. In this context, paraphrasing AI technology may contribute to the student's supervision process. According to Fandl and Smith (2014), a paraphrasing tool is a software application that allows users to change text to contain other words without altering the original meaning. The copied text one uses and the original text are the two sources the paraphrasing tool uses. According to Kinkead (2016), the software starts by reading the text that serves as the source and then creates a new text with the same meaning. One such tool, QuillBot, takes existing phrases and makes minor adjustments to them, making it possible for one to revise and rewrite information effortlessly. The tool's purpose is to rewrite information by changing the structure of sentences and replacing words with synonyms while preserving the sense of the original content. QuillBot can enhance grammar, condense lengthy passages, eliminate plagiarism, and paraphrase writing to be concise and sound professional (Dale, 2020). According to Nur Fitria (2021), the AI technique integrates deep learning with several approaches to natural language analysis. QuillBot provides a solution by assisting with paraphrasing when teachers and students cannot paraphrase (Nur Fitria, 2021). QuillBot rewrites texts after the user has written or pasted text and has pressed the 'Paraphrase' icon (Kinga & Gupta, 2021). Gupta, Jason, and Silin, three individuals studying computer science, were responsible for the development of QuillBot in 2017. Given the challenges of writing in English, it is not unusual for students to resort to dishonest practices such as plagiarism (Nur Fitria, 2021). In addition to providing a tool for paraphrasing, QuillBot also has tools for summarising and checking for grammatical errors, all in one location. As this application can replace words with synonyms or change word order, it can potentially reduce plagiarism in student writing, where a supervisor has not picked this up.

In the following sections, we provide examples of how generative AI and paraphrasing AI could contribute to active engagements between supervisors and students and thus improve the communicative process of student supervision.

Social generative AI and student supervision

In a recent article by Mike Sharples (2023), titled "Towards social generative AI for education: Theory, practice and ethics", generative AI is described as a component in an education system in which humans and AI act as language agents. Gordon Pask (Sharples, 2023), a pioneer in using AI in education, argues for conversation to be a fundamental process in learning, much like Vygotsky did. Pask argues that, through conversation, we can reflect on existing understandings of knowledge and question underlying assumptions as we reach a consensus. Through a conversational learning system, the potential exists to explore differences continually, gain experience, and reach agreements (Sharples, 2023). Here, generative AI can enable such conversations. Although Pask did not foresee AI as a participant in a dialogical space, much potential exists here to support student supervision, an inherently communicative process.

Sharples (2023) references six different roles of generative AI supporting cooperative and social learning and, consequently, active engagement in the student supervision process. These roles are a possibility engine, Socratic opponent, collaboration coach, co-designer, Exploratorium, and storyteller. Sharples (2023) suggests that generative AI may broaden perspective. A student may explore an open question, prompting generative AI to generate multiple responses. The implication here is that by using generative AI, students and supervisors can explore different perspectives. By rephrasing prompts, more extensive replies can be identified using AI. This can assist in identifying gaps within existing research or build on existing AI knowledge. The responses generated by AI can help foster active discussions between supervisors and students.

When prompted with the research question, "Write me a summary essay of how AI has improved teaching and learning in no more than 150 words?", generative AI, for example, generated this text:

> Over the past decade, AI has significantly enhanced the teaching and learning landscape. Personalised learning has become a reality as AI-driven platforms assess individual student needs, adapting content in real-time to suit varying learning paces and styles. Virtual tutors provide instant feedback, ensuring students grasp concepts before progressing. For educators, AI tools help in curriculum planning, grading, and identifying students who may be at risk, enabling timely intervention. Through natural language processing, language barriers are diminished, opening up global learning avenues. Moreover, AI-powered simulations and virtual labs provide hands-on experiences, especially in STEM [science, technology, engineering, and mathematics] fields, transcending the limitations of physical classrooms. These advances have fostered more engaged, effective, and inclusive educational environments while simultaneously freeing teachers to focus more on fostering critical thinking and creativity rather than routine administrative tasks.

This was followed by the prompt, "In no more than [a] 150-word essay, which of the above are not well researched?", and generative AI then generated the following text:

> While AI's impact on education is undeniable, certain claims demand more rigorous research. Specifically, the efficacy of AI-driven personalized learning platforms in consistently improving learning outcomes across diverse student populations remains an area of contention. While these platforms show promise, studies offer mixed results about their universal effectiveness. Similarly, while AI tools claim to help in curriculum planning and identifying at-risk students, their accuracy and effectiveness in diverse, real-world settings need more empirical validation. The claim that AI diminishes language barriers is largely attributed to translation tools, but these aren't flawless and can sometimes misinterpret nuances. Additionally, AI-powered simulations and virtual labs, though innovative, need further research to gauge how effectively they can replace or augment traditional hands-on learning. While the trajectory is promising, it's crucial to approach these claims with cautious optimism, ensuring that technology is deployed based on robust evidence of its efficacy.
>
> (OpenAI, 2023)

It is evident that by using AI, supervisors and students could converse in active discussions with the AI to help plan research.

Furthermore, Sharples (2023) proposes that generative AI could be used as an opponent in an argument. As academic writing transcends the presentation of information or summarising content, students can improve their arguments by entering ideas into generative AI and asking questions beyond the confines of what is known. In this way, writing can become more persuasive, with a greater degree of credibility and validity. When prompted with the research question, "Yes or no, is the knowledge produced on ChatGPT inclusive?", generative AI for instance generated the following text:

> OpenAI aims to make models like ChatGPT as neutral and unbiased as possible. However, the model is trained on vast amounts of internet text, and it's possible for biases in those texts to be reflected in the model's responses. While the intent is to create a model that is inclusive, knowledgeable, and representative of diverse viewpoints, no model can be perfectly unbiased or universally inclusive. It's important to approach AI models with a critical mindset and understand that they can inadvertently produce biased or non-inclusive information. OpenAI is constantly working to improve the fairness and inclusivity of its models, but perfection in this domain remains a challenging goal.
>
> (Sharples, 2023: 87)

This was followed by the prompt, "Is much of the data from Africa?" to which generative AI generated this text:

> OpenAI has not disclosed the specific breakdown of data sources by region for the GPT models. However, GPT models like ChatGPT are trained on a mixture of licensed data, data created by human trainers, and publicly available data. Given the vast amount of data used to train these models, it's likely that they include information from all over the world, including Africa.
>
> (Sharples, 2023: 87)

The internet is however not yet evenly representative of global voices. Since my last training cut-off in September 2021, internet penetration and online content creation in many parts of Africa were still significantly lower than in regions such as North America, Europe, or East Asia. This means that, while there is content from Africa in the training data, it might be underrepresented compared to content from other regions. OpenAI is aware of the importance of diverse and representative training data, and they aim to improve the models in this aspect continuously. If one has specific questions about Africa or its many cultures, histories, and contexts, I will do my best to provide accurate and informative answers.

This was followed by the prompt, "Since you have not disclosed where your data comes from, how can we trust you? Answer in a short essay [of] 150 words.", and generative AI generated the following text in response:

> Trust in artificial intelligence, particularly in models like ChatGPT, hinges on several factors beyond just the disclosure of data sources. Firstly, OpenAI operates under a charter committed to ensuring that AI benefits all of humanity. The organisation is driven by transparency, ethical considerations, and continuous research to make models better and fairer. Secondly, while exact data breakdowns aren't provided, OpenAI has been forthright about its intent and the general nature of its training data. Thirdly, trust is also built through utility and consistency. Users worldwide find value in using ChatGPT for a range of purposes, from education to entertainment. However, it's crucial for users to exercise critical thinking and verify information when needed. Ultimately, trust in any tool, be it AI or otherwise, is a blend of its track record, the principles of the organisation behind it, and the user's individual experiences and judgments.
>
> (OpenAI, 2023)

Based on this example, it is evident that supervisors and students can use generative AI to engage in active discussion to improve students' arguments in their writing, using different prompts from supervisors or students.

Sharples (2023) also suggests that generative AI can be used as a co-designer. There are already instances of generative AI being used in collaborative design tasks such as designing websites, videos, games, and other tangible products (Sharples, 2023). During these processes, AI is called on to research user needs, outline problems, challenge known assumptions, brainstorm ideas, and generate prototypes or test solutions. By implication, AI can support students and supervisors in a co-design process, where research is being conducted on developing a product or approach. For example, when prompted with the question to assist in research on the use of blogs for teaching and learning, "Write me a 150-word essay on the main aspects of designing a blog", generative AI generated this text:

> Creating an educational blog tailored for students demands a keen understanding of their unique needs and preferences. At the forefront is simplicity. With the vast amount of academic information students process daily, the blog should serve as a respite, offering content in an organised, digestible manner. An intuitive structure, with content grouped by subject or grade level, can facilitate ease of access. Interactivity is another vital component. Incorporating multimedia, like videos, infographics, and quizzes, can cater to varied learning styles and make complex concepts more comprehensible. The design palette should be conducive to focus, using muted colours that minimise distractions and highlighting important points

through bold or coloured text. Moreover, considering the tech-savviness of today's youth, the blog should be optimised for mobile and tablet viewing. This means clean layouts, touch-friendly buttons, and swift load times. In summary, designing an educational blog for students means merging simplicity, interactivity, and mobile optimisation to foster an effective learning environment.

(OpenAI, 2023)

From the above quotes, it can be summarised that generative AI can assist in brainstorming ideas and generate potential prototypes or test solutions when supervisors and students engage in discussion with generative AI.

As an Exploratorium, generative AI can support both students and supervisors in exploring, visualising, and interpreting databases or design spaces. There are instances of how generative AI can take spreadsheets and convert these data sources into visual interpretations, such as graphs. Generative AI can support the presentation of data in different ways to support students and supervisors in interpreting data in ways that offer opportunities for deeper analysis.

When prompted, for example, with the question to assist in the research on global warming, "Write me a 150-word essay on the temperature rise in recent years", generative AI generated text in response:

The global temperature rise in recent years has emerged as a pivotal concern, signaling a disturbing shift in the Earth's climate system. Rooted predominantly in human activities, especially the burning of fossil fuels, deforestation, and industrial processes, the increased concentration of greenhouse gases in the atmosphere has magnified the natural greenhouse effect. The repercussions of this escalation are manifold. Melting ice caps and glaciers not only lead to rising sea levels, threatening coastal regions and small island nations but also disrupting habitats and freshwater sources. Enhanced heatwaves, more intense storms, and prolonged droughts wreak havoc on ecosystems, economies, and human health. Furthermore, the intertwined complexities of modern life – from food production to urban infrastructure – become increasingly vulnerable. In essence, the upsurge in global temperatures underscores an urgent need for sustainable strategies and international cooperation to mitigate potential catastrophes and secure a viable future.

(OpenAI, 2023)

Furthermore, using the prompt, "Can you tabulate the temperature rises in recent years and identify if there is a trend?", AI was able to express the data in the form of the table below and to generate this response:

Overall, the data underscores the scientific consensus that the Earth is experiencing accelerated global warming. The increasing temperature anomalies are consistent with other evidence pointing towards human-induced climate change, primarily driven by the emission of greenhouse gases like carbon dioxide and methane.

(OpenAI, 2023)

This is a good illustration of how generative AI can express and interpret data in various forms. The data can provide an opportunity for active discussion between supervisors and students as they attempt to identify trends in data.

Finally, as a storyteller, Sharples suggests that generative AI can be used to create stories representing diverse views, orientations, and cultures. Sharples (2023) exemplifies how generative AI can engage in conversation and, when prompted with specific questions, avoid racial and sexual stereotypes and clichéd language. For example, when prompted with the question to develop a story, "Write me 200-word story involving the concept of Ubuntu", generative AI responded as follows:

In the heart of the Namibian desert, Nala, a young girl, stumbled upon a lost tourist, James, sunburnt and dehydrated. Instead of passing by, she guided him to her village, offering him water from her own canteen. James, touched by her kindness, asked, "Why are you helping me, a stranger?"

Nala replied, "In our culture, we believe in 'Ubuntu' – the essence of being human. Ubuntu tells us that my well-being is intrinsically linked to yours. If you suffer, I suffer."

Touched by her words, James decided to stay in the village for a few days. The villagers taught him their dances, songs, and shared their stories around evening fires. In return, James, an engineer, helped them set up a rudimentary water purification system.

As he prepared to leave, Nala handed him a necklace, saying, "Take this. It's a reminder of our shared humanity and interconnectedness."

Years later, James would often share the story of the young girl in the Namibian desert and the profound lesson of Ubuntu. The necklace became more than just an accessory; it was a testament to the idea that in our shared humanity, we find our truest selves.

(OpenAI, 2023)

This was followed by the prompt, "Make all the characters originate from China" to which generative AI generated the following text:

In the heart of the Gobi Desert, Li, a young girl from a remote village, found a lost tourist, Han, sunburnt and dehydrated. Instead of passing by, she guided him to her village, sharing the water she carried.

"Why help me, a stranger?" Han whispered, his throat parched.

Li smiled, "In our culture, we believe in a philosophy akin to 'Ubuntu'. We say, '人之初,性本善', meaning 'people are born good at heart'. Your well-being is bound to mine. If you suffer, I suffer."

Touched by her kindness, Han decided to stay a few days. The villagers introduced him to their traditional dances, songs, and tales told under the canopy of stars. Han, skilled in technology, set up a simple water filtration system for the village in gratitude.

When it was time for him to leave, Li gave him a pendant, saying, "Keep this. It's a symbol of our shared human spirit and connection."

Years later, wherever Han travelled, he'd share the story of the young girl in the Gobi Desert and the profound lesson of interconnectedness. The pendant wasn't just an ornament; it was a beacon of the belief that in our shared humanity, we discover our true essence.

(OpenAI, 2023)

It is evident that by using generative AI, supervisors and students can be supported while conducting research in areas characterised by a diversity of views, orientations, and cultures beyond those of which a supervisor or student may be cognisant. This can offer rich opportunities for discussion between students and supervisors.

These exemplars illustrate the potential of generative AI to support active discussion in student supervision. There is much potential for AI to foster rich discussion, as students and supervisors engage with generative AI in their justifications, sharing, assessment, reflection, negotiation, and implementation in any given research area. In this way, there is the potential to enact DCE.

Paraphrasing AI and student supervision

The previous section outlined how generative AI can augment the communicative aspects of student supervision. In this section, it is argued that paraphrasing AI tools can also augment these communicative aspects, especially when students struggle with aspects of language, such as vocabulary, grammar, structure, and coherence. A paraphrasing AI tool, QuillBot, can rephrase a piece of text using several different ways, such as employing the use of synonyms, changing the form of the word, changing the use of active or passive sentences, and changing the sequence of words within sentences. This ensures that the text is not altered drastically when users edit it while at the same time preventing such editing from altering the true (or original) meaning of the text. As one aspect of academic writing is paraphrasing existing research into a writer's own words and referencing the original author, this tool may also be valuable in supporting students' academic writing abilities on which supervisors advise during discussions.

When prompted with the question to write a 200-word essay on AI using deliberately incorrect English, generative AI for instance generated the following text:

AI be this thing what computers use for think smart-like. You ever see a phone who can talk back? That be AI. Many peoples thinks AI be magic, but actually it be just lot of numbers and code things. Computers be real fast in the brain, so they do lots of things quicker than us. But, they don't got feelings, even if they talk like they do. They just follow what the programmers done told them. Some humans be scared of AI. They watch too many films where robots take over everything! But in the real world, AI help us lots. It make cars go without driver, help doctors find the sick, and even play that chess game real good. But we gots to be careful. If AI get too smart and we don't watch it, maybe it cause problems. In ending, AI be super cool tech stuff, but also we needs to be using it careful-like. It ain't human, it's machine, but it can do big thinks if we teach it right.

(OpenAI, 2023)

The text quoted above has vocabulary, grammar, structure, and coherence issues. However, all these issues were addressed using the QuillBot AI. The paraphrasing AI generated the following text:

Artificial intelligence (AI) is a computational system utilised by computers to enhance their cognitive capabilities and enable intelligent decision-making processes. Have you ever encountered a mobile device that can engage in verbal communication? This refers to artificial intelligence (AI). There is a prevalent belief among individuals that artificial intelligence (AI) possesses magical qualities, yet it is important to note that AI mostly comprises intricate numerical computations and complex coding structures. Computers possess remarkable processing capabilities, enabling them to do tasks faster than human beings. However, it is important to note that despite their ability to communicate in a manner that resembles human speech, OpenAI, 2023stems do not possess emotions. They adhere to the instructions provided by the programmers. Certain individuals exhibit a fear towards artificial intelligence (AI). They consume excessive cinematic productions in which robots assume control of all aspects of society. However, in practical applications, artificial intelligence provides significant assistance to humanity. Autonomous vehicles can operate without human intervention, aiding in transportation. Additionally, they possess the potential to assist medical professionals in diagnosing illnesses and exhibit exceptional performance in strategic board games such as chess. However, we must exercise caution. If artificial intelligence becomes excessively intelligent and is poorly monitored, it may lead to many issues. In conclusion, artificial intelligence (AI) is a highly advanced technological field with remarkable capabilities. However, we must exercise caution and prudence in its utilisation. The entity in question is not of human origin but rather a machine. However, with appropriate instruction, it can engage in complex cognitive processes.

(OpenAI, 2023)

For a supervisor, comprehending the initial output from generative AI can be challenging, mirroring the struggles of a student grappling with language aspects, such as vocabulary, grammar, structure, and coherence. It is, however, evident in the 'corrected' text that paraphrasing AI technologies can address these challenges. In this way, paraphrasing AI can augment the engagements between supervisors and students and reduce instances of accidental plagiarism.

Conclusion

Currently, there are rapid developments in EdTech, specifically with regard to AI. These developments have implications for student supervision practices.

The teachings of Vygotsky, who underscored strong social interaction in terms of cognitive evolution, illuminated my journey while supervising a student for whom English was not a first language. Furthermore, this student also initially grappled with the rudimentary facets of academic research. In navigating these challenges with the student, the advantages of AI technologies, namely generative AI and QuillBot, became indisputable assets. These tools facilitated in two ways. Firstly, the tools enabled active discussion by alleviating communication barriers in their research endeavour. Secondly, AI guided paraphrasing, citation, and effective academic writing, thus ensuring authentic research output and addressing the pitfalls of plagiarism. This improved the way I was able to engage with my students.

My role as a supervisor was characterised by empathy, guidance, and understanding as I actively engaged with my student, supported by AI. AI allowed me to support the students throughout their study without being hampered by language barriers or a lack of initial research skills, which could break down the active engagement. With active engagement, there exists the potential to enact democratic citizenship education (DCE), as active engagement requires actively engaging in discussions and interactions with others, whereas 'belonging' refers to the state of being a community member where individuals actively engage with one another (Waghid, 2008).

With the rapid developments in AI in shaping, refining, and advancing the field of educational technology, there exists the potential for engagement in the supervision relationship between supervisor and students to be augmented towards the enactment of DCE. As AI is having a transformative effect on our everyday lives, the approach to student supervision, augmented by AI, could play an important role in producing graduates who can contribute effectively to society, which is the goal of DCE.

In this chapter on the use of artificial intelligence (AI) to augment student supervision, a critical examination reveals a nuanced perspective on the potential and limitations of AI in educational settings. The chapter emphasises the integrative role of generative and paraphrasing AI technologies in enhancing student supervision through active dialogue and improved academic writing. This integration aligns with Benhabib's concept of intercultural dialogue and Vygotsky's social dimension of learning, aiming to cultivate democratic citizenship education (DCE) through active engagement and mutual respect among diverse perspectives. My narrative illustrates AI's potential to democratise the educational process, allowing for a more inclusive and accessible learning environment. Generative AI models can simulate human-like interactions, facilitating nuanced exchanges between supervisors and students, thus enhancing the supervisory process. Similarly, paraphrasing tools like QuillBot help students overcome language barriers and maintain academic integrity, further enriching their research experience.

However, the chapter's optimistic view on AI's role in education warrants a critical analysis. The reliance on AI technologies raises concerns about the authenticity of learning and the potential erosion of critical thinking skills. While AI can facilitate discussion and provide language support, it is essential to question whether this assistance could lead to over-dependence, potentially diminishing students' ability to engage deeply with academic content and develop independent thought. Moreover, the notion of AI as an unbiased and equitable tool in education must be scrutinised. AI systems, including generative AI and QuillBot, are trained on vast datasets that may contain biases, which can be inadvertently perpetuated in their outputs. This risk of bias highlights the importance of a critical approach to using AI in education, ensuring that these technologies support rather than undermine the diversity of thought and perspective that is essential to a democratic educational environment.

While the chapter seems biased towards the implementation of AI in education, some critical reflection invariably highlights several concerns: Firstly, the over-reliance on AI could undermine the authenticity of learning and student independence. Students may become too reliant on AI, which may be detrimental to their critical thinking and problem-solving capabilities. While AI can provide language assistance and facilitate discussion, more nuanced understanding and critical engagement from deep interaction with academic writing and the supervisory relationship is needed; secondly, generative AI technologies are trained on datasets that can lead to the perpetuation of existing biases, inadvertently influencing students' research perspectives and academic outputs. The challenge is to ensure that the use of AI tools is unbiased and representative; and thirdly, issues on data privacy, intellectual property, and the potential for AI to exacerbate educational inequalities should be considered. Supervisors and students need to consider how they use AI, ensuring that these tools are used ethically without compromising the integrity of the students' output. Thus, while AI presents significant opportunities for enhancing student supervision, it must be implemented with careful consideration of its limitations and potential impacts on higher education.

In this chapter, I attempted to provide an argument for the potential of AI to transform student supervision, promoting more active and inclusive educational experiences. However, this optimistic perspective must be balanced with a critical examination of the challenges and ethical considerations associated with integrating AI into the educational process. By navigating these complexities, educators and technologists can harness the power of AI to enhance student supervision while upholding the values of democratic citizenship education (DCE).

References

Benhabib, S. 2002. *The claims of culture*. Princeton, NJ: Princeton University Press. https://doi.org/10.1515/9780691186542

Dale, R. 2020. Natural language generation: The commercial state of the art in 2020. *Natural Language Engineering*, 26:481–487. https://doi.org/10.1017/S1351324920000025X

Fandl, K.J. & Smith, J.D. 2014. *Success as an online student: Strategies for effective learning*. New York: Routledge, https://doi.org/10.4324/9781315721316

Kinga, S. & Gupta, G. 2021. Platforms as foundation of sharing economy. *Delhi Business Review*, 22:1–13. https://doi.org/10.51768/dbr.v22i1.221202101

Kinkead, J. 2016. *Researching writing: An introduction to research methods*. Logan Utah: Utah State University Press.

Laurillard, D. 2013. *Rethinking university teaching: A conversational framework for the effective use of learning technologies*. London and New York: Routledge, https://doi.org/10.4324/9781315012940

Murray, N. 2012. *Writing essays in English language and linguistics: Principles, tips, and strategies for undergraduates*. Cambridge: Cambridge University Press, https://doi.org/10.1017/CBO9781139035347

Nur Fitria, T. 2021. QuillBot as an online tool: Students' alternative in paraphrasing and rewriting of English writing. *Englisia Journal*, 9:183–192. https://doi.org/10.22373/ej.v9i1.10233

OpenAI. 2023. *ChatGPT based on GPT-4 architecture* [Computer software]. Retrieved from www.openai.com/?> [Accessed 28 December 2023].

Sharples, M. 2023. *Towards social generative AI for education: Theory, practices and ethics*. Retrieved from https://arxiv.org/abs/2306.10063 [Accessed 20 January 2024].

Vygotsky, L.S., Cole, M., John-Steiner, V., Scribner, S., & Souberman, E. (eds.). 1978. *Mind in society*. Boston, MA: Harvard University Press. https://doi.org/10.2307/j.ctvjf9vz4

Waghid, Y. 2008. Democratic citizenship, education and friendship revisited: In defence of democratic justice. *Studies in Philosophy and Education*, 27:197–206. https://doi.org/10.1007/s11217-007-9090-y

3 Dialectical reasoning and communicative rationality as emancipatory forces in African higher education

A reflection on my doctoral encounters

Lester Brian Shawa

Introduction

Doctoral studies are often rigorous and require serious intellectual pursuit. In fact, doctoral studies constitute an *adventure* – that intellectual experience that allows one to articulate one's thoughts based on one's encounters with knowledge and interests guided by whatever rationale (Waghid, 2023). My doctoral adventure was guided by the belief that both democratic citizenship higher education and an African philosophy of higher education are concerned with the resolution of problems that have implications for higher education on the African continent. While the term 'democratic citizenship higher education' is broad, it also entails the development of responsible citizens through the higher education (HE) sectors. This means that higher education must be a site for democratic action in all its facets, including in emancipatory research. For Nussbaum (1997:269–270), a responsible citizen has the capability to cultivate humanity by attending to three capacities:

- the capacity for critical self-examination and critical thinking about one's own culture and traditions;
- the capacity to see oneself as a human being who is bound to all humans with ties of concern; and
- the capacity for narrative imagination – the ability to empathise with others and to put oneself in another's place (Nussbaum, 1997:269–270).

In advancing democratic citizenship higher education and an African philosophy of higher education, Nussbaum's sentiments are pertinent and, if enacted by HE actors, could contribute to solving African HE challenges.

Drawing on Waghid's (2023) understanding of the notion of adventure, my doctoral study, titled *Exploring anti-democratic practices in university policy-steerage, management and governance in Malawi: A critical theory approach*

DOI: 10.4324/9781003530091-4

(2011), was an intellectual experience with built-in impetus to confront problems in the university sector and provide ways towards change. In this way, the study was in line with both democratic citizenship higher education and an African philosophy of higher education concerned with the resolution of problems that have implications for higher education on the African continent. In other words, my doctoral adventure and encounters with knowledge and my interests culminated in a philosophical pursuit aimed at enhancing the notion of democratic citizenship higher education while advocating for critique and disruption of the status quo – emancipation. It is for this reason that my study posed two critical theory-related questions:

- *What is the nature of anti-democratic practices in university policy-steerage, management, and governance in Malawi at international, university, and government level?*
- *What nature of social change or emancipation is required in university policy-steerage, management, and governance in Malawi at international, university, and government level?*

It is not my intention to rewrite the thesis in this chapter but rather to show my interests that have remained philosophical, democratic, and emancipatory in nature and how my study provided space for adventure and encounters with knowledge. These experiences have shaped my current post-graduate teaching and learning, post-graduate supervision, HE researches, HE community service as well as HE governance style – simply put, they have shaped my professional world view.

Two philosophical ideas informed my doctoral adventure and encounters with knowledge and my interests: *dialectical reasoning* (Adorno, 1982) and *communicative rationality* (complemented by the theory of lifeworld (Habermas, 1984, 1987)). Dialectical reasoning entails understanding things as they are now and what they might be in future. It is therefore a useful idea for emancipation in that it fosters constant questioning (reflexivity) on the part of actors to make things better (Adorno, 1982; Carr, 2000; How, 2003). Communicative rationality entails that actors seek to reach common understanding and coordinate actions by reasoned arguments, consensus, and cooperation rather than instrumental reasoning and is useful for attaining social change (Habermas, 1984, 1987). The phrase 'instrumental reasoning' was coined by Horkheimer (1895–1973) to mean purposive reason, oriented towards means to the exclusion of ends (Habermas, 1984, 1987; Rasmussen, 2004). Instrumental reasoning is therefore used to explain the deliberate use of reason to manipulate society and exert power for social control (Shawa, 2011, 2012, 2013).

Drawing on the belief that both democratic citizenship higher education and an African philosophy of higher education are concerned with the resolution of problems that have implications for higher education on the African continent, my doctoral study revealed challenges of policy-steerage, management, and governance of the university in Malawi and suggested ways to enact change (Shawa, 2011, 2012, 2013).

I present this chapter in five sections with the introduction first followed by a section on my doctoral adventure and encounters with knowledge and my interests. In this section, I briefly explain the nature of the problems my doctoral study confronted. In the third section, I briefly explain my doctoral adventure, my encounters with knowledge, and my interests related to the approach I used to resolve the problems. The fourth section is dedicated to a discussion of how my doctoral adventure, my encounters with knowledge, and my interests have shaped my professional world view. Finally, I present the conclusion.

Doctoral adventures and encounters: The problems

During my doctoral adventure, literature was clear that most studies on African higher education experienced a number of challenges, such as those dealing with access to university education, teaching and learning, growth of private universities, financing, ageing teaching staff as well as outdated curricula (see Assié-Lumumba, 2005, 2006; Banya, 2001; Banya & Elu, 2001; Bloom & Rosovsky, 2007; Ishengoma, 2004; Johnstone, 2004; Levy, 1999, 2007; Ramphele, 2004; Teferra & Altbach, 2004). While African HE researchers and scholars confront these challenges, most of them pay little attention to problems that are beyond nomothetic stances of positivist theorising. In other words, the researchers and scholars tend to reduce the problems to measurability, and those problems that do not fit within the measurability lens were neglected.

My doctoral adventure was thus positioned within critical theory to go beyond positivist measurability and interpretivist theorising to suggesting change. Drawing on critical theory, the study revealed problems related to policy-steerage, management, and governance in Malawi at both international and national policy-steerage levels as well as at university level (Shawa, 2011, 2013). For example, at international policy-steerage level, university policymaking in Malawi was affected by the global neoliberal logic while at national level, policy-steerage was interventionist and characterised by both neopatrimonial[1] aspects of the 'big-man syndrome'[2] and patron–client relationships that led to instrumental use of reason (Shawa, 2011, 2012, 2013). At university level, the neopatrimonial modes were apparent along with a rivalry relationship among academics and administrators, which constrained collegial governance (Shawa, 2011, 2012, 2013).

Doctoral adventures and encounters: Approach to resolve problems

Given the challenges indicated, my doctoral adventures and encounters were anchored in changing the status quo, drawing on Horkheimer's (1976) suggestion summarised by Bohman (1996) that critical theory is adequate only if it meets three criteria:

> [I]t must be explanatory, practical, and normative, all at the same time. That is, it must explain what is wrong with current social reality, identify actors to change it, and provide both clear norms for criticism and practical goals for the future.
>
> (Bohman, 1996:190)

My study thus explained what was wrong with policy-steerage, management, and governance in the Malawian HE context, identified actors to change it, and provided both clear norms for criticism and practical goals for the future. I identified, for example, university administrators or managers, government policymakers, Malawian civil society leaders, leaders of staff, and student unions in Malawian universities as well as international policymakers as actors to resolve the challenges encountered and to provide social change. After delineating clear norms for criticisms, I developed a theory of university management and governance based on critical theory as a way of achieving emancipation in the university sector in Malawi. The theory was based on the notions of dialectical reasoning and communicative rationality as noted earlier.

Dialectical reasoning as an emancipatory force to resolve the problems

Given the challenges of the university policy-steerage, management, and governance I encountered during my doctoral adventure, I needed to provide solutions that could offer new ways of thinking and doing. These required a change of attitudes as well as solutions that were not quick positivist fixes but rather theoretically grounded. Dialectical reasoning provided one way of assisting identified actors of change to bring about social change. As noted, the idea of dialectical reasoning entails understanding things as they are now, and what they might be in future (Adorno, 1982; Carr, 2000; How, 2003). The idea was to assist actors of change to be reflexive and to imagine that things could be better than they were. For example, they were expected to challenge neopatrimonial attitudes that permeate policy-steerage, governance, and management of the university sector in Malawi. Carr (2000) provides insight into how such problems could be challenged using dialectical reasoning:

> The dialectical process begins with a thesis, any definable reality that is the starting point from which all further developments precedes ... reflection progresses and this thesis is seen to encompass its opposite or antithesis as part of its very definition. One moment of the dialectic process gives rise to its own negation ... what emerges from the dialectic of affirmation and negation is a transcendent moment that at once negates, affirms, and incorporates all the previous moments.
>
> (Carr, 2000:212–213)

Dialectical reasoning thus demands constant questioning or reflexivity conceived as involving three moments: thesis, antithesis, and synthesis. As delineated by Carr (2000), if actors of change could go through the dialectical process on a matter such as neopatrimonialism that permeate the university system, the actors would allow for rigorous critique to improve the situation. The idea is that, utilising this constant questioning, reality embodies the reflexive mind that negates the self-evident nature of reality to imagine or re-imagine the future – the better future. The understanding of imagination or re-imagination of the better future is well encapsulated by Adorno's (1982) description of the notion of dialectal reasoning:

> Dialectics is the quest to see the new in the old instead of just the old in the new. As it mediates the new, so it preserves the old as the mediated. If it were to proceed according to the schema of sheer flow and indiscriminate vitality, then it would degrade itself to a replica of the amorphous structure of nature, which it should not sanction through mimicry, but surpass through cognition. Dialectics gives its own to the old as reified and consolidated, which dialectic can move only by realising the force of its own weight.
>
> (Adorno, 1982:38–39)

Adorno's reflection here is quite useful in that dialectical reasoning entails seeing the new in the old – not just the new but the better new by avoiding mimicry – and to just come up with the same reality (e.g. policy) but engage through cognition to bring about change (e.g. better policy). Applied to the identified actors of change in the university sector in Malawi, the actors needed to see the new in the old university policies and governance systems, and to avoid mimicry while providing necessary social change through cognition. The other tenet is communicative rationality, which is discussed next.

Communicative rationality as an emancipatory force to resolve the problems

Communicative rationality (Habermas, 1984) complemented dialectical reasoning (Adorno, 1982) as theoretical contributions to confront the challenges the university in Malawi faced. Since the theory of communicative rationality is against instrumental reasoning (manipulative behaviour using reason) in its quest for actors to seek to reach common understanding and coordinate actions by reasoned arguments, consensus, and cooperation (Habermas, 1984), it was useful in conceiving social change in policy-steerage, management, and governance in Malawian universities.

The theory of communicative rationality is itself complemented by the idea of *lifeworld* – a cultural, social, and shared meaning context (Habermas, 1984). The "lifeworld provides context in which actors come to know themselves, where they ask questions of each other raising validity claims about what is true or force, right or wrong, about what should or should not happen" (How, 2003:128). A lifeworld thus ought to have provided university administrators or managers, government policymakers, Malawian civil society leaders, members of staff, and student unions in Malawian universities as well as international policymakers a context for valid claims through argumentation to make policy-steerage, management, and governance better. Argumentation was therefore not used just to support the status quo but also to help provide what Adorno (1982) refers to as the new that results from cognition rather than mimicry.

Overall, a combination of dialectical reasoning, communicative rationality (together with the notion of lifeworld) is pertinent to be employed for social change or emancipation. While I have fully developed the theory of university management and governance based on these theoretical positions in my PhD thesis, there is no space to repeat the positions in this chapter. Suffice to argue that my doctoral adventure and encounters with knowledge and my interests highlight that both democratic citizenship higher education and an African philosophy of higher education are concerned with the resolution of problems that have implications for higher education on the African continent. As noted earlier, in this chapter, my intention is to show how my study provided space for adventure and encounters with knowledge and my interests that have remained philosophical, democratic, and emancipatory in nature. These experiences have shaped my current HE teaching and learning, HE research, post-graduate supervision, HE community service as well as HE governance style.

Doctoral adventures and encounters with knowledge and my interests: Shaping my current professional practice

My doctoral adventures and encounters with knowledge and my interests have shaped my current professional practice. The idea is that in enacting these, I draw on my world view that democratic citizenship higher education and an African philosophy of higher education are concerned with the resolution of problems that have implications for higher education on the African continent.

Doctoral adventures and encounters with knowledge and my interests: Lessons for my post-graduate teaching and learning

Since completing my doctorate, I have mostly taught and facilitated post-graduate teaching and learning (master's and doctoral students). While drawing on philosophy (and sociology) of higher education, I delve into several subjects in the field of higher education touching on HE context and policy, HE leadership and governance, teaching and learning in higher education, designing and evaluating curricula for higher education, and the philosophy of education research. At this level, these subjects require thorough philosophical thought, as students need to see the new in the old (dialectical reasoning) and exercise argumentation (communicative rationality).

Drawing on my professional world view, I therefore help students to approach learning as dialectical. This means facilitating students to question and provide an assessment of their learning – the quest to see the new in the old, instead of just the old in the new. This is an invitation to students to be reflexive in their approach and to imagine the possibility of the new. Students need to know that they just do not have to accept class work as given but they may challenge it to think about making things better. Students are, for instance, invited to analyse and evaluate HE policy, curricula design, teaching and learning, university leadership and governance as well as research, and they may also act as agents of change in the African HE landscape. Drawing on communicative rationality, I invite students to deliberate, that is to seek to reach common understanding and coordinate actions by reasoned arguments, consensus, and cooperation, rather than instrumental reasoning or strategic action aimed at manipulation (Habermas, 1984). In this way, students learn to share knowledge, shape each other's knowing, and help each other to correct misconceptions.

One way to support dialectical reasoning as well as communicative rationality has been my use of the socio-cultural theory in the classroom. The socio-cultural theory – also referred to as the social constructivist perspective (Vygotsky, 1978) – posits that reality is socially constructed (Shunk, 2012; Subban, 2006). Socio-cultural theory maintains that the social context is vital for higher-order learning. In utilising the socio-cultural theory, Shawa (2020a:196) posits:

> Particular teaching methods are needed such as working in teams (to facilitate social learning), attention to diversity in engaging with participants (to facilitate learning from different perspectives), understanding students' prior knowledge … and reflecting on experiences (to facilitate one's construction of reality).

Working in teams to facilitate social learning helps students to engage in dialectical reasoning and be reflexive. They therefore use cognition to imagine and re-imagine better new knowledge. When teams are organised with attention to diversity, communicative rationality is enhanced and enriched by various perspectives. Students thus learn to substantiate their talk, taking into consideration varied views.

Doctoral adventures and encounters with knowledge and my interests: Lessons for my post-graduate supervision

Post-graduate supervision (master's and doctoral) requires understanding of students' background, the nature of knowledge production to be engaged in, as well as the context of the production of knowledge. This means that post-graduate supervision is not some kind of laissez-faire activity by the academic; it is genuine guidance provided to students to bring about students' adventures and encounters with knowledge and their interests. As a supervisor, I help students to own their studies by encouraging them to engage freely in their adventures (i.e. intellectual pursuit) as they encounter knowledge and their interests.

Understanding or getting to know my students' backgrounds helps me to understand their lifeworlds, including those aspects of their lifeworlds that could negatively influence their world views in relation to their doctoral study. This provides a starting point to our journey, which entails constant questioning and reflexivity. Drawing on dialectical reasoning, I therefore start by inviting students to read around their topics and to begin to question their own knowledge. This helps students to challenge their lifeworlds, and they begin to engage with the literature in the belief that new things could emerge. In other words, what they read points to something worthwhile but not to finality (i.e. rather seeing the new in the old) and therefore constant evaluation and assessment are necessary.

Drawing on communicative rationality, I invite post-graduate students to share their knowledge and arguments through seminars, debates, conference presentations, and whole class discussions. From time to time, students learn from invited guest lecturers who share thoughts on topical issues surrounding the students' work. Engagement in these platforms – which are typical of the socio-cultural theory methodology – helps students to learn to substantiate their claims through reasoned arguments, consensus, and cooperation and to guard against instrumental reasoning. As the students grow and eventually develop their theses, they address the challenges facing African higher education and their advocacy for critique.

Doctoral adventures and encounters with knowledge and my interests: Lessons for my research

As is evident by now, my research is embedded in (post-)critical theory with connotations of social justice, social change, and emancipation in African higher education. To reiterate, this translates into the belief that both democratic citizenship higher education and an African philosophy of higher education are concerned with the resolution of problems that have implications for higher education on the African continent. In undertaking my research, I therefore constantly seek to identify problems, seek actors to effect social change, and provide ways of change. Anchoring my research in dialectical reasoning and communicative rationality, I also constantly draw on reflexivity and deliberation. Since this chapter already exemplifies the nature of the research that I do, I now turn to three examples from my recent research to clarify the nature of my research further.

My recent HE research centred on *ubuntu* ethics in African higher education, transformation of higher education in South Africa, the role of middle managers in African higher education, teaching and learning in higher education, decolonisation of higher education, ontological and epistemological dimensions in higher education, and development effectiveness, especially within the realms of international development. In these research works, I have constantly applied my professional world view in executing the studies.

For example, my research on an *ubuntu* ethic (the interconnectedness of humanity – we exist because of others) has drawn on *ubuntu* to advocate for a (post-)critical theory application in African higher education to conceive social change or emancipation (see Waghid et al., 2023). Such an understanding proposes that universities ought to draw on *ubuntu* values, such as compassion, reciprocity, dignity, humanity and mutuality, to make teaching and learning, research, governance, and community service better – especially if enacted within dialectical reasoning and communicative rationality.

My research on HE transformation in South Africa (see Shawa, 2019a) makes a poignant point that the SA HE sector emphasises the epistemological dimension (learning and knowledge production) rather than the ontological (being, what one becomes), and that in this way, genuine transformation is impeded. The idea is that knowledge alone is not enough to lead to transformation without considering what students eventually become in society. In this research, I argued that any meaningful HE transformation in South Africa requires balancing the epistemological and the ontological dimensions.

My research on African higher education and decolonisation was also conceived with a need for social change (see Shawa, 2019b). Drawing on lenses of solving problems, Shawa (2019b) advances:

> [D]ecolonisation is a necessary project in society and especially the South African higher education context. However, that merely changing pedagogic styles and content to reflect context without a robust conceptualisation of the notion of education cannot lead to decolonisation. I draw on Aristotelian notions of practical reason, phronäsis (conceiving the end to be as well as correct deliberation on how to achieve it), and potentiality, dynamis (that people have the potential to become what they can or not). I further draw on the Platonic idea espoused in the allegory of the cave (the liberating power of education) to propose a concept of education woven within practical reasoning, potentiality and liberation that has intrinsic power to decolonise or which could prepare people better to decolonise.
> (Shawa, 2019c:90)

These three examples, together with what this chapter espouses, provide examples of how my world view has shaped the nature of the research that I do in African higher education.

Doctoral adventures and encounters with knowledge and my interests: Lessons for my community engagement

My professional world view has also influenced the way I theorise community engagement. In my professional work, community engagement is not a way of getting data for research; it is rather about engaging the community in identifying challenges, identifying actors of change, and theorising change or enacting social change. I provide an example of how I understand community engagement within the realms of my world view.

For example, in a recent study (Shawa, 2020b), realising the challenges universities in South Africa face in conceptualising and enacting community service, I developed a combined epistemological-ontological conception of community engagement that could help solve the challenges in the SA HE sector. I argued that first, university induction programmes, which tend to prioritise the teaching and researching roles of staff members, should consider community engagement as equally important. Second, just as the teaching and researching roles tend to be well planned and/or incentivised, so too should community engagement. Third, community engagement should adopt a mode 2 knowledge production lens where community members reflexively produce knowledge together with members of the university staff and contribute to holistic human development.

I argued for the need to embed the epistemological-ontological conception of community engagement at all three levels (induction, planning, and enactment). The epistemological-ontological conception has five activities.

- First is the need to provide space for knowledge production or epistemological growth, where activities should aim to introduce or increase staff members' knowledge of community engagement.
- Second, there is a need for self-intellectual engagement, where academics embrace self-criticism and are assisted to use community engagement as a way of learning new ways of solving problems or engaging with knowledge.
- Third, concern for social justice where community service is seen as an arena for promoting social justice should be promoted.
- Fourth, dispositions of empathy, respect, and deliberation should be developed to assist staff to learn to engage with communities with respect, while encouraging a deliberative spirit that could allow all to engage freely, listen to one another, assess one another, and be able to make decisions together.
- Lastly, a sense of agency should be developed among staff to correct social injustices in the communities.

Doctoral adventures and encounters with knowledge and my interests: Lessons for my university governance style

After my doctoral studies, I have held governance responsibilities in universities. For example, I have served as a deputy dean of an education faculty and as a coordinator of post-graduate studies. As a leader in an African university, one experiences several challenges that include student activism, access to university education, a lack of resources, and poverty. Mediating such problems within the university can be daunting. In enacting my university governance-related responsibilities, I have applied my professional world view – seeing the new in the old and promoting deliberation. As an academic administrator (deputy dean) and programme coordinator, I paid special attention to leading in relation to curriculum planning and pedagogical dimensions, communicating with members of the faculty, communicating with students, communicating with administrators and university managers, and the need for capacity development for academic programme leaders (Shawa, 2019d).

My governance style could be said to be democratic and draws on dialectical reasoning as I strive to be reflexive about my actions related to others within the university as well as about governance responsibilities prescribed to the office that I hold. Drawing on communicative rationality, I strive to work with others as well as through university committees by paying attention to the tenets of reason, inclusivity, domination-free environment (establishing an environment where everyone can freely contribute), equality, and consensus.

Conclusion

In this chapter, I have argued that my doctoral study provided space for adventure and encounters with knowledge and my interests that have remained philosophical, democratic, and emancipatory in nature. I have shown that my study was in line with both democratic citizenship higher education and an African philosophy of higher education concerned with the resolution of problems that have implications for higher education on the African continent. In other words, my doctoral adventure and encounters with knowledge and my interests culminated into a philosophical pursuit aimed at enhancing the notion of democratic citizenship higher education while advocating for criticism and disruption of the status quo. Further, I have shown how these experiences have shaped my current professional practice. Most pertinent, I have shown how the notions of dialectical reasoning, communicative rationality (with the idea of lifeworld) guided my doctoral adventures and remain plausible with (post-)critical theory theorising in bringing about social change in African higher education.

Key lessons learned

Through my doctoral adventures and encounters, I have learned that doctoral students should be open to critique. In this way, doctoral students do not hold any knowledge as static (in finality); rather, knowledge and its production remain in-becoming. It is only through constant critique and reflexivity that knowledge could contribute to making the world better, that is, making the human condition better. Further, a deliberative approach that is the heart of communicative rationality is important for doctoral students to shape or refine their thoughts. Most importantly, my doctoral adventures and encounters have helped me to reflect on the importance of applying what we learn from the adventures and encounters to our professional life.

Notes

1 Neopatrimonialism refers to government systems in which formal structures and rules exist, although in practice the separation of the private and the public sphere is not always observed. The patrimonial of the personal relations and the legal-rational of the bureaucracy exist and permeate each other (Engel & Erdmann, 2007).
2 The 'big-man syndrome' refers to the domination of one individual or groups of individuals who strive to exert absolute rule over others (Bratton & van de Walle, 1997).

References

Adorno, T. 1982. *Against epistemology: A metacritique*. Oxford: Basil Blackwell.
Assié-Lumumba, N. 2005. Critical perspectives on the crises, planned change and the prospects for transformation in African higher education. *JHEA/RESA*, 3(3):1–29.
Assié-Lumumba, N. 2006. *Higher education in Africa: Crisis, reforms and transformation*. Dakar: CODESRIA.
Banya, K. 2001. Are private universities the solution to the higher education crisis in sub-Saharan Africa? *Higher Education Policy*, 14(16):161–174.
Banya, K. & Elu, J. 2001. The World Bank and financing higher education in sub-Saharan Africa. *Higher Education*, 42(1):1–34.
Bloom, D. & Rosovsky, H. 2007. Higher education in developing countries. In J. Forest & P. Altbach (eds.). *International handbook of higher education*. Volume 18. Dordrecht: Springer, 443–459.
Bohman, J. 1996. Critical theory and democracy. In D. Rasmussen (ed.). *The handbook of critical theory*. Cambridge: Blackwell, 190–215.
Bratton, M. and van de Walle, N. 1997. *Democratic experiments in Africa: Regime transitions in comparative perspective*. Cambridge: Cambridge University.
Carr, A. 2000. Critical theory and the management of change in organisations. *Journal of Organisational Change*, 13(3):208–220.
Engel, U. & Erdmann, G. 2007. Neoptarimonialism reconsidered: Critical review and elaboration of an elusive concept. *Commonwealth & Comparative Politics*, 45(1):95–119.
Habermas, J. 1984. *The theory of communicative action: Reason and the rationalisation of society*. Boston, MA: Beacon.
Habermas, J. 1987. *The theory of communicative action: Lifeworld and system: A critique of functionalist reason*. Boston, MA: Beacon.
Horkheimer, M. 1976. Traditional and critical theory. In P. Connerton (ed.). *Critical sociology: Selected readings*. Harmondsworth: Penguin, 206–224.
How, A. 2003. *Critical theory*. New York: Palgrave Macmillan.
Ishengoma, M.J. 2004. Cost-sharing in higher education in Tanzania: Fact or fiction. *JHEA/RESA*, 2(2):101–133.
Johnstone, B.B. 2004. Higher education finance and accessibility: Tuition fees and student loans in sub-Saharan Africa. *JHEA/RESA*, 2(2):11–36.
Levy, D. 1999. When private higher education does not bring organisational diversity. In P. Altbach (ed.). *Private Prometheus: Private higher education and development in the 21st century*. London: Greenwood Press, 15–44.
Levy, D. 2007. A recent echo: African private higher education in an international perspective. *JHEA/RESA*, 5(2/3):197–220.

Nussbaum, B. 1997. *Cultivating humanity: A classical defence for reform in liberal education*. Cambridge, MA: Harvard University.
Ramphele, M. 2004. The university as an actor in development: New perspectives and demands. *JHEA/RESA*, 2(1):15–33.
Rasmussen, D. 2004. Critical theory and philosophy. In D. Rasmussen & J. Swindal (eds.). *Critical theory*. London: Sage, 3–28.
Shawa, L.B. 2011. Exploring anti-democratic practices in university policy-steerage, management and governance in Malawi: A critical theory approach. Unpublished thesis. Stellenbosch: Stellenbosch University.
Shawa, L.B. 2012. The big-man syndrome as a security threat in Malawi: A critical theory perspective. *Southern African Peace and Security Studies*, 1(2):44–56.
Shawa, L.B. 2013. Governance in Malawian universities: The role of dialectical reasoning and communicative rationality. *South African Journal of Higher Education*, 27(1):221–238.
Shawa, L.B. 2019a. Academic programme leadership in African higher education: A phenomenological reflection. *Journal of Higher Education in Africa*, 17(1/2):129–144.
Shawa, L.B. 2019b. Beyond epistemology: Ontological transformation in South African universities. In E. Ivala & D. Scott (eds.). *The status of transformation in higher education institutions in post-apartheid South Africa*. New York: Routledge, 109–120.
Shawa, L. B. (2019c). Knowledge Production and epistemic justice in African Higher Education. In T. Halvorsen & J. Nossum (eds.), *North-south knowledge networks: Towards equitable collaboration between academics, donors and universities* (pp. 75–95). African Minds, Cape Town, South Africa.
Shawa, L.B. 2019d. In defence of education that embodies decolonisation. In C. Manthalu & Y. Waghid (eds.). *Education for decoloniality and decolonisation*. Springer: Palgrave Macmillan, 89–109.
Shawa, L.B. 2020a. Advancing the Scholarship of Teaching and Learning (SoTL) using learning theories and reflectivity. *Centre for Educational Policy Studies Journal*, 10(1):191–208.
Shawa, L.B. 2020b. The public mission of universities in South Africa: Community engagement and the teaching and researching roles of faculty members. *Tertiary Education and Management*, 26:105–116.
Shunk, D. 2012. *Learning theories: An education perspective*. Boston, MA: Pearson Education.
Subban, P. 2006. Differentiated instruction: A research basis. *International Education Journal*, 7(7):935–947.
Teferra, D. & Altbach, P. 2004. African higher education: Challenges for the 21st century. *Higher Education*, 47(1):21–50.
Vygotsky, L. 1978. *Mind and society*. Cambridge, MA: Harvard University.
Waghid, Y. 2023. *Philosophical, educational and moral openings in doctoral pursuits and supervision: Promoting the values of wonder, wander, and whisper in African higher education*. London: Routledge.
Waghid, Y., Terblanche, J., Shawa, L.B., Hungwe, J.P., Waghid, F. & Waghid, Z. 2023. An African university and claims of democratic citizenship education. In Y. Waghid, J. Terblanche, L.B. Shawa, J.P. Hungwe, F. Waghid & Z. Waghid (eds.). *Towards an ubuntu university: Africa higher education reimagined*. Cham: Palgrave Macmillan, 77–84. https://doi.org/10.1007/978-3-031-06454-8_1

4 Democratic citizenship education and its effects on employability
A reflection of my doctoral encounters

Sithobile Priscilla Dube

Introduction

In Zimbabwe, employability is at an extremely low level (Tapfuma, Chikuta, Ncube, Baipai, Mazhande, & Basera, 2021), making it difficult to find work, even with the highest qualifications, while universities consistently produce graduates, and industries struggle to fill open positions (Tapfuma *et al.*, 2021). Graduates from African higher education institutions (HEIs) have undoubtedly increased due to the massification of university students and rising enrolment (Mohamedbhai, 2014; Wildschut, Rogan, & Mncwango, 2020). The manufacturing sector is fighting low-capacity utilisation as the Zimbabwean economy struggles to recover from the hyperinflation era, and human capital management is crucial in helping businesses regain their productive capacities (Mohamedbhai, 2014; Ngwenya & Pelser, 2020). Reviewing democratic actions in higher education both before and after independence, as well as the implications for employment difficulties, was the focus of the study reported here. Since the declaration of independence in Zimbabwe on 18 April 1980 (Kufakurinani, 2021), several developments have taken place. Further discussion addresses the ongoing educational changes that have been in place since independence in 1980, focusing on their potential to affect the economy. The role of universities and their participation as stakeholders are heavily emphasised. The democratic educational initiative in Zimbabwe is anticipated to significantly enhance the country's economy in the long term (Chirisa, Mhlanga, Matamanda, & Ncube, 2021).

Democratic citizenship education defined

As I reflect on my experience as an educator and my doctoral studies, I have observed that students require the freedom and skills necessary to participate in unrestricted debate and critique in democratic citizenship education (DCE) (Monicah, 2018). Davids and Waghid (2020:4) articulate the importance of university teachers to lead activities because of their position of authority. Teachers at universities should, however, encourage their students to interact with their peers in a way that benefits both students and teachers. University

DOI: 10.4324/9781003530091-5

teachers accomplish the aforementioned by recognising their student's intellectual potential. Previous studies purport that DCE is purposeful involvement, compassionate imagination, and connection with others through *ubuntu* (i.e. human dignity and collective participation) (Chiroma, 2015; Monicah, 2018). Additionally, Yitzhaki, Gallagher, Aloni, and Gross (2022:72) advocate that forgiveness and respect in DCE are essential. In support of the notion of forgiveness and respect, to interact, people should have respect for one another. People must be able to put aside their differences and show compassion for one another to communicate and be amicable. Violence would be eliminated because of the respect and forgiveness that would grow from DCE. The DCE principles state that when people are educated following their principles, even opposing factions can begin to live in harmony and peace (Waghid, Waghid, & Waghid, 2018).

Furthermore, in DCE, there is active participation and a sense of belonging to create connections with one another (Waghid & Davids, 2017:3). People are therefore allowed to interact freely and on an equal footing here. Individuals consequently support the mission of education and feel a sense of belonging. DCE is an educational process that develops people into democratic citizens with a sense of community and the creation of educational places that are both physically and virtually conducive to the development of individuals (Waghid & Davids, 2017). Learning areas serve as places for communication. Learning how to coexist, share, and find common ground as well as these spaces aid individuals in respecting one another's differences when there are disagreements (Ellis & Goodyear, 2016; Finkelstein, Ferris, Weston, & Winer, 2016). People are protected from violence and can forgive the unforgivable where there are areas for refuge and calm (Waghid, 2013). They are made aware of their political participation, and the environment is set up to educate them to become democratic citizens (Chinyonga & Kurebwa, 2023). Ultimately, people are taught to embrace the fact that they cannot be excluded from positions, that they have a right to be heard, and that they may participate in their community (Ngubane & Makua, 2021).

Since gaining its independence in 1980, Zimbabwe has made significant efforts to achieve DCE by ensuring that all individuals have access to education at all levels of primary, secondary, and higher education (Monicah, 2018; Zembere, 2018). Zimbabwe has, however, faced significant difficulties in its quest to achieve democracy to address social evils and inequalities (Chapfika, 2023; Nhapi, 2022).

Prior research substantiates the belief that people need education that incorporates all groups of people, allowing students, parents, teachers, and employees to participate in the creation of a new educational system that aids in the development of democratic persons and actively engages in addressing issues that arise (Bailey, 2014; Tibbitts, 2015; Zembylas & Keet, 2018). Universities have the responsibility of developing places where people can interact and connect (Ferri, Grifoni, & Guzzo, 2020). To avoid fostering inequality, public education should continue to offer opportunities to both rich and less privileged students (Lumadi, 2020; Muridzo, Mukurazhizha, & Simbine, 2022).

What is democracy?

Democracy is a form of representative government and a setting for social and political life where individuals have access to equal opportunities, and where they can pursue their own personal development, fulfillment, and self-determination (Waghid, 2014). The democratic process is a political process that allows citizens to have a say in how their government operates. In a democracy, citizens can vote for their representatives, who are responsible for making decisions on their behalf. Overall, a democratic process is based on the principle of equality and fairness for all (Christiano, 2018). Democracy can be a kind of representational governance in which only elected officials and voters who have already cast their ballots can make decisions. This is also viewed as a form of representative government that engages in political decision-making and has an influence on several facets of the nation, including the educational system (Mutamiri, 2019). Democracy is also referred to as a social connection space that rejects class divisions and opportunity equality for all citizens (Waghid, 2014). The goal will be to guarantee that all citizens:

- participate based on equality and liberty;
- have the freedom to live the lives they choose;
- are capable individuals actively participating in economic, political, and social life; and
- are included and no one is left silent (Waghid, 2014:15).

Everyone can take part, develop his or her ability to make reasoned decisions and participate as much as possible. A strong democracy illustrates how people can come together and find the will to accomplish goals in common (Cheeseman & Sishuwa, 2021).

University education before Zimbabwean independence in 1980

Research shows that, during the colonial period, there were significant educational disparities (Garwe, 2014) and not much was said about democratic university education (Garwe, 2014). Before independence in 1980, the bulk of black people in Zimbabwe had to work on farms and in mines while the white minority had access to education. The colonial system that split education along racial lines and which was operated on a racial basis was complex (Garwe, 2014; Maylette & Wride, 2017). According to Mawere (2015), Zimbabwean traditional knowledge and educational objectives focus on the growth of the entire individual. When examining the educational objectives before independence, it becomes clear that they were solely directed towards the white minority, which influenced the black majority. According to Shizha

(2013b), the colonial administration restricted education and suppressed knowledge in schools to control the populace.

Shizha (2013a) adds that the educational policy was to prevent the indigenous people from entering the modern industrial economy, which belonged to the European settlers. As a result, Africans were denied advanced skills for self-sufficiency and self-determination in the new socio-economic order (Shizha, 2013a). People who attended colonial schools were not exposed to practical knowledge that was appropriate for realities in their community (Muzira & Bondai, 2020). Missionary schools, for instance, continued to oppress the indigenous population on social and economic level by decreasing their prospects of obtaining high-paying employment or influential positions, and by providing them with a meagre education and basic skills that allowed them to be used as cheap labour (Shizha, 2013a). Because the colonial authority limited entrance to reputable institutions based on race and socio-economic class, Europeans received disproportionately more educational resources than the majority black population (Blakemore & Cooksey, 2017).

Msila (2013) examines the fight for democratic education in South Africa; Msila articulates and offers a survey of pertinent literature that reveals how democracy in education benefits the vast majority of (black) South Africans. The study for Msila (2013) provided an excellent opportunity to examine the factors that affected the level of schooling among Africans. Poverty in South Africa can result from a variety of variables that influence educational attainment, such as teachers who lack the necessary training and experience to impart skills to pupils and curriculum changes that occur frequently (Olawale, 2023). Moreover, Msila (2013) examines a variety of subjects, including power dynamics, post-apartheid educational alternatives, and other writers' viewpoints on post-independence politics. Msila (2013) keeps referring to the idea that Africans were regarded as less superior and impoverished, and they therefore perceived the colonisers as their providers. All these problems highlight the negative effects of democratic legislation passed by the white majority on the black majority. It is evident from the discussion above that, under the apartheid educational system, learners' difficulties were related to inequality in access to education and resources (Msila, 2013).

University education reforms after Zimbabwean independence in 1980

After independence, education changed for the better (Kufakurinani, 2021). Both the education and the employment sectors saw changes from the 1980s to the 1990s (Kufakurinani, 2021). In his history of Zimbabwean education, Stoneman (2018) together with other researchers note that, after Zimbabwe had gained independence from colonial authority in April 1980, many of its citizens were denied access to opportunities and resources for high-quality secondary education. Just a small percentage was able to complete primary school, while others only completed a few years of it (Ndlovu, 2013). The enhancement of resources, teacher preparation, and school growth all advanced dramatically in Zimbabwe after 1980. Many Zimbabweans reside in rural areas, and there are still big differences in the educational opportunities available to them compared to those who live in the major cities (Nera & Nyikadzino, 2023). Furthermore, because of the improvement in education, Zimbabwe continues to have the highest literacy rate in sub-Saharan Africa and sends the fourth highest number of students from Africa to the United States (Mills, 2014; Nera & Nyikadzino, 2023).

Rather than the predicted democracy and trust, education was around the period of 2003 a source of mistrust and risk, when graduates started to migrate to neighbouring countries and the students would question whether they should take a chance on attending college (Kanonge, 2021; Kołczyńska, 2020). The majority of people preferred to take a chance on expanding backyard markets or leave the nation (Mashaya & Tafirenyika, 2017; Southall, 2020). As a result, they were ready to handle the risks of coming across hazards and effects related to the brain drain that began in 2003 due to a lack of job possibilities and inability to manage businesses (Kanonge, 2021). The two sets of hazards would obviously be: people moulded by industry and research together; and people who are poor or who reside in underdeveloped areas (Kanonge & Bussin, 2022).

It is evident, however, that new policies were put in place to address the past in Zimbabwe once the country had gained its independence in 1980. In addition, Moyo (2019) stipulates that, in 1980, the Mugabe administration altered the constitution to identify primary and secondary public education as free and required and declared it to be a fundamental human right. Looking at the rules that governed education in the era before independence, this was done with the intention of helping the black population (Moyo, 2019). When black people took control of the education system after independence, many things changed. 'Education for all' was made possible by new legislation that governed education (Keche, 2021; Mundy, 2016).

Public schools had large student populations, necessitating many teachers. Even though the infrastructure could not support everyone, it was the responsibility of schools to ensure that everyone had access to education (Pacho, 2017). School had to offer a set of morning classes and a different group of lessons in the afternoon because of the implementation of double-session schooling. This was done to address the problem that had emerged and is still in use today. However, the school system today is still working on finding other options that possibly will be satisfactory (Pacho, 2017; Singh & Mukeredzi, 2024). As a result, by offering in-service teacher training, the Ministry of Education quickly increased the number of teacher education colleges. There was an urgent need for more infrastructure and teachers because of the rising number of learners in schools in order to guarantee that democratic education was taking place. The situation however needed time to improve before reforms took effect (Pacho, 2017).

Contrary to the mentioned case above of in-service training and colleges, one might also conclude that there is still lack of trained teachers in secondary schools and it has an influence on educational quality (Goronga, 2014; Singh & Mukeredzi, 2024). Trained teachers migrate to seek for greener pastures in other countries. Due to the high demand for labour and a lack of attention to quality, I have observed from my experience as a teacher that many teachers in rural regions lack training (also see Moyo & Hadebe, 2018; Singh & Mukeredzi, 2024). Given this, the quality of education is greatly impacted by the shortage of qualified teachers and other staff. The employment sector remained affected because skills are crucial in the sector. The consequent brain drain of human resources in the period from 2003 to current date was one consequence of the crisis (Singh & Mukeredzi, 2024).

Over time, the expense of education and tuition had risen. As a result, fewer persons were able to receive tertiary education. Additionally, because tertiary education costs increase, fewer individuals may be able to complete their degrees and find employment (Oreopoulos & Petronijevic, 2013; Singh & Mukeredzi, 2024). It is also clear that most black people ended up working on farms and in mines rather than in other sectors where white people predominately worked before independence. Despite government funding for education, many families were unable to pay tuition fees due to the added costs of building projects, transport, levies and stationery for the students. Due to government spending on educational infrastructure and the effects of the global economic crisis, education cannot be free in Zimbabwe (Hwami, 2024; Shizha, 2013a). Attaining universal 'education for all' was one of the Zimbabwean Millennium Development Goals (MDGs) (Mudyanadzo, 2017). In terms of achieving the Sustainable Development Goal (SDG) of providing universal and free education to all pupils by 2030, the nation is currently making progress (Muchenje, 2024). Zimbabwe continues to have the highest literacy rate in Africa, thanks to significant investments in education. According to Makou and Wilkinson's (2018) report, the literacy rate was 90% by the time of their study. Although the World Bank (2022) states that the regional literacy level is 67%, Zimbabwe has continuously maintained a literacy rate above 90% since 2012 (Mahone, 2022). The literacy rate has been high in recent years; according to Zimstat (2020) and Mahone (2022), it was 96% in 2012 and 2019. However, in 2022, it dropped to 93.7% (Muchenje, 2024).

For a very long time, it had been anticipated that Zimbabwean university education would produce a workforce that is sufficiently skilled and competitive, giving the nation competitive chances in the globalised market economy (Maireva & Mabika, 2022). For the underprivileged, it is however difficult to obtain higher education. The government offers opportunities for students to borrow from banks and financial institutions than ever before to pay for a university education because of rising tuition fees and a decrease in state financial help for students (Massimo, Mavima, & Kurebwa, 2024). Even though university tuition fees are high, most people who have completed their university studies and who have graduated are not able to find employment. This has increased unemployment, which in turn has increased poverty and suffering among people, as funds had been during their studies while hoping for a positive outcome (Chinyoka & Mutambara, 2020). It further appears that colleges have evolved into commercial enterprises. Students are considered as customers who interact with the HE markets, and universities compete with one another to produce and market their courses to students (Mukwambo, 2019).

By disrupting the normal mistrust and criticism of the educational system, which students perceive as being insufficiently relevant to produce employable graduates or job creators, students and educators ultimately succeed in changing students' perceptions. In what Waghid (2014) refers to as 'friendship', democratic individuals would be active participants. The next section highlights the importance of maintaining high standards of education in order to preserve this friendship. It was necessary to revisit the question of whether the education provided was of high quality in light of the debate on considering high-quality education.

Quality education revisited

'Quality' is a vague and ambiguous concept. It is challenging to accomplish because it is dependent on one's own emotions, preferences, or ideas. According to Mawere and Rambe (2013), the concept is debatable with some people interpreting it to signify good performance on benchmark examinations, successful completion of learning curricula, as well as low dropout and repetition rates. Surur *et al.* (2020) claim that quality refers to satisfying predetermined requirements and indicators, including appropriate inputs, a successful process, high-quality outputs, and successful results. In schools, 'success' is defined as a recognisable output or score on a test, the completion of the learning curriculum, and low dropout and repetition rates (Fomba, Talla, & Ningaye, 2023). These are merely quantifiable results of different indicators used to assess the effectiveness of the teaching and learning process. According to Marongedza, Hlungwani, and Hove (2023), the school atmosphere, teaching and learning procedures that entail learning and teaching time, as well as student outcomes are elements influencing quality. Supporting input from parents, communities, and the educational system is also a component. Higher education can however result in both public and private advantages. Compared to not having such an education, the private benefits include better work chances, higher salaries, and a stronger opportunity to save and invest (Corak, 2013; Muwaniki, Wedekind, & McGrath, 2024). Good health and a high quality of life may also be outcomes of the advantages, and public benefits may encourage a nation's improvement and technical and economic growth (Bloom, Canning, Chan, & Luca, 2014).

Zimbabwe, an African nation, has the potential to speed up technological dissemination, reducing knowledge gaps and contributing to the reduction of poverty in the area. Modern policies are implemented in Zimbabwe to support tertiary education systems (Garwe & Thondhlana, 2019). In comparison to other parts of the world, progress is however still lacking. The absence of awareness of the benefits that higher education could have on economic development might be to blame (Succi & Canovi, 2020). Students' contentment with their education, ongoing advancements in current standards, and the ability to keep them in educational institutions are all used to measure and judge the quality of education (Stephenson, 2013). In turn, students can choose their courses freely, and course providers do not have to work as hard to sell their courses when institutions provide high-quality education to students. When it comes to the topic of employment, universities do not inform graduates what will happen to them. Zimbabwe and South Africa both face high rates of unemployment (Chikoko, Naicker, & Mthiyane, 2015; Singh & Mukeredzi, 2024). In terms of substance, universities and other educational institutions make an attempt to offer what may be called 'quality education', as we live in a dynamic world that is constantly evolving (Nyakotyo & Goronga, 2024).

Conclusion

As a way of concluding this chapter, it should be mentioned that the definition of education can be understood in two different ways: firstly, as instrumental in that it views education as a tool for achieving specific goals, such as economic productivity, national development, or social mobility (Mpofu, Mpofu, Mantula, & Shava, 2024); and secondly, as consummatory in that it focuses on developing the individual's full potential and providing a fulfilling learning experience, purpose to develop the individual's ability to think critically, appreciate beauty, and live a fulfilling life (Kalyani, 2024) for both personal and for social benefits (Kalyani, 2024). The role that education plays is for personal achievements, i.e. economically, socially, politically, to have a good job, have more money, be employed in a good office, gain political influence for some individuals, and have an educated citizenry (Lengrand, 2016). The scope of education therefore refers to the subject of its advantages and might connect personally to the influence education has on an individual's life or socially in terms of groups or other people (Spiel *et al.*, 2018).

In my opinion, knowledge is beneficial for the sake of education as a necessary precondition for becoming a good person and participating in society. Socially, a person's education is for the benefit of the country. Well-educated citizens make for a good society. Using people's opinions to better the country, making rulers rule, and providing people the freedom to develop the country are, for instance, all benefits that many regard as associated with acquiring education. The connotations of education vary depending on priorities. One person may appreciate education from both the instrumental and consummatory (personal and social) points of view, while another person may only hold one of these perspectives. Education, which relates expectations of work, prestige, and the capacity to fulfilling commitments to parents and relatives thus appears to have a significant role in learners' long-term personal aspirations.

As a result, it should be noted that the employability of democratic citizens after graduation is a concern. On the one hand, graduates are expected to demonstrate sustained participation and engagement in industry as employees or as entrepreneurs and job creators. On the other hand, the demand for universities and educators to produce democratic citizens ready to meet the demands of the market creates competition among universities and the marketplace. Graduates are expected to provide skilled and competitive labour. Universities however experience difficulties in terms of a lack of staff, resources, and money as well as difficulties with teaching and training. Graduates are expected to have the knowledge, traits, and abilities necessary to participate actively in their communities as democratic citizens and to work as professionals for their personal and professional growth.

References

Bailey, R. 2014. *Teaching values and citizenship across the curriculum: Educating children for the world*. New York: Routledge.

Blakemore, K. & Cooksey, B. 2017. *A sociology of education for Africa*. Volume 8. London: Routledge.

Bloom, D.E., Canning, D., Chan, K.J. & Luca, D.L. 2014. Higher education and economic growth in Africa. *International Journal of African Higher Education*, 1(1):22–57.

Chapfika, B. 2023. Critique of education reforms in Zimbabwe: Challenges and prospects. *Journal of African Education*, 4(1):283–313.

Cheeseman, N. & Sishuwa, S. 2021. African studies keyword: Democracy. *African Studies Review*, 64(3):704–732.

Chikoko, V., Naicker, I. & Mthiyane, S. 2015. School leadership practices that work in areas of multiple deprivation in South Africa. *Educational Management Administration & Leadership*, 43(3):452–467.

Chinyoka, A. & Mutambara, E. 2020. The challenges of revenue generation in state universities: The case of Zimbabwe. *Cogent Social Sciences*, 6(1):1–10.

Chinyonga, B.C. & Kurebwa, J. 2023. Effectiveness of transitional justice processes in peacebuilding in Zimbabwe: The case of national peace and reconciliat. *Journal of African Studies and Development*, 15(2):23–25. [Online]. Available at: https://academicjournals.org/journal/JASD/article-full-text-pdf/15FA4FC70685 [Accessed 6 April 2024].

Chirisa, I., Mhlanga, G., Matamanda, A.R. & Ncube, R. 2021. Education and knowledge under the impact of economic stress: Rhodesia 1965–1979 vis-a-vis Zimbabwe since 2002. In N. V. Lopes & R. Baguma (Eds.), *Developing knowledge societies for distinct country contexts* (pp. 180–205). Hershey, PA: IGI Global.

Chiroma, J.A. 2015. Democratic citizenship education and its implications for Kenyan higher education. Unpublished PhD dissertation. Stellenbosch: Stellenbosch University.

Christiano, T. 2018. The authority of democracy. In *Political philosophy in the twenty-first century* (pp. 199–215). Routledge.

Corak, M. 2013. Income inequality, equality of opportunity, and intergenerational mobility. *Journal of Economic Perspectives*, 27(3):79–102.
Davids, N. & Waghid, Y. 2020. *Teaching, friendship and humanity*. Singapore: Springer.
Ellis, R.A. & Goodyear, P. 2016. Models of learning space: Integrating research on space, place and learning in higher education. *Review of Education*, 4(2):149–191.
Ferri, F., Grifoni, P. & Guzzo, T. 2020. Online learning and emergency remote teaching: Opportunities and challenges in emergency situations. *Societies*, 10(4):1–18.
Finkelstein, A., Ferris, J., Weston, C. & Winer, L. 2016. Informed principles for (re)designing teaching and learning spaces. *Journal of Learning Spaces*, 5(1):26–34.
Fomba, B.K., Talla, D.N.D.F. & Ningaye, P. 2023. Institutional quality and education quality in developing countries: Effects and transmission channels. *Journal of the Knowledge Economy*, 14(1):86–115.
Garwe, E.C. 2014. Quality assurance challenges and opportunities faced by private universities in Zimbabwe. *Journal of Case Studies in Education*, 5:2–8.
Garwe, E.C. & Thondhlana, J. 2019. Higher education systems and institutions, Zimbabwe. In Teixeira, P.N. & Shin, J.C. (Editors-in-Chief). *Encyclopedia of international higher education systems and institutions* (pp. 1–11). Dordrecht: Springer.
Goronga, P. 2014. Teachers' and students' perceptions of double session schooling on ordinary level students' performance in Geography. *The International Asian Research Journal*, 02(03):10–16.
Hwami, M. 2024. The challenge for university teaching and research practice in Zimbabwe: An empirical study. *Teaching in Higher Education*, 29(1):266–285.
Kalyani, N. 2024. Philosophy of education: Structuring and perspectives. *International Journal of Research in Social Sciences*, 14(03).
Kanonge, T.T. 2021. *A framework to curb the academic brain drain in Zimbabwean universities*. University of Johannesburg (South Africa).
Kanonge, T.T. & Bussin, M.H.R. 2022. Pre-conditions for employee motivation to curb Zimbabwe's academic brain drain. *SA Journal of Human Resource Management*, 20:18–19.
Keche, K. 2021. Relevancy of new higher education approaches in 'Second Republic Zimbabwe'. In Waller, L. & Waller, S. (Eds). *Higher education: New approaches to accreditation, digitalization, and globalization in the age of Covid*. IntechOpen. Available at: http://dx.doi.org/10.5772/intechopen.99934. 1–11.
Kołczyńska, M. 2020. Democratic values, education, and political trust. *International Journal of Comparative Sociology*, 61(1):3–26.
Kufakurinani, U. 2021. Political history of Zimbabwe since 1980. In *Oxford research encyclopedia of African history*. Oxford: Oxford University Press. https://oxfordre.com/africanhistory/display/10.1093/acrefore/9780190277734.001.0001/acrefore-9780190277734-e-450 (Accessed: 16 July 2024).
Lengrand, P. (Ed.). 2016. *Areas of learning basic to lifelong education*. Volume 10. Oxford: UNESCO Institute for Education Hamburg FRG and Pergamon Press
Lumadi, M.W. 2020. Fostering an equitable curriculum for all: A social cohesion lens. *Education as Change*, 24(1):1–20.
Mahone, T. 2022. '2022 Population and Housing Census Preliminary Results on Education' [Zimstat report] Available at: www.zimstat.co.zw/wpcontent/uploads/2022/10/2022_PHC_Education_Presentation.pdf (Accessed: 8 April 2024).
Maireva, C. & Mabika, P. 2022. Role of the higher and tertiary institutions in human capital development in Zimbabwe. In Lengrand, P. (Ed.), *Areas of learning basic to lifelong education* (Vol. 10, pp. 1–234). Oxford: UNESCO Institute for Education Hamburg FRG and Pergamon Press.

Makou, G. & Wilkinson, K. 2018. Validating 'the truth' about SA's education system. *News24*, 26 April. Retrieved from www.news24.com/news24/opinions/columnists/validating-the-truth-about-sas-education-system-20180426 [Accessed 26 April 2023].

Marongedza, L., Hlungwani, P.M. & Hove, P. 2023. Institutional constraints affecting secondary school student performance: A case study of rural communities in Zimbabwe. *Cogent Education*, 10(1):1–14.

Mashaya, B. & Tafirenyika, M. 2017. New curriculum unworkable. *Nehanda Radio*, 15 February. Retrieved from https://nehandaradio.com/2017/02/15/new-curriculum-unworkable/ [Accessed 8 April 2024].

Massimo, C., Mavima, P. & Kurebwa, J. 2024. Evolution of public-private partnerships in Zimbabwe's state universities. In I. Chirisa, E. Chigudu, & M. Masvaure (Eds.), *Higher education and lifelong learning in Zimbabwe* (pp. 85–102). Springer. Retrieved from https://link.springer.com/book/10.1007/978-3-030-76205-2

Mawere, M. 2015. Indigenous knowledge and public education in sub-Saharan Africa. *Africa Spectrum*, 50(2):57–71.

Mawere, M. & Rambe, P. (Eds). 2013. *Leveraging educational quality in southern African educational systems: A practitioners' perspective*. Cameroon: Langaa RPCIG.

Maylett, T. & Wride, M. 2017. *The employee experience: How to attract talent, retain top performers, and drive results*. London: Wiley.

Mills, G. 2014. *Africa's third liberation*. South Africa: Penguin Random House South Africa.

Mohamedbhai, G. 2014. Massification in higher education institutions in Africa: Causes, consequences and responses. *International Journal of African Higher Education*, 1(1):2–5.

Monicah, Z. 2018. Democratic citizenship education in Zimbabwe's higher education system and its implications for teaching and learning. Unpublished PhD dissertation. Stellenbosch: Stellenbosch University.

Moyo, D. 2019. Sharpening the minds of opponents in opposition movements? Mugabe's education policies in Zimbabwe. In Nhemachena, A. & Warikandwa, T.V. (Eds). *From African peer review mechanisms to African queer review mechanisms? Robert Gabriel Mugabe, empire and the decolonisation of African orifices* (p. 245). Cameroon: Langaa RPCIG.

Moyo, L. & Hadebe, L.B. 2018. The relevance of teacher education as a trajectory in developing and sustaining inclusivity in the digital classroom. *European Journal of Open Education and E-Learning Studies*, 3(1):1–12.

Mpofu, F.Y., Mpofu, A., Mantula, F. & Shava, G.N., 2024. Towards the attainment of SDGs: The contribution of higher education institutions in Zimbabwe. *International Journal of Social Science Research and Review*, 7(1):474–493.

Msila, V. 2013. Democratic education through the eyes of the poor: Appraising the post-apartheid experience. *Universal Journal of Educational Research*, 1(3):191–199.

Muchenje, A. 2024. Effects of declining income and improving education standards on Green Consumerism in Zimbabwe's FMCG Sector. Doctoral dissertation. Dublin Business School.

Mudyanadzo, W. 2017. The post-colonial challenges of nation-building through international engagement: An analysis of Zimbabwe's international relations from 1980 to 2016. Unpublished PhD dissertation. Gweru: Midlands State University.

Mukwambo, P. 2019. *Quality in higher education as a tool for human development: Enhancing teaching and learning in Zimbabwe*. London: Routledge.

Mundy, K. 2016. "Leaning in" on education for all. *Comparative Education Review*, 60(1):1–26.
Muridzo, N., Mukurazhizha, R. & Simbine, S. 2022. Social work in Zimbabwe: From social control to social change. *International Journal of Social Work Values and Ethics*, 19(2):227–243.
Mutamiri, P. 2019. The impact of electoral boundaries on youth participation in governance: Case study of Gweru District in Zimbabwe. *Case Study of Gweru District in Zimbabwe*, 1:1–20.
Muwaniki, C., Wedekind, V. & McGrath, S. 2024. Agricultural vocational education and training for sustainable futures: Responsiveness to the climate and economic crisis in Zimbabwe. *Journal of Vocational Education & Training*, 76(1):1–17.
Muzira, D.R. & Bondai, B.M. 2020. Perception of educators towards the adoption of education 5.0: A case of a state university in Zimbabwe. *East African Journal of Education and Social Sciences*, 1(2):43–53.
Ndlovu, M.E. 2013. Zimbabwe's educational legacy from the 1980s: Was it all so rosy? *The Zimbabwean*, 24 May. Retrieved from www.thezimbabwean.co/2013/05/zimbabwes-educational-legacy-from-the/ [Accessed 7 April 2024].
Nera, G.R. & Nyikadzino, T. 2023. Factors hampering the realization of equity and quality education in Zimbabwe's rural schools: Experiences of Chipinge central circuit, Manicaland. *Journal of Asian and African Studies*, 58(3):341–357
Ngubane, N.I. & Makua, M., 2021. Intersection of Ubuntu pedagogy and social justice: Transforming South African higher education. *Transformation in Higher Education*, 6(0):a113. https://doi.org/10.4102/the.v6i0.113?>
Ngwenya, B. & Pelser, T. 2020. Impact of psychological capital on employee engagement, job satisfaction and employee performance in the manufacturing sector in Zimbabwe. *SA Journal of Industrial Psychology*, 46(1):1–12.
Nhapi, T. 2022. An exploration of the domains of the inequality trajectory in Zimbabwe. *Contemporary Social Science*, 17(2):84–98.
Nyakotyo, C. & Goronga, P. 2024. Resilience strategies for higher education institutions. In *Rebuilding higher education systems impacted by crises: navigating traumatic events, disasters, and more* (pp. 1–18). Hershey, PA: IGI Global.
Olawale, B.E. 2023. Teacher Quality and Learner Achievement in South African Schools. In A. Amara, B. Arasaratnam-Smith, & C. Zhou (Eds.), *Rebuilding higher education systems impacted by crises: Navigating traumatic events, disasters, and more* (pp. 19–36). Hershey, PA: IGI Global.
Oreopoulos, P. & Petronijevic, U. 2013 *Making College Worth It: A Review of Research on the Returns to Higher Education*, NBER working paper series Making college... Available at: www.nber.org/system/files/working_papers/w19053/w19053.pdf [Accessed 5 April 2024].
Pacho, T. 2017. Service-learning in higher education in Zimbabwe. Unpublished PhD dissertation. Germany: Staats- und Universitätsbibliothek Hamburg Carl von Ossietzky.
Shizha, E. 2013a. Reclaiming our indigenous voices: The problem with postcolonial Sub-Saharan African school curriculum. *Journal of Indigenous Social Development*, 2(1):1–14.[Online]. Available at: https://scholarspace.manoa.hawaii.edu/server/api/core/bitstreams/24a9b689-1a2a-4f41-88b2-c41c748c465 [Accessed 5 April 2024].
Shizha, E. (Ed.). 2013b. *Restoring the educational dream: Rethinking educational transformation in Zimbabwe*. Pretoria, South Africa: Africa Institute of South Africa.

Singh, M. & Mukeredzi, T. 2024, February. Teachers' experiences of continuous professional development for citizenship and social cohesion in South Africa and Zimbabwe: Enhancing capacity for deliberative democracies. In In M. A. Peters & R. Heraud (Eds.), *Frontiers in education* (Vol. 9, pp. 1–15). Lausanne, Switzerland: Frontiers Media SA.

Southall, R. 2020. Flight and fortitude: The decline of the middle class in Zimbabwe. *Africa*, 90(3):529–547.

Spiel, C., Schwartzman, S., Busemeyer, M., Cloete, N., Drori, G., Lassnigg, L., Schober, B., Schweisfurth, M. & Verma, S. 2018. The contribution of education to social progress. In: International Panel on Social Progress (Ed). *Rethinking society for the 21st century: Report of the international panel for social progress* (pp. 753–778). Cambridge: Cambridge University Press, https://doi.org/10.1017/978110 8399661.006.

Stephenson, J. 2013. The concept of capability and its importance in higher education. In J. Stephenson & M. Yorke (Eds.), *Capability and quality in higher education* (pp. 1–13). London: Routledge.

Stoneman, C. 2018. *Land reform in Zimbabwe: Constraints and prospects*. London: Routledge.

Succi, C. & Canovi, M. 2020. Soft skills to enhance graduate employability: Comparing students and employers' perceptions. *Studies in Higher Education*, 45(9):1834–1847.

Surur, M., Wibawa, R.P., Jaya, F., Suparto, A.A., Harefa, D., Faidi, A., Triwahyuni, E., Suartama, I.K., Mufid, A. & Purwanto, A. 2020. Effect of education operational cost on the education quality with the school productivity as moderating variable. *Psychology and Education*, 57(9):1196–1205.

Tapfuma, M., Chikuta, O., Ncube, F.N., Baipai, R., Mazhande, P. & Basera, V. 2021. Graduates' perception of Tourism and Hospitality Degree program relevance to career attainment: A case of graduates from three state universities in Zimbabwe. *Journal of Tourism, Culinary and Entrepreneurship (JTCE)*, 1(2):190–207.

Tibbitts, F. 2015. *Curriculum development and review for democratic citizenship and human rights education*. Paris, France: UNESCO Publishing.

Waghid, Y. 2013. *African philosophy of education reconsidered: On being human*. Cape Town: Routledge.

Waghid, Z. 2014. (Higher) Education for social justice through sustainable development, economic development and equity. *South African Journal of Higher Education*, 28(4):1448–1463.

Waghid, Y. & Davids, N. (Eds). 2017. *African democratic citizenship education revisited*. Cape Town: Springer.

Waghid, Y., Waghid, F. & Waghid, Z. 2018. *Rupturing African philosophy on teaching and learning: Ubuntu justice and education*. Cape Town: Springer.

Wildschut, A., Rogan, M. & Mncwango, B. 2020. Transformation, stratification and higher education: Exploring the absorption into employment of public financial aid beneficiaries across the South African higher education system. *Higher Education*, 79(6):961–979.

World Bank. 2022. Global Literacy Trends 2022. World Bank Group. www.worldbank.org/en/research

Yitzhaki, D., Gallagher, T., Aloni, N. & Gross, Z. 2022. *Activist pedagogy and shared education in divided societies: International perspectives and next practices*. Volume 17. Leiden, The Netherlands: Brill.

Zembere, M. 2018. Democratic citizenship education revisited in Zimbabwean higher education. In Waghid, Y. & Davids, N. (Eds). *African democratic citizenship education revisited. Palgrave studies in global citizenship education and democracy.* Cham: Palgrave Macmillan, https://doi.org/10.1007/978-3-319-67861-0_10

Zembylas, M. & Keet, A. 2018. *Critical human rights, citizenship, and democracy education: Entanglements and regenerations.* London: Bloomsbury Academic.

Zimbabwe National Statistics Agency. 2020. Zimbabwe Statistical Yearbook 2020. Zimstat. www.zimstat.co.zw

5 An analysis of critical thinking skills and its link to democratic citizenship education within the South African chartered accountancy higher educational landscape

A reflection on my doctoral encounter

Elton Pullen

Introduction

Attaining a Doctor of Philosophy (PhD) signifies the pinnacle of educational attainment and is accordingly widely acknowledged as a representation of intellectual accomplishment and unwavering commitment to a specific academic discipline. Notwithstanding the elevated prestige associated with obtaining a PhD, it is imperative to acknowledge that the pursuit of doctoral education comes with numerous challenges. Some of these include not getting the right promoter, a long-term time commitment, feelings of isolation, research uncertainty, and a lack of work–life balance. I briefly elaborate on the challenges.

Encountering difficulties in finding an appropriate PhD promoter can be a considerable obstacle on one's doctoral journey. A lack of alignment between one's own research interests and the expertise of one's supervisor might result in digression in terms of research direction. This could lead to feelings of irritation and diminished excitement about one's research topic, thus posing challenges to maintaining motivation. The support of an appropriate supervisor is therefore crucial for ensuring a satisfactory PhD journey and successful progress towards PhD completion. Failure to secure an appropriate promoter might affect the overall quality of one's PhD thesis and impede progress towards graduation and, in severe instances, cause the discontinuation of one's doctoral studies.

The PhD pursuit notably also entails substantial and protracted dedication, generally spanning multiple years until its fulfilment. This extended timeline could pose difficulties, particularly when attempting to strike a balance between work and other professional commitments, family obligations, as well as other responsibilities. Advancing through the PhD process thus invariably entails the

DOI: 10.4324/9781003530091-6

necessity of relinquishing quality time spent with loved ones, as well as time for self-care. Furthermore, the pursuit of a doctoral degree necessitates a considerable degree of independence and autonomy and may engender feelings of isolation. Individuals may find themselves dedicating extensive periods to engage in reading and/or writing activities, potentially resulting in feelings of seclusion or exhaustion. Moreover, due to the inherent unpredictability of research, one may confront various challenges, setbacks, or the necessity to alter one's research direction. This uncertainty can be emotionally and intellectually challenging.

Throughout the course of my PhD studies, I was certainly not exempted from the challenges highlighted above. Firstly, as someone possessing the designation of a chartered accountant (CA), I encountered a notable constraint throughout my pursuit of the CA qualification. This constraint pertained to the absence of exposure to research during my CA qualification journey, which encompassed the acquisition of an undergraduate degree in accounting as well as an honours in accounting. My initial encounter with research only occurred with the completion of the half-thesis for my master's degree (coursework) in Financial Management. Being only a half-thesis, this did not equip me adequately for the substantial undertaking of a whole doctoral thesis, let alone doing research in the social sciences, which is an area in which I lacked expertise and exposure. Moreover, it is common for CAs in the South African (SA) higher educational (HE) landscape not to have a doctoral degree, and even if they possess one, it is usually not in the field of Philosophy of Education. Given my strong interest in teaching and learning within the context of the chartered accountancy educational landscape in South Africa, I had significant challenges in locating a supervisor who had a doctoral degree as well as an understanding of the nuances associated with chartered accountancy education. Consequently, I experienced a profound sense of gratitude upon being formally introduced to my promoter, Distinguished Professor Yusef Waghid, who upon our first meeting instilled in me the belief that pursuing a doctorate in Philosophy of Education would foster the development of interdisciplinary and integrated thinking. This way of thinking closely aligned with my research interest of developing critical thinking (CT) skills within students pursuing the CA designation.

In addition to initially struggling to find an appropriate promoter, as discussed above, I also faced the additional responsibility of balancing my full-time position as a senior lecturer in Management Accounting and Financial Management (MAF) at the University of the Western Cape (UWC). The educational programme in which I am a lecturer holds accreditation from the South African Institute of Chartered Accountants (SAICA), and SAICA-accredited programmes are known for their emphasis on teaching, due to the overloaded SAICA syllabus (Venter & De Villiers, 2013). This results in limited time for research pursuits. The period of my PhD studies also coincided with the Covid-19 pandemic in the years 2020 and 2021. At the beginning of 2020, my wife and I also found that we were expecting our second child, which was an absolute blessing. At the same time, we were also informed that, as a result of the financial limitations imposed by the Covid-19 pandemic, my wife's employer unfortunately had to terminate her employment. This event elicited emotions of financial insecurity, prompting me to seek extra contractual employment in order to mitigate the reduction in our household earnings while awaiting the arrival of a new member to our family. This circumstance inevitably intensified the time constraints for conducting my PhD research, while it simultaneously heightened the challenges associated with finding a work–life balance.

Nevertheless, despite encountering several hurdles as highlighted above, I am grateful to have completed my PhD successfully with the assistance of my family and the exceptional mentorship provided by Distinguished Professor Yusef Waghid.

In this chapter, I present a background to the SA chartered accountancy HE landscape with a focus on the need to advance the notions of CT and democratic citizenship education (DCE). within the chartered accountancy pedagogy. I also touch on the relationship between CT and DCE and briefly show how the current prevailing chartered accountancy pedagogy falls short of advancing these competencies optimally. Lastly, this chapter presents how the chartered accountancy pedagogy could be reimagined to develop CT and citizenship competence within aspiring CAs more optimally.

Background to the South African chartered accountancy higher educational landscape

SAICA is entrusted with the task of overseeing the education of CAs in South Africa. SAICA has however delegated the entirety of its academic obligations to accredited universities, while retaining substantial influence over the accountancy curriculum in higher education. This significant control is mostly accomplished through the utilisation of continuing monitoring and accreditation standards by SAICA in accrediting accountancy programmes offered by universities. A crucial aspect for a university to uphold its continuous SAICA accreditation is the achievement rate of its graduates in the SAICA Initial Test of Competence (ITC) examination (Venter & De Villiers, 2013). The SAICA ITC examination is the first of two qualifying examinations set by SAICA and is written by prospective CAs after completing a SAICA-accredited academic programme. This academic programme typically comprises a three-year undergraduate degree in accounting as well as a one-year Post-Graduate Diploma in Accounting (PGDA) or otherwise known as a Certificate in the Theory of Accounting (CTA) (SAICA, 2019). The SAICA ITC examination assesses the academic curriculum, which had also been developed by the professional body. This curriculum is known as the SAICA Competency Framework (see Wood & Maistry, 2014).

The SAICA Competency Framework has traditionally prioritised the technical and vocational aspects of accountancy, despite the prevailing demand for accountancy education to encompass the contextual, social, environmental, ethical, and cultural dimensions of the field (Terblanche, 2019; Terblanche

& Waghid, 2021; Wood & Maistry, 2014). Since 2019, however, SAICA has introduced a new competency framework, known as CA2025 (SAICA, 2021). The new CA2025 framework puts special emphasis on CT skills and citizenship competence as important skills for future CAs to have, and this caught my attention as I worked on my PhD thesis. The new framework requires prospective CAs to have an advanced level (Level 3) of proficiency in citizenship competence as well as CT competence. The CA2025 levels of proficiencies are categorised from Level 1 (being the foundational level of competence) to Level 3 (being the most advanced level of competence for a particular competency or learning outcome). The CA2025 framework regards citizenship competence as a professional value and attitude. In terms of all competencies listed under professional values and attitudes, a Level 3 competency level implies that prospective CAs need to display these values and attitudes: "Always under all circumstances. In a difficult context with complex situations and/or circumstances" (SAICA, 2021:8). Critical thinking is regarded as an enabling competency within the CA2025 framework. In terms of all competencies listed under enabling competencies, a Level 3 competency level implies that prospective CAs need to:

> [D]isplay an advanced level of task understanding (clear problem identification, thorough analysis/evaluation and useful recommendations are made). Integrating multiple knowledge sources and skills in all areas, to perform a task. Relying on own actions complemented by actions of others for which formal responsibility is carried
>
> (SAICA, 2021:8)

Considering the new CA2025 framework, my thesis focused on whether chartered accountancy higher education is achieving this requisite degree of CT and citizenship competency. This was especially interesting to me because the chartered accountancy curriculum has always been known for being focused on technical skills. This is at odds with the advanced levels of citizenship competence and CT required by the new framework. My study followed a conceptual-deconstructive analysis approach, with an overarching eclectic paradigm, incorporating broad philosophical perspectives based on interpretivism, critical theory, and deconstruction to evaluate the related meanings of CT and DCE. My analysis then delved deep into the extent to which these fundamental concepts are being promoted (or not) through the educational practices implemented by SAICA-accredited programmes.

The relationship between critical thinking and democratic citizenship education

While conducting my literature review to gain a thorough understanding of CT, it became clear that there is limited consensus on a clear definition of the term "critical thinking", and the concept can therefore be interpreted in many different ways. As a result, CT is often not well understood and consequently applied inconsistently (Kataoka-Yahiro & Saylor, 1994). Even though a universally accepted definition of CT seemed not to exist, it was nevertheless important for me to state the definition of CT precisely, as this would form the foundation of my study. In this regard, I chose the definition of CT conceptualised by the American Psychological Association (APA) Delphi study (Facione, 1990), as the working definition of CT for my study. My reason for choosing the APA definition was the fact that it has been cited by several seminal articles on CT and is regarded as a leading CT definition (Abrami et al., 2008, 2015; Brudvig, Dirkes, Dutta & Rane, 2013; Carter, Creedy & Sidebotham, 2015).

The conceptualisation of CT by the APA Delphi study, which ran from February 1988 to November 1989, was summarised in a document entitled *Critical thinking: A statement of expert consensus for purposes of educational assessment and instruction – Executive summary of "The Delphi Report"* (Facione, 1990).

The expert panel arrived at the following consensus statement (definition) concerning CT and the ideal critical thinker (Facione, 1990:3):

> We understand critical thinking to be purposeful, self-regulatory judgement which results in interpretation, analysis, evaluation and inference, as well as explanation of the evidential, conceptual, methodological, criteriological [the science of criteria] or contextual considerations upon which that judgement is based. Critical thinking is essential as a tool of inquiry. As such, critical thinking is a liberating force in education and a powerful resource in one's personal and civic life. While not synonymous with good thinking, critical thinking is a pervasive and self-rectifying human phenomenon.
>
> The ideal critical thinker is habitually inquisitive, well-informed, trustful of reason, open-minded, flexible, fair-minded in evaluation, honest in facing personal biases, prudent in making judgements, willing to reconsider, clear about issues, orderly in complex matters, diligent in seeking relevant information, reasonable in the selection of criteria, focused in inquiry and persistent in seeking results which are as precise as the subject and the circumstances of inquiry permit.

Educating good critical thinkers thus means working towards the idea of the ideal critical thinker, as elucidated by the APA Delphi study (Facione, 1990). Such an education combines developing CT skills with nurturing those dispositions which consistently yield useful insights and which are the basis of a rational and democratic society.

Importantly, the APA panel also determined that CT comprises two dimensions, namely a cognitive skills dimension and a dispositions dimension (Facione, 1990). For the panel, it was apparent that these two dimensions are important to conceptualise CT. My understanding of the literature is that the focus is very often on the development of cognitive skills within the pedagogy but not on the development of CT dispositions (see Halpern, 1998). The APA panel argued that good critical thinkers should have "a critical spirit which provides them with an eagerness to search for trustworthy evidence, devotion to reason as well as a keen and inquisitive mind" (Facione, 2011:11). This 'critical spirit' can also be seen as a disposition towards CT (Terblanche, 2018).

In my study, I argued that, if the advanced levels of CT and DCE, as required by the new CA2025 framework are going to be actualised, pedagogical environments, which foster DCE notions, such as equality and tolerance, are vital, as these democratic values are synonymous with many of the CT dispositions as espoused by the APA Delphi study (Pullen, 2022).

In the paragraphs below, I elucidate some of these discussions, starting with a brief conceptualisation of DCE.

Benhabib (2002:169) suggests that democracy and citizenship can coexist, as education emphasises active consent and involvement, while 'citizenship' refers to the sense of belonging that people exhibit through socialisation in educational processes. I engage with others when I participate in a conversation or belong to a group where members are conversing; therefore, I engage with them by becoming involved in the conversation. Benhabib (2002:133–134) defines active participation as people being free and equal moral beings who try to influence each other's opinions by engaging in public dialogue where they examine and assess each other's positions (civilly and considerately) and explain their own. Conversely, 'belonging' refers to people's commitment to education by increasing accountability and attachment to the process. A prevalent thread in Benhabib's (2002) articulation of DCE is the importance of the democratic values of equality and tolerance. These democratic values are synonymous with the following CT dispositions, as espoused by the APA Delphi study (Facione, 1990:13):

- open-mindedness regarding divergent world views;
- flexibility in considering alternatives and opinions;
- understanding the opinions of other people;
- fair-mindedness in appraising reasoning;
- honesty in facing one's own biases, prejudices, stereotypes, egocentric or socio-centric tendencies;
- prudence in suspending, making, or altering judgements; and
- willingness to reconsider and revise views where honest reflection suggests that change is warranted.

The actualisation of critical thinking and democratic citizenship education within the South African chartered accountancy landscape

In light of the high levels of proficiency required by the new CA2025 for CT skills and citizenship competence, my analysis identified three major weaknesses within current pedagogical practices in terms of chartered accountancy education, which hinder optimal development of these competencies:

- a lack of pedagogical environments that foster intellectual equality;
- a lack of critical deliberation within the classroom; and
- a lack of explicit cultivation of humanity within the curriculum.

In the paragraphs below, I elucidate each of these.

CAs often transition into the academe without substantial pedagogical training. Despite possessing extensive technical knowledge gained through a specialised accountancy curriculum, CAs generally lack familiarity with a wide range of educational approaches. Moreover, academics in the fields of accountancy and finance and chartered accountancy possess specialised technical expertise, which enables them to elucidate complex concepts effectively. Consequently, students are often not seen as intellectual equals but rather as recipients of the knowledge imparted by their master teachers, i.e. the chartered accountancy academics. As a result, the pedagogical approach is seldom characterised by active student engagement.

Rancière (1991) refers to this way of teaching by instruction as "explication" and views it as "enforced stultification" (Rancière, 1991:7). Most importantly, for Rancière (1991), the ideal learning environment is one where educators regard students as possessing equal intelligence and, as a result, are able 'to come to know' with only minimal intervention on the part of the educator. The democratic value of equality within the pedagogy is therefore critical for Rancière (1991), as he sees equality not as an outcome to be achieved but rather as a value to be maintained always and in all educational settings.

My inference from Rancière (1991) is that the democratic value of equality is key to optimal CT development as it fosters the development of both cognitive skills and dispositions as espoused in the APA Delphi study (see Facione, 1990). Engaging with students from the vantage point of equality is something that is not prevalent in chartered accountancy education pedagogy, as chartered accountancy academics are often seen as master explicators, and their students are the recipients of their knowledge. Co-learning between students and teachers are thus often scant within the chartered accountancy pedagogy.

I shall now move to discuss why I regard a lack of critical deliberation in the classroom as hindering the development of CT. Benhabib advocates for a "deliberative model of democracy" (Benhabib, 1996:69) to attain a legitimate and rational democracy. According to Benhabib, this entails "collective deliberation conducted rationally and fairly among free and equal citizens" (Benhabib, 1996:69).

My rationale for highlighting the deliberative model of democracy proposed by Benhabib (1996) lies in the possibilities this model creates for the development of CT. Benhabib (1996) also points out that it is a matter of impossibility for any single individual to predict the variation in perspectives relating to ethics and politics, which different individuals may hold. Similarly, one individual is unlikely to have all the information relevant to a decision affecting all other individuals. I therefore agree with Benhabib (1996) when she states that deliberation allows for an "enlarged mentality" (Benhabib, 1996:72), as it creates the platform to be informed more fully.

The deliberative model of democracy argued for by Benhabib (1996) relates to the CT in the following ways:

- It is deliberation among free and equal citizens and thus requires the CT disposition of "open-mindedness" as espoused by the APA Delphi study panel of experts (Facione, 1990:25).
- Given, as stated by Benhabib (1996:71), "no single individual can possess all the information deemed relevant to a decision affecting all"; deliberation also allows for the CT disposition of developing "a concern to become and remain generally well-informed" (Facione, 1990:25).

My analysis revealed that pedagogical environments, which foster critical deliberations, are scant within chartered accountancy HE programmes.

Finally, I shall now discuss why a lack of explicit cultivation of humanity within the curriculum could hinder the development of CT by reflecting on the work of Nussbaum (2022). Nussbaum (2002:290) essentially argues for three abilities vital to such cultivation in the modern world, where people are interconnected, namely:

- the Socratic ability to criticise one's own traditions and to keep an argument going in terms of mutual respect for a reason;
- the ability to think as a citizen of the whole world, not just of some local region or group; and
- the "narrative imagination" in other words, the ability to imagine what it would be like to be in the position of someone very different from oneself (Nussbuam, 2022:290).

A discussion of these abilities and their relationship to CT follows below.

Firstly, the ability to criticise oneself and one's own tradition is essentially living what Socrates called the "examined life" (Reich, 1998:68). This involves a mind-set that questions everything – even passed-down beliefs – and accepts beliefs that have been rationally justified. In order to develop this ability, Nussbaum (2002:293) holds the view that one needs to develop the capacity "to reason logically, to test what one reads or says for consistency of reasoning, the correctness of fact, and accuracy of judgment". This first ability advocated by Nussbaum (2002:293), i.e. the ability to live the "examined life", essentially calls for the development of CT abilities, namely "interpretation", "analysis", "evaluation", and "inference", as advocated by the APA Delphi study (see Facione, 1990:19).

In my view, Nussbaum's (2002) second and third abilities are similar in their relationship to CT dispositions as espoused by the APA Delphi study experts. In my view, the "ability to think as a citizen of the whole world" and "the ability to imagine what it would be like to be in the position of someone very different from oneself", require the CT dispositions of:

- "open-mindedness regarding divergent world views";
- "flexibility in considering alternatives and opinions"; and
- "understanding the opinions of other people" (Facione, 1990:19).

Sadly, my analysis revealed that pedagogical environments, which foster this reimagining, are scant within chartered accountancy education.

Reimaging the development of citizenship and critical thinking competence within the chartered accountancy educational landscape

In my doctoral encounter, I found the development of citizenship and CT competence to be minimal when viewed along a continuum of minimal CT development to maximal CT development. One of the main reasons for my low evaluation was that the pervasive pedagogy at SAICA-accredited universities was to focus on success in the SAICA ITC examination, which is a technically focused examination. In preparing students for the SAICA ITC examination, SAICA-accredited universities place much emphasis on monitored and timed assessments, throughout a student's academic journey. Using Foucauldian thought, I argued that the current assessment practices prevalent within SAICA-accredited universities can be regarded as a strong power mechanism related to knowledge and knowledge transfer, first from academic teacher to student and then with knowledge extraction from the student (Foucault, 1991a). The SAICA ITC examination and the assessments adopted in accredited accountancy programmes, which are aimed at preparation for the ITC, could be seen as one of the techniques used to exercise disciplinary power. Terblanche (2019:164) argues:

> [T]he purpose of discipline is often to programme individuals to think that what they see and experience or a specific method of conduct, is the norm, and it is difficult to see a new tomorrow without these behaviours.

Similarly, Mills (2003:43) explains:

> Discipline consists of a concern with control which is internalised by each individual; it consists of a concern with time-keeping, self-control over one's posture and bodily functions, concentration, sublimation of immediate desires and emotions – all of these elements are the effects of disciplinary pressure and at the same time they are all actions which produce the individual as subjected to a set of procedures which come from outside of themselves but whose aim is the disciplining of the self by the self.

Following from the perspectives of Terblanche (2019) and Mills (2003), the SAICA ITC and the related assessment practices can be seen as a form of exercising disciplinary power. A further example of disciplinary power related to the SAICA ITC and assessments in SAICA-accredited accountancy programmes is that these assessments are often based on the perceived understanding of the SAICA knowledge list by the master explicator (i.e. the teacher or examiner). Students however have no input into how the SAICA knowledge list and competencies will be assessed. Put differently, students are passive receivers of how they will be assessed. The examiner's explication of the knowledge contained in the SAICA Competency Framework constitutes the norm against which students writing these assessments are benchmarked (Pullen, 2022). My argument is that, in preparing for the SAICA ITC and assessments at SAICA-accredited universities (SAUs), students are, in fact, currently preparing to be tested according to a norm in which they have no input. According to Terblanche (2019), this provides another example of the disciplinary power of the current assessment practices at SAUs.

While power is often perceived negatively, according to Foucault (1998), the power-knowledge relationship can however be both restrictive (negative) and productive (positive). I now move to focus on the possibility of power being productive and thus conducive to maximal CT and citizenship development.

In *Discipline and Punish: The Birth of a Prison*, Foucault (1991a:194) states:

> We must cease once and for all to describe the effects of power in negative terms: it 'excludes', it 'represses', it 'censors', it 'abstracts', it 'masks' it 'conceals'. In fact, power produces; it produces reality; it produces domains of objects and rituals of truth. The individual and the knowledge that may be gained of him [or her] belong to this production.

My understanding of the above statement by Foucault (1991a) is that power is not limited to ideas of domination or politics but is also embedded within the individual and how he or she wishes to exercise that power, which gives it its negative or positive connotation. Based on this positive connotation of power, Waghid and Davids (2017) argue for assessment *within* teaching and learning.

Assessment *within* teaching and learning requires deliberative encounters between teachers and students and allows students to be part of the grading process. The notion of deliberative encounters, as advocated by Benhabib (1996), fosters notions of "open-mindedness" and "fair-mindedness", which are synonymous with CT, as espoused by the panel of experts in the APA Delphi study when reaching their consensus on the definition of CT (Facione, 1990:3). Furthermore, inviting students to be part of the grading process creates opportunities for "reasoning between equals" (Rancière, 1991:45). My argument is that pedagogical encounters based on the premise of 'equal intelligence' are conducive to an environment in which both students and teachers gain new insights and hence acquire increased knowledge. This also creates the potential for assessments *within* teaching and learning as a form of deliberative encounters, promoting CT development. In advancing this argument, I reflect on the fact that the cognitive level of 'create' is regarded as the highest cognitive level of Bloom's Revised Taxonomy (see Anderson &

Krathwohl, 2001). This, according to Ennis (1993), is synonymous with the concept of CT. In short, assessments *within* teaching and learning, which are based on the premise that students and teachers have equal intelligence, foster an environment conducive to DCE in which CT can be developed.

The potential for assessments *within* teaching and learning to influence the development of CT positively lies in the fact that assessments *within* teaching and learning offers "the possibilities of action and *resistance*" (Waghid & Davids, 2017). Furthermore, assessments *within* teaching and learning create the potential for both resistance and CT development. This is supported by Foucault, for whom *resistance* to power is about "detaching the power of truth from the forms of hegemony, social, economic, and cultural, within which it operates at the present time" (Foucault, 1991b:75). Elsewhere Foucault (1980:97) explained that "forms of resistance against different forms of power" suggest that power exists within the individual's freedom to oppose that which he or she meets.

My argument that the possibility of resistance through negotiated assessments offers the potential for developing CT derives from the fact that Foucault's (date) resistance is synonymous with critical theory. Critical theorists argue that our experiences and perceptions are manipulated by power structures or rather 'relations of power', following Foucauldian thought. As pedagogical encounters are therefore relationships of power, the possibility exists in these relationships for students to be manipulated by teachers. Critical theory essentially aims to critique and challenge social structures, power dynamics, cultural norms, and ideologies to promote social justice and emancipation (Ryan, 2018). In the case of Foucault's (1980) resistance, I argue that critical theory extends to the student challenging the teacher's views in an assessment *within* teaching and learning.

A further benefit of resistance made possible through assessments *within* teaching and learning for CT development is the possibility of encouraging independent thought. Waghid and Davids (2017) contend that a crucial aspect of assessments *within* teaching and learning is that teachers cannot simply expect that students will agree with and support their own viewpoints. Waghid and Davids believe that such compulsion would probably prevent willing and independent learning. They elucidate their argument that *resistance* in negotiated assessments encourages independent thought by stating:

> The point is, students (in negotiated assessments) are imbued with power to contest and scrutinize critically what they learn and, in a Foucauldian sense, this means even resisting the thoughts teachers expect them to make their own. Such a form of non-indoctrination is commensurable with the notion that power relationships are inherently connected to resistance.
> (Waghid & Davids, 2017:35)

Following this comment by Waghid and Davids (2017), my argument is that CT is also developed through resistance in power relationships such as assessments *within* teaching and learning due to the potential it creates for independent thought. One of the hallmarks of the ideal critical thinker, according to the APA Delphi study, was identified as the propensity to be "habitually inquisitive" (Facione, 1990:30), which I argue is synonymous with independent thought. In short, my argument is, therefore, that resistance in negotiated assessments creates the potential to develop independent thought, which is synonymous with notions of CT.

An opportunity exists for SAICA-accredited accountancy programmes to make use of alternative assessment methods, such as problem-based learning (PBL) case studies, to assess the competencies required within the new CA2025 framework. PBL case studies have a greater potential for assessment *within* teaching and learning than the current monitored and timed assessments adopted within the chartered accountancy pedagogy. One of the many benefits of PBL case studies is the fact that it requires students to work collaboratively. As students engage in groups or with their teachers, the potential for developing the CT dispositions of 'fair-mindedness' and 'open-mindedness' exists (Facione, 1990). Typically, PBL case studies do not have a set solution; thus, the student is aware that the teacher is not going to provide the solution to a given problem. The student therefore needs to think independently and adopt an inquisitive mind-set that is again consistent with CT.

Conclusion

In this chapter, I presented my doctoral encounter with reference to the development of citizenship and CT competence within SAICA-accredited accountancy programmes, against the background of the new CA2025 curriculum laid down by SAICA. I highlighted how the current technically focused pedagogy and the focus on success in the SAICA ITC examination are at odds with the development of the fundamental competencies, namely CT and citizenship competence. I also discussed how the current prevailing pedagogy could be reimagined to develop these fundamental competencies at a maximal level. In particular, chartered accountancy programmes should explore strategies that foster assessment *within* teaching and learning, as an alternative to the current assessment practices of sit-down monitored and timed assessments.

I would like to conclude by highlighting that, while the chartered accountancy pedagogy has been known to be very technically focused, the explicit requirement to develop citizenship competence and CT at such advanced levels within the CA2025 framework indicates a written intent on the part of SAICA to develop prospective CAs who are well-rounded rather than just being technically astute. This written intent should be embraced by chartered accountancy academics.

Key lessons learned

While the development of CT and citizenship competence may be at a minimal level across SAICA-accredited accountancy programmes, a significant opportunity exists to reimagine the prevailing pedagogy, especially in light of the new CA2025 framework. It is, however, important to note that notions of CT and citizenship competence cannot simply be viewed as outcomes to be achieved. Instead, chartered accountancy academics, in particular, should endeavour to foster notions of CT and DCE as ongoing pedagogical pursuits. It is only through such ongoing pedagogical pursuits that one can create the potential to produce CAs who, while still being technically competent, are also ethically and socially aware.

References

Abrami, P.C., Bernard, R.M., Borokhovski, E., Waddington, D.I., Wade, C.A. & Persson, T. 2015. Strategies for teaching students to think critically: A meta-analysis. *Review of Educational Research*, 85(2):275–314.

Abrami, P.C., Bernard, R.M., Borokhovski, E., Wade, A., Surkes, M.A., Tamim, R. & Zhang, D. 2008. Instructional interventions affecting critical thinking skills and dispositions: A stage 1 meta-analysis. *Review of Educational Research*, 78(4):1102–1134.

Anderson, L.W. & Krathwohl, D.R. 2001. *A taxonomy for learning, teaching and assessing: A revision of Bloom's taxonomy of educational objectives.* Abridged edition. New York: Longman.

Benhabib, S. 1996. *Democracy and difference: Contesting the boundaries of the political.* Princeton, NJ: Princeton University Press.

Benhabib, S. 2002. *The claims of culture: Equality and diversity in the global era.* Princeton, NJ: Princeton University Press.

Brudvig, T.J., Dirkes, A., Dutta, P. & Rane, K. 2013. Critical thinking skills in health care professional students: A systematic review. *Journal of Physical Therapy Education*, 27(3):12–25.

Carter, A.G., Creedy, D.K. & Sidebotham, M. 2015. Evaluation of tools used to measure critical thinking development in nursing and midwifery undergraduate students: A systematic review. *Nurse Education Today*, 35(7):864–874.

Ennis, R.H. 1993. Critical thinking assessment. *Theory into Practice*, 32(3):179–186.

Facione, P.A. 1990. *Critical thinking: A statement of expert consensus for purposes of educational assessment and instruction – executive summary of "The Delphi report".* Oakland, CA: California Academic Press.

Facione, P.A. 2011. *Critical thinking: What it is and why it counts.* California: Insight Assessment.

Foucault, M. 1980. Power and strategies, in C. Gordon (ed.). *Power/knowledge.* New York: Pantheon. 134–145

Foucault, M. 1991a. *Discipline and punish: The birth of the prison.* London: Penguin.

Foucault, M. 1991b. Governmentality, in G. Burchell, C. Gordon, & P. Miller (eds). *The Foucault effect: Studies in governmentality.* Chicago, IL: University of Chicago Press. 87–104.

Foucault, M. 1998. *The history of sexuality: The will to knowledge.* London: Penguin.

Halpern, D.F. 1998. Teaching critical thinking for transfer across domains: Dispositions, skills, structure training, and metacognitive monitoring. *American Psychologist*, 53(4):449–455.

Kataoka-Yahiro, M. & Saylor, C. 1994. A critical thinking model for nursing judgment. *Journal of Nursing Education*, 33(8):351–356.

Mills, S. 2003. *Michel Foucault*. London: Routledge Taylor & Francis Group.
Nussbaum, M. 2002. Education for citizenship in an era of global connection. *Studies in Philosophy and Education*, 21(4–5):289–303.
Nussbaum, M. C. 2022. *Citadels of pride: Sexual abuse, accountability, and reconciliation*. W.W. Norton & Company, New York, NY.
Pullen, E. 2022. *An analysis of critical thinking skills and democratic citizenship education in the South African higher education system and its implications for teaching and learning*. Doctoral dissertation. Stellenbosch: Stellenbosch University.
Rancière, J. 1991. *The ignorant schoolmaster* (Vol. 1). Stanford, CA: Stanford University Press.
Reich, R. 1998. Confusion about the Socratic method: Socratic paradoxes and contemporary invocations of Socrates. *Philosophy of Education Archive*, 68–78 [Online]. Available: https://educationjournal.web.illinois.edu/archive/index.php/pes/article/view/2086.pdf [Accessed 15 October 2021].
Ryan, G. 2018. Introduction to positivism, interpretivism and critical theory. *Nurse Researcher*, 25(4):41–60.
South African Institute of Chartered Accountants (SAICA). 2019. *SAICA competency framework 2018: Detailed guidance for the academic programme* [Online]. Available from: www.saica.co.za/Portals/0/LearnersStudents/documents/CompetencyFramework2019b.pdf [Accessed 28 May 2021].
South African Institute of Chartered Accountants (SAICA). 2021. *CA2025*. Available from: www.saica.org.za/initiatives/competency-framework/ca2025 [Accessed 14 May 2022].
Terblanche, E.A.J. 2018. *Developing critical thinking in auditing students through technology-based educational interventions: A conceptual framework*. Doctoral dissertation. Pretoria: University of South Africa.
Terblanche, J. 2019. *Cultivating socially just responsible citizens in relation to university accounting education in South Africa*. Doctoral dissertation. Stellenbosch: Stellenbosch University.
Terblanche, J. & Waghid, Y. 2021. Chartered accountancy and resistance in South Africa. *South African Journal of Higher Education*, 35(3):239–253.
Venter, E.R. & De Villiers, C. 2013. The accounting profession's influence on academe: South African evidence. *Accounting, Auditing & Accountability Journal*, 26(8):1246–1278.
Waghid, Y. & Davids, N. 2017. *Education, assessment, and the desire for dissonance*. Bern, Switzerland: Peter Lang Incorporated, International Academic Publishers.
Wood, N. & Maistry, S.M. 2014. Professional accounting associations' influence on higher education accounting pedagogy. *Alternation*, 12:198–239.

6 Reflections on a doctoral journey in DCE

Deliberative encounters and the transformational potential

Judith Terblanche

Introduction

In this chapter, I offer my reflections on my doctoral journey. In part, this chapter focuses on the doctoral study itself, but it also focuses on the transformation that occurred within me due to my doctoral journey. There are several tools available to facilitate reflexive exercises for researchers, e.g. autoethnography (see Miyahara & Fukao, 2022), *currere* as an autobiographical method (see Le Grange, 2021), and the futures triangle (see Inayatullah, 2008). These tools share commonality as both require a look at the past, the present, the interrelatedness of the past and present, and, therefore, the possible plausible future. It is through this lens that I offer my reflections in this chapter.

In reflecting on some aspects that have led me to my doctoral studies, my studies originated from my choice of career. My interests were always broad and very diverse – seen from the outside, perhaps, seemingly incompatible. Participation in sports, my love for nature, and my love for books are by far the most pressing. Yet, I enrolled for an accounting degree at Stellenbosch University to qualify as a chartered accountant (CA). Indeed, being part of a highly esteemed profession that would allow for job security, adequate financial remuneration, and the possibility of travelling abroad – and working overseas – were all factors that drew me to the accountancy profession. In a sense, however, it was also because of the elimination of other possibilities.

I visited Onderstepoort, the only veterinary training facility in South Africa in the early 1990s. Upon exiting the car, I noticed that some assistance was required at the stables. I ran instinctively to assist in keeping the horse calm while the veterinary student administered the required medicine. When we later entered the theatre however, and saw the dog on which they were operating, I knew that studying to become a veterinary surgeon had just been eliminated.

Similarly, considering becoming a physiotherapist for a sports team sounded thrilling. After several conversations, I realised one would do endless hours

DOI: 10.4324/9781003530091-7

in a hospital. The thought of people coughing around me was enough to eliminate another possible profession. I, therefore, opted for the accountancy qualification, for which I had no passion or interest per se; yet, I perceived it to be the perfect foundation from where I would launch my career and adult life.

There is no denying that many business transactions are closed on the golf course. For a sport-loving person, taking up golf was a natural fit. Upon qualification as a CA(SA), I intended to move abroad and work as a finance person in the golfing industry, which would have been perfect for me. Instead, as was becoming the norm, I was once again invited to stand in the tension of a paradox. To be drawn to and experiencing discomfort simultaneously. I ended up working in the finance team at a learning disability charity in the United Kingdom called Mencap. That was the first time in my life that I experienced the transformational power of a deliberative encounter. Up until that point, I was a well-protected white female from South Africa who could mostly speak only Afrikaans (my home language). At Mencap, amongst many other factors, I faced three distinctive disrupting factors that propelled me into reflexivity and transformed thinking.

Firstly, as a white female from South Africa with its apartheid past, where I attended a predominantly white school and university and all my friends were Afrikaans-speaking, I faced a genuinely diverse workforce. In the finance team, everyone was from a different ethnicity, and we shared stories of our past, our traditions, and our beliefs. Secondly, several people with learning disabilities worked in the head office. At first, I was filled with anxiety when I found myself in the lift or kitchen with a colleague with a learning disability as I was unsure what I should talk about. Over the months, I slowly grew more comfortable, and I started to look forward to the endless analysis of football matches and banter about the teams we all supported. Thirdly, my direct line manager (the finance director), and the person I was at that stage, were complete opposites. I wanted to get the job done, meet deadlines, and manage all teams against a strict monthly programme with tasks to ensure a smooth yearly audit. The finance director, on the other hand, was more interested in the 'why' of what we do. In addition, he believed the role of the head office was to enable the widespread finance teams rather than being seen as an instructional entity based on a hierarchical organogram. In his view, a head office warrants its existence only through service and enabling measures. At that stage, that notion was foreign to me. Yet, I could see the difference it made when I started to focus predominantly on building relationships with all the various finance teams across the United Kingdom. The time at Mencap was rich and rewarding, and I will forever be thankful for the transformational process that started in me because of my employment there.

From this basis, I returned to South Africa to pursue in career in academia. I found the environment and people largely how I left it a few years back, but

I was not the same person anymore, and it felt as if I did not truly belong in my profession. Hansen (1998:650) argues, "[t]eaching embodies the human endeavour of moving human beings closer to the good, or, posed differently, closer to rather than farther from the prospect of a flourishing life". Intuitively, I felt we were getting it wrong in the chartered accountancy educational landscape in South Africa.

CAs registered with the South African Institute of Chartered Accountants (SAICA) disproportionately dominate the business landscape in South Africa. Not only are the majority of chief financial officers (CFOs) of entities listed on the Johannesburg Stock Exchange (JSE) CAs, but CAs also make up the majority of directorships in companies (Deloitte, 2018). Consequently, it would be negligent to disregard the latent effect of this influential profession on the SA economy, the potential for job creation, the possibility of poverty alleviation, and the road to greater equality. CAs in the SA business context are, therefore, regularly fulfilling a strategic role with decision-making authority and can therefore influence the effect of the corporate business milieu on all stakeholders and the environment. Such influence could either lead to policies and practices that perpetuate inequality or to those that purposefully eliminate unjust consequences.

In South Africa – a country known for exorbitant levels of inequality, often still along racial lines because of the legacy of apartheid (Leibbrandt, Woolard & Woolard, 2007; World Bank, 2021) – it is paramount that citizens are provoked to notice inequality. It is often only through compassionate care and by noticing social difficulties that changed action, behaviour, and decision-making become possible (Greene, 2001; Naudé, 2017). This is of importance to South Africa, as the skewed levels of inequality threaten social cohesion (and peace): "[g]rowing inequality in the economic realm threatens divisions within nations and between nations" (Desjardins, Torres & Wiksten, 2020:6).

In recent years, the accountancy profession has however been in the news because members contravened the fundamental principles of the profession as contained in the SAICA Code of Professional Conduct for chartered accountants, namely integrity, objectivity (independence), professional competence and due care, confidentiality, and professional behaviour (SAICA, 2016), and tarnishing the reputation of the profession and bringing it into disrepute. Being aware of the social reality within a particular context (i.e. being 'conscientised' [see Freire, 1974:23]) and developing a social consciousness are significantly more comprehensive than a mere ethical code of conduct intending to protect the image of the profession (Hellsten & Larbi, 2006). The significant contravention of the narrow ethical code is indicative of the vast amount of work required to develop CAs who can make socially responsible and just business decisions.

In the next section, I explain and discuss my research study, i.e. the chartered accountancy educational landscape in South Africa, through the lens of democratic citizenship education (DCE).

The doctoral study: The chartered accountancy educational landscape in South Africa

It is well-documented knowledge that SAICA, the custodian of the CA(SA) designation, influences the HE landscape (see Pullen & Waghid, 2022; Terblanche & Waghid, 2021).

The pathway to qualifying as a CA(SA) can be summarised as follows (SAICA, n.d.). Firstly, a student starts the academic part of the journey and needs to enrol for an undergraduate accounting degree. This is followed by a Certified Theory in Accounting (CTA) post-graduate qualification. Both these qualifications should be obtained from a SAICA-accredited institution. SAICA regularly conducts accreditation monitoring visits to ensure that higher education institutions (HEIs) adhere to the accreditation requirements. SAICA also prescribes a detailed competencies framework (CF) (see SAICA, 2019) listing the competencies that should be developed by and in students at HEIs. Upon graduating from the HEI with a CTA, students write their first external examination facilitated by SAICA, namely the Initial Test of Competence (ITC). The results of this examination are released per HEI cohort and have a direct financial influence on the academics teaching on the SAICA-accredited programmes through financial reward (more or less depending on how students of a particular HEI perform in the examinations). The outcome of the ITC, teaching and assessing the content as per the SAICA CF, and having appropriate staff (narrowly interpreted as CA(SA)s) to teach on the SAICA-accredited programmes are among the accreditation conditions to be met (Terblanche, 2019; Venter & De Villiers, 2013).

Secondly, graduates start with the training part (three-year learnership contract) of the journey at a registered training office. Again, very briefly – like the academic part – training officers are registered with SAICA, and SAICA prescribes a CF. Trainees also need to complete a professional programme at a SAICA-registered entity in preparation for the second external examination that trainees write twenty months into their trainee contract. This examination is called the Assessment of Professional Competence (APC). Successful candidates in this assessment will earn the right to use the CA(SA) designation upon completion of their training contract.

In the genealogical work, *Discipline and Punish: The Birth of the Prison*, Foucault (1995) explicates how power and knowledge are dispersed throughout society, particularly in the development of various disciplines, e.g. the field of accountancy. Disciplinary power, Foucault (1995) argues, uses three mechanisms to remain in control of the status quo (or changes): hierarchical observation, normalising judgement, and examination. In short, *hierarchical observation* is associated with a particular way of surveillance that internalises behaviour because of the possible threat of observation. *Normalising judgement* is associated with the internalisation of a set of rules that becomes part of the identity of individuals, and in this manner, conformity is achieved. Lastly, the *examination* is a measurement tool based on what is constituted as knowledge or the truth. Stehr and Adolf (2018:196) summarise this notion of disciplinary power as follows:

> The term discipline is understood in a double sense: on the one hand, it is the practice of *disciplining* workers and citizens; on the other hand, it is the *discipline-based knowledge* that enables power holders to discipline workers, which means that it does not make sense to separate knowledge and power. Both are fused, one cannot be exercised without the other. There is no truth that speaks to power, only knowledge that has been created by the powerful to serve their purposes. [original emphasis]

Elsewhere, Terblanche (2019) argues how the three mechanisms of disciplinary power, as proffered by Foucault (1995), are evident in the South African chartered accountancy educational landscape, namely –

- accreditation of HEIs by SAICA (as hierarchical observation);
- the issuing of a prescriptive CF by SAICA (as normalising judgement); and
- utilisation by SAICA of examinations – specifically the ITC – as a measurement tool to determine access into the profession (in the form of the examination).

The above analysis highlighted several consequences for South Africa because of these mechanisms of disciplinary power.

Firstly, chartered accountancy academics are appointed for their professional and technical skills and on account of the CA(SA) designation. Chartered accountancy academics obtained this designation in an environment that frequently assessed them in written examinations, where those deemed to have mastered the technical content, were awarded a pass. The academic environment that shaped them (as chartered accountancy academics) was primarily void of diverse learning and teaching pedagogy. The focus was overwhelmingly on the mastery of technical content, expounded by lecturers as experts, and students were responsible for demonstrating their knowledge in an examination.

In an educational environment where the focus is on pure technical content without embedding such knowledge within a broader social reality through diverse pedagogical approaches or considering the concept of conscientisation, teaching often becomes the mere transfer of technical knowledge from the so-called expert (i.e. the chartered accountancy academic) to the student. Such a teaching style is what Freire (1996) refers to as the 'banking' approach. A teaching approach such as this falls short of establishing the appropriate conditions to cultivate "a whole person who is capable of thinking critically, behaving responsibly, building peace, and engaging in issues of common concern as a global citizen" (Adeto, 2019:29).

The 'banking' approach to teaching keeps dominant world views in power, as the approach does not encourage inquiry. Consequently, knowledge is not sufficiently and appropriately shaped (see Freire, 1996). Juxtaposed against a 'banking' approach to teaching that conditions students to accept the status quo, Freire (1996) offered a problem-posing (participatory) model where teachers and students "discuss and analyse their experiences, feelings and knowledge of the world together" (Rugut & Osman, 2013:24) with the aim of students cultivating a form of critical thinking (CT) ('conscientisation') (Freire, 1996). For this reason, "learning can best be achieved through critical thinking and analysis of one's experiences and feelings" (Rugut & Osman, 2013:24), referring to learning that invites the embodied knowledge of students (and teachers) into the learning space.

"[T]he philosophy and its ideals, which constitute the essence of Africa and its people as well as their indigenous knowledges and history, are lacking in the education policies and systems of this continent" (Takyi-Amoako & Assié-Lumumba, 2018:11). In South Africa, this plight for decoloniality of the HE landscape came to the fore during violent protests that spread throughout university campuses during 2015–2017. Decoloniality is however not necessarily a project of replacing all Western knowledge (Mbembe, 2015) with African knowledge, nor is it the "dogmatic inclusion of whatever is deemed African" (Manthalu & Waghid, 2019:43). Instead, it is about a call that "the dominant ways of being of a selected few should be ruptured in order for education to become reflective of the knowledge interests of all a society's people" (Waghid, Waghid & Waghid, 2018:148). One example could be the chartered accountancy educational landscape, where the curriculum primarily focuses on the private sector and new-market profit-oriented ideologies (Segall, 2013; Terblanche, 2019). Swanson (2015:33) aptly warns, "[i]n the wake of global capitalism's common-sense mechanisms that render other options irrational, unviable or irrelevant, it is often a difficult task to assert alternatives in the spaces left behind". Such exclusionary practices of non-Western views and traditions are intrinsically unjust (Manthalu & Waghid, 2019).

The chartered accountancy educational landscape is therefore unlikely to consider and apply the required decolonial shift. Shultz (2010:20) defines such a required decolonial shift as:

> [T]he need to shift the westernised world views and structures of hierarchy (racialised, classed, gendered, etc.) towards those where ethical intercultural, inter-spatial relationality becomes the central organising principle allowing for reciprocity and mutual exchange of knowledge for the common good.

The decolonial shift, therefore, does not imply replacing the capitalistic Westernised world views with local African perspectives but instead suggests an "integration and validation" of diverse knowledge systems (Waghid, 2021:3).

Secondly, when chartered accountancy academics join the academe, they often associate with the profession and focus on the mastery of technical skills that can be measured in an examination. Although several SAICA-accredited institutions are research-led public entities, chartered accountancy academics rarely incorporate research as a learning and teaching pedagogical strategy. This is partly the case because chartered accountancy academics are overly confident in their ability to explain technical content and believe in the value of a written examination, as they have never fully developed the required skills themselves as students to incorporate research. Very seldom, therefore, will chartered accountancy academics utilise any other diverse learning and teaching practices, such as narrative reflection, deliberation, or research assignments with community interaction. Furthermore, due to the pressure of delivering all the learning content in the CF, which is significant in volume and complexity, chartered accountancy academics will rarely incorporate other (diverse) learning material – for example, material from the fields of the humanities and of the arts that might be especially suitable to provoke critical reflective thought for deliberation. As a result, they are not utilising a participative approach to learning (Freire, 1996) that could result in the 'conscientisation' of future business leaders (i.e. CA(SAs)) for decision-making that would promote the ideals of DCE, and of social transformation premised on the values of respect, equality, and dignity: recognising, therefore, our shared humanity and henceforth value. Participative pedagogy validates students' being, and consciousness is provoked through the presentation of embodied knowledge (see Auth.).

Thirdly, the obsession that an examination is the most appropriate (and almost exclusive) measurement tool to measure the development of competencies often leads to the stultification of thinking. Students' performance in the ITC is so over-emphasised that the pressure exists to 'coach' students to pass written examinations rather than to provoke CT or cultivate social awareness. Such an emphasis on 'teaching-to-the-test' "distracts the learning process from student-centred instruction and places the emphasis on the content" (Snyder & Snyder, 2008:92). This type of teaching does not lead to developing CT skills or competencies to solve societal challenges. "The premise that critical thinking is to knowing as listening is to hearing implies that critical thinking is a learned skill that must be developed, practiced, and continually integrated into the curriculum to engage students in active learning" (Snyder & Snyder, 2008:91).

These students have seemingly mastered the technical content when they pass an examination, but the question remains whether they have developed the necessary CT competency. Or were students with greater social awareness silenced if they did not conform to the pure capitalistic thinking underpinning the technical curriculum? For any significant economic change to address the inequality conundrum in South Africa, our business decision-makers need skills beyond mere technical competence. In a diverse environment, deliberation is often required to provoke new thinking and to notice the lived reality of those other than oneself. An examination therefore rarely develops the conditions for dignified and ethical human engagement.

In the next section, I reflect on my own transformation as a result of the deliberative encounter during my doctoral research, and I offer a possible remedy for the chartered accountancy educational landscape to teach towards the cultivation of the full humanity of students. This includes assisting students "to learn and think more critically and creatively in a way that develops an understanding of self, others and surroundings, and to participate as active global citizens for the greater good" (Giles, 2019:14).

The doctoral study: The being of the chartered accountancy academic

In struggling to find a 'home' for my doctoral studies, I explored various options and possibilities. Combining social justice, philosophy, accountancy, and education in one coherent product that makes sense to a traditional SAICA-accredited Department of Accounting is difficult. In the end, I registered for a PhD in Philosophy of Education at Stellenbosch University. During my studies and subsequent involvement in research projects, my lens and paradigm of how I viewed education – specifically chartered accountancy education and my ability to notice the voices of those silenced through systemic practices and policies – shifted significantly. Reading endless articles and books on education and the philosophy of education, conversations with other scholars, attending webinars, and participating in research workshops made me find the chartered accountancy academic space restrictive.

Because of my shift in perceptions, views, and beliefs after the deliberative encounter, I found the tension of discomfort in the accountancy educational space rather strong. Throughout the years, I became calm in my discomfort – knowing that I often have a different perspective than the dominant views and that my position could often be described as the dissonant voice on the periphery. I, therefore, have no doubt that my stance is to remain grounded within the profession and the chartered accountancy educational space but also that I will continue to challenge the status quo. That will require of me to –

- stand in the gap between discomfort and accepting the status quo;
- attempt to open the eyes of colleagues by challenging them to:
  - start noticing the richness that diverse educational practices and transformational pedagogy offer;
  - accept the practice of critical reflection in their lives; and
  - understand the responsibility foremost to teach towards the full humanity of students who could lead justly in the business world.

The CA profession is trying to make changes, and the adoption of the CA2025 CF is an example. The problem, though, is that these frameworks and policies are often compiled using accountants and chartered accountancy academics. Both groups are largely unfamiliar with the philosophy of education, which results in frameworks dominated by the importance of technical knowledge. It will also require that chartered accountancy academics implement this framework. Chartered accountancy academics are technical experts, not educational experts, meaning they can explicate and assess technical content. They are, however, unfamiliar with and experience discomfort when considering diverse teaching and learning practices.

My doctoral thesis re-imagined a chartered accountancy educational landscape premised on DCE, decoloniality, and *ubuntu*, focusing on the transformational potential of deliberative encounters. The possibility for education to achieve the required transformational potential depends mainly on the capacity of the (chartered accountancy) academic staff to translate the theoretical underpinnings of DCE and decoloniality into pedagogical practice. I argued that this is particularly true when an academic teaches on a market-driven programme, such as an accounting degree chosen by aspiring CAs in South Africa. The transformative potential of engendering values in students (i.e. aspiring business leaders) through pedagogical practices, therefore, compels the focus on the notion of ways of doing (the how of pedagogy) and the ways of being (i.e. of the chartered accountancy academic specifically).

The emphasis should, therefore, be on theorising towards the appropriate re-education of chartered accountancy academics in South Africa. Smith (2016) argues that changed behaviour in terms of deep-rooted habits might not happen due to new theoretical knowledge or awareness of dominant powers. Rather, Smith (2016) suggests counter formative practices as a possible solution towards the transformation of habits, actions, and being. "Therefore, the being (identity) of an individual changes through deliberate doing, and as a result of the being that is transformed, future doing (newly formed habits) will be different" (Gwadiso & Terblanche, 2024: forthcoming).

By looking at the ability and willingness to teach values and higher-order thinking skills through participatory learning approaches, we already identified that most chartered accountancy academics would not feel comfortable or confident in deviating from their lecturing styles (Wood & Maistry, 2014). The appropriate re-education of chartered accountancy academics will disrupt the identity and being of the individual(s) (Papastephanou, 2017). Gwadiso and Terblanche (2024) claim that chartered accountancy academics should choose discomfortable counter formative practices to transform deep-rooted habits by choosing:

- courageous vulnerability over comfort by including a diverse array of learning material from the arts and humanities, such as research activities and engagement with communities in the curriculum and assessment;
- embracing teaching practices that are premised on deliberation rather than the mere explicating of technical content; hence, acknowledging that the lecturer can learn from the embodied knowledge of students; and
- compassionate care (cultivation of the full humanity of the student) over the mere objective 'mastery' of technical content that can be measured through a time-measured written examination.

The re-education of the chartered accountancy academic necessitates a rupturing of the self to transform.

In the next and last section, I reflect on the supervisory relationship and how it contributed to my being and in-becoming.

The doctoral journey: The supervisory relationship premised on democratic citizenship education

The supervisor–student relationship during doctoral studies plays a significant role in the success of the student in completing the research output, his or her transformation and growth, and the overall satisfaction or disillusion of the doctoral process for the participants (i.e. the supervisor and the student). Malfroy (2005) reports on some of the challenges in the doctoral journey:

- there is an underlying hierarchical nature to supervision evident in the word 'supervisor' that could be perceived as the overseer, controller, superior;
- students need to listen to suggestions from the supervisor and have to respond suitably; and
- there is a paradox and tension in following the guidance of a supervisor, yet needing to become a self-directed scholar in own right.

"The practices of doctoral writing simultaneously produce not only a dissertation but also a doctoral scholar"; hence, the doctoral journey has to do with formation of the identity or the being and transformation of the student (Kamler & Thomson, 2008:508).

Lee (2008) reports on some supervisory approaches to doctoral supervision: functional, enculturation, critical thinking, emancipation, and relationship development. Below is a brief description of each approach (Lee, 2008:270):

- The *functional* approach focuses on rational progression through the tasks associated with producing a thesis.
- The *enculturation* approach focuses on 'gatekeeping', or, put differently, encouragement of the student to enter the disciplinary community.
- The *critical thinking* approach focuses on evaluating and challenging students to question and analyse their work.
- The *emancipation* approach focuses on encouraging the students to question and develop themselves.
- The *relationship development* approach focuses on inspiring the student through emotional intelligence.

By reflecting on these approaches to supervision, it becomes evident that there is a risk that 'supervision' could inherently come into conflict with some of the fundamental principles underpinning DCE – especially when perceived from the relationship aspect. In a Rancièrian sense, and in line with *ubuntu*-inspired education, DCE is premised on equality between the student and lecturer. In contrast, the underlying principle in a supervisor–student relationship is that the supervisor is the expert, and the student, the novice. Equally so, DCE invites the student to find his or her voice through a participatory learning style, while there is a risk that, under the supervisor's strict opinions, the doctoral student only finds his or her voice after acceptance of the supervisor's judgement. This is often the case as the students "carry the weight of expectation with them" since they are aware that their "[t]exts literally put the self and the work in the public domain to be judged by expert others" (Kamler & Thomson, 2008:508).

My supervisory journey was a very positive experience and perhaps unique. Intuitively or perhaps premised on emotional intelligence, my supervisor offered me the opportunity to find my voice. He has done this by delaying judgement and allowing me to grow in confidence and to realise, through self-reflection, how flawed my initial thinking was. That does not mean that the journey was not hugely disruptive. My supervisor provoked me by asking probing questions: 'refusing' to present answers until I had done additional readings, after which I re-articulated my thoughts; and by unreservedly treating me as if I do have a voice. Waghid's (2019) pedagogy of rhythmic care during our supervisor–student doctoral journey demonstrated to me the significant value of deliberative encounters in education and the transformational potential of such encounters – a key outcome and focus area of my thesis.

Based on exploring the dominant approaches to doctoral supervision and reflecting on my unique journey of rhythmic care as utilised by my supervisor, there is perhaps another framework to consider as a possible approach to PhD supervision that shares the underpinnings associated with DCE – that of coaching. Socrates influenced the modern-day coaching profession significantly and true to a Socratic method, a coach keeps asking intentional questions that will allow the opportunity for deeper self-reflection (Stout-Rostron, 2013).

Coaching is about a collaborative and participatory relationship that functions within a psychological space of safety (Bluckert, 2006), similar to the way students will only feel they belong and are cared for if the educational interactions create those boundaries for dignified human interactions. According to the International Coaching Federation (ICF) (n.d.:n.p.), coaching can be defined as "partnering with clients in a thought-provoking and creative process that inspires them to maximize their personal and professional potential". The emphasis on the potential within a client attests to the notion that "[c]oaches assume that their clients are whole and healthy human beings who can discover many of their own answers" (Rock & Page, 2009:344). Coaches and Mentors of South Africa (COMENSA, n.d.:n.p.) defines coaching as "a professional, collaborative and outcome-driven method of learning that seeks to develop an individual and raise self-awareness so that he or she might achieve specific goals and perform at a more effective level".

As a result, it can be said, "a coach does not diagnose nor does a coach offer treatment", as coaching has to do with performance, growth, and development (Hullinger & DiGirolamo, 2018:7). It is also significantly different to mentoring. COMENSA (n.d.: n.p.) refers to mentoring as that instance when the "mentor's wisdom is utilised by the mentee to facilitate and enhance new learning" and can be associated with the supervisor or academic as the 'expert'. Instead, the role of the coach is to serve as a reflective surface. Terblanche and Van der Walt (2019) argue that mediums, such as film or the arts, or material from the humanities, can be used as a reflective surface in educational encounters to provoke awareness and instigate changed behaviour. Likewise, the coach becomes a reflective surface for the client when he or she actively listens to ask appropriate questions, paraphrase the client's answers, and provide summaries of what was shared (Stout-Rostron, 2013). This allows the client to reflect truly and increases self-awareness, which my supervisor offered me. Put differently by Bluckert (2006:81), "the objective is to encourage them [the client] to see and hear themselves better by acting as a sounding board for them". Such an interpretation is closer to my lived experience of supervision through rhythmic caring – caring that offers a disruption and delayed judgement.

Not only is the coaching profession influenced by Socratic thinking but also by Dewey's (1938) interpretation of experiential learning. In the educational landscape, we refer to this subjective experience or reality of students as the embodied knowledge of the student. Educational practices that exclude the student-self in the classroom are violent in nature (see Galtung, 1969). Coaching is a practice that deliberatively invites the client to bring his or her own and whole self into the safe space. It is a profoundly personal journey and premised on a safe relationship where a connection of trust has been established. Coaching focuses on the not-yet present but the already-within potential of individuals. To my mind, that should be the aim of supervision premised on the principles of DCE.

In envisioning a plausible future, I hope that an awakening, an initiation, so to speak, into critical self-reflection, reflexivity, dignified human interactions, and consciousness of prospective chartered accountancy students will continue as they transition into various leadership positions in the business world. Perhaps not only would coaching be a possible source of direction for an approach for doctoral supervision, but it could also be a space where future business leaders could continue to grow into their full potential of leading just and responsibly in South Africa, leading us collectively to pronounced social cohesion and human flourishing.

In this section, I briefly explored some approaches to doctoral supervision and provided some reflection on my doctoral supervisory journey. I also reflected on how doctoral supervisors could possibly explore the field of coaching as a framework for supervision that is aligned with DCE.

Conclusion

This chapter focused on my reflections on my doctoral journey, including my study, which looked at the chartered accountancy educational landscape through the lens of DCE. It was presented that the chartered accountancy educational landscape is significantly affected by power relations that have led to the belief that measuring the mastery of technical content through an examination equates to education. Consequentially, chartered accountancy academics often explicate technical knowledge and teach towards the test. I further argued that, through re-education, chartered accountancy academics could contribute significantly towards social transformation in South Africa if they are willing to step into some area of discomfort by choosing courageous vulnerability over comfort, deliberation over explication, humility over superiority, and compassionate care over a supposed mastery of technical content measured via an examination. The chapter also focused on broad aspects associated with the doctoral journey – specifically in relation to the supervisor–student relationship. I also suggested exploring how the supervisory relationship could potentially benefit from the field of coaching.

Key lessons from the doctoral journey

It is an (almost) impossible task to highlight key lessons from the doctoral journey. Yet, if I must, the following words come to mind: equality, deliberative encounters, belonging, reflexivity, and transformational.

Firstly, the idea to see the student as 'equal intelligence' is a notion that I will carry forward in my daily activities and in future research concerning curriculum design. The invitation to a student to find his or her voice and to articulate his or her ideas is a dignified human engagement that has the potential for the emancipation of the self, the restorative justice of the self, and possible future responsible actions. Secondly, deliberative encounters create the opportunity for change and transformation of the self when the self is provoked to challenge dearly held beliefs through reflexivity. Encounters that delay judgement are premised on the conditions for dignified interactions and offer the potential for belonging in a diverse environment. For humanity to live in peace in a diverse world, it is imperative that deliberation and acceptance, irrespective of differences, lead to responsible and justified actions. My doctoral journey demonstrated the promise of the not-yet – although possible – future.

References

Adeto, Y.A. 2019. Transformative pedagogy for building peace. In APCEIU, *Reconciliation, peace, and global citizenship education: Pedagogy and practice*. Seoul: APCEIU, 28–35.

Bluckert, P. 2006. *Psychological dimensions of executive coaching*. Berkshire: McGraw-Hill Education.

COMENSA (Coaches and Mentors of South Africa). n.d. *Coaching vs mentoring: Understanding the difference*. Retrieved from www.comensa.org.za/ [Accessed 8 April 2024].

Deloitte. 2018. *The Audit Committee report: Analysing the trends in South Africa*. Retrieved from www2.deloitte.com/content/dam/Deloitte/za/Documents/audit/za_ Deloitte_The_Audit_Committee_Report_240418.pdf [Accessed 1 March 2019].

Desjardins, R., Torres, C.A. & Wiksten, S. 2020. *Social contract pedagogy: A dialogical and deliberative model for global citizenship education.* Background paper for the Futures of Education Initiative. Retrieved from https://unesdoc.unesco.org/ark:/48223/pf0000374879 [Accessed 8 April 2024].

Dewey, J. 1938. *Experience and education.* New York: MacMillan.

Foucault, M. 1995. *Discipline and punish: The birth of the prison.* New York: Vintage Books.

Freire, P. 1974. Conscientisation. *CrossCurrents*, 24(1):23–31. www.jstor.org/stable/24457877

Freire, P. 1996. *Pedagogy of the oppressed.* Second edition. London: Penguin Education.

Galtung, J. 1969. Violence, peace, and peace research. *Journal of Peace Research*, 6(3):167–191. www.jstor.org/stable/422690.

Giles, L. 2019. Learning to live together and a life worth living. In APCEIU, *Reconciliation, peace, and global citizenship education: Pedagogy and practice.* Seoul: APCEIU, 20–27.

Greene, M. 2001. *Variations on a blue guitar. The Lincoln Center Institute lectures on aesthetic education.* New York: Teachers College Press.

Gwadiso, S. & Terblanche, J. 2024. Cultivating socially responsible and ethical chartered accountant business leaders through learning and teaching. In M. Drinkwater & P. Deane (eds.). *The Bloomsbury handbook of context and transformative leadership in higher education.* London: Bloomsbury Academic (forthcoming).

Hansen, D.T. 1998. The moral is in the practice. *Teaching and Teacher Education*, 14(6):643–655.

Hellsten, S. & Larbi, G.A. 2006. Public good or private good? The paradox of public and private ethics in the context of developing countries. *Public Administration and Development*, 26(2):135–145. https://doi.org.10.1002/pad.406?>

Hullinger, A.M. & DiGirolamo, J.A. 2018. *Referring a client to therapy: A set of guidelines.* International Coaching Federation. Retrieved from www.coachingfederation.org/app/uploads/2021/01/ReferringaClienttoTherapy.pdf [Accessed 8 April 2024].

ICF (International Coaching Federation). n.d. *What is coaching?* Retrieved from https://coachingfederation.org/about#:~:text=What%20is%20Coaching%3F,of%20imagination%2C%20productivity%20and%20leadership [Accessed 8 April 2024].

Inayatullah, S. 2008. Six pillars: Futures thinking for transforming. *Foresight*, 10(1):4–21. https://doi.org.10.1108/14636680810855991?>

Kamler, B. & Thomson, P. 2008. The failure of dissertation advice books: Toward alternative pedagogies for doctoral writing. *Educational Researcher*, 37(8):507–514. https://doi.org.10.3102/0013189x08327390?>

Le Grange, L. 2021. (Individual) responsibility in decolonising the university curriculum. *South African Journal of Higher Education*, 35(1):4–20. https://doi.org.10.20853/35-1-4416?>

Lee, A. 2008. How are doctoral students supervised? Concepts of doctoral research supervision. *Studies in Higher Education*, 33(3):267–281. https://doi.org.10.1080/03075070802049202?>

Leibbrandt, M., Woolard, I. & Woolard, C. 2007. *Poverty and inequality dynamics in South Africa: Post-apartheid developments in the light of the long-run legacy.* Retrieved from https://ipcig.org/conference/ems/papers/ENG/Leibbrandt_Woolard_Woolard_ENG.pdf [Accessed 8 April 2024].

Malfroy, J. 2005. Doctoral supervision, workplace research and changing pedagogic practices. *Higher Education Research and Development*, 24(2):165–178. https://doi.org.10.1080/07294360500062961?>

Manthalu, C.H. & Waghid, Y. 2019. Decoloniality as a viable response to educational transformation in Africa. In C.H. Manthalu & Y. Waghid (eds.). *Education for decoloniality and decolonisation in Africa*. Cham: Palgrave Macmillan, 25–46.

Mbembe, A. 2015. *Decolonising knowledge and the question of the archive*. WISER. Retrieved from https://wiser.wits.ac.za/system/files/Achille%20Mbembe%20-%20Decolonizing%20Knowledge%20and%20the%20Question%20of%20the%20Archive.pdf [Accessed 1 May 2019].

Miyahara, M. & Fukao, A. 2022. Exploring the use of collaborative autoethnography as a tool for facilitating the development of researcher reflexivity. *System*, 105:1–9. https://doi.org.10.1016/j.system.2022.102751?>

Naudé, P.J. 2017. Toward justice and social transformation? Appealing to the tradition against the tradition. *HTS Teologiese Studies/Theological Studies*, 73(3):1–8. https://doi.org.10.4102/hts.v73i3.4350?>

Papastephanou, M. 2017. Learning by undoing, democracy and education, and John Dewey, the colonial traveller. *Education Sciences*, 7(20):1–13. https://doi.org.10.3390/educsci7010020?>

Pullen, E. & Waghid, Y. 2022. Towards global citizenship education: Implications for the South African higher education accounting system. *Progressio*, 43:13 pages. https://doi.org/10.25159/2663-5895/13517

Rock, D. & Page, L.J. 2009. *Coaching with the brain in mind: Foundations for practice*. Hoboken: Wiley.

Rugut, E.J. & Osman, A.A. 2013. Reflection on Paulo Freire and classroom relevance. *American International Journal of Social Sciences*, 2(2):23–28.

SAICA (South African Institute of Chartered Accountants). n.d. *How to become a CA(SA)*. Retrieved from www.saica.co.za/Training/BecomingaCA/tabid/157/language/en-US/Default.aspx [Accessed 7 April 2019].

SAICA (South African Institute of Chartered Accountants). 2016. *SAICA student handbook 2020/2021*. Volume 2B. Durban: LexisNexis.

SAICA (South African Institute of Chartered Accountants). 2019. *SAICA Competency Framework 2018: Detailed Guidance for the Academic Programme*. Retrieved from www.saica.co.za/Portals/0/LearnersStudents/documents/CompetencyFramework20 19b.pdf [Accessed 28 May 2021].

Segall, A. 2013. Revitalizing critical discourses in social education: Opportunities for a more complexified (un)knowing. *Theory & Research in Social Education*, 41:476–493.

Shultz, L. 2010. What do we ask of global citizenship education? A study of global citizenship education in a Canadian university. *International Journal of Development Education and Global Learning*, 3(1):1–22. https://doi.org.10.18546/IJDEGL.03.1.02?>

Smith, J.K.A. 2016. *You are what you love. The spiritual power of habit*. Ada, MI: BrazosPress.

Snyder, L.G. & Snyder, M.J. 2008. Teaching critical thinking and problem solving skills. *The Delta Pi Epsilon Journal*, 50(2):90–99.

Stehr, N. & Adolf, M.T. 2018. Knowledge/power/resistance. *Society*, 55(2):193–198. https://doi.org.10.1007/s12115-018-0232-3?>

Stout-Rostron, S. 2013. *Business coaching: Wisdom and practice*. Second edition. Johannesburg: Knowledge Resources.

Swanson, D.M. 2015. Ubuntu, indigeneity, and an ethic for decolonizing global citizenship. In A.A. Abdi, L. Schultz & T. Pillay (eds.). *Decolonizing global citizenship education*. Rotterdam: Sense, 27–38.

Takyi-Amoako, E.J. & Assié-Lumumba, N.T. 2018. Introduction: Re-visioning education in Africa: Ubuntu-inspired education for humanity. In E.J. Takyi-Amoako & N.T. Assié-Lumumba (eds.). *Re-visioning education in Africa: Ubuntu-inspired education for humanity*. London: Palgrave Macmillan, 1–18.

Terblanche, J. 2019. Cultivating socially just responsible citizens in relation to university accounting education in South Africa. Unpublished PhD dissertation. Stellenbosch: Stellenbosch University.

Terblanche, J. & Van der Walt, C. 2019. Leaning into discomfort: Engaging film as a reflective surface to encourage deliberative encounters. In C.H. Manthalu & Y. Waghid (eds.). *Education for decoloniality and decolonisation in Africa*. Camden: Springer Nature Switzerland, 203–224.

Terblanche, J. & Waghid, Y. 2021. Chartered accountancy and resistance in South Africa. *South African Journal of Higher Education*, 35(3):239–253. https://doi.org/10.20853/35-3-3894

The World Bank. 2021. *The World Bank in South Africa*. Retrieved from www.worldbank.org/en/country/southafrica/overview [Accessed 8 April 2024].

Venter, E.R. & De Villiers, C. 2013. The accounting profession's influence on academe: South African evidence. *Accounting, Auditing & Accountability Journal*, 26(8):1246–1278. https://doi.org.10.1108/AAAJ-06-2012-01027?>

Waghid, Y. 2019. *Towards a philosophy of caring in higher education. Pedagogy and nuances of care*. Camden: Palgrave Macmillan.

Waghid, Y. 2021. Why the decolonisation of higher education without critique is not possible? *South African Journal of Higher Education*, 35(2):1–3. https://doi.org.10.20853/35-2-4621?>

Waghid, Y., Waghid, F. & Waghid, Z. 2018. *Rupturing African philosophy on teaching and learning: Ubuntu justice and education*. London: Palgrave Macmillan.

Wood, N. & Maistry, S.M. 2014. Professional accounting associations' influence on higher education accounting pedagogy. *Alternation*, Special edition(12):198–239.

7 Reflections on an academic voyage
Encounters with a democratic citizenship education praxis

Monica Zembere

Introduction

This chapter is an extension of the PhD reflections that I presented at the National Institute of Humanities and Social Sciences conference in 2022. It reflects a thesis journey from the position of experiencing writing the thesis and, in doing so, considering what this voyage might offer fellow doctoral candidates. The reflection considers the individual experiences I had during the conceptualisation and assemblage of my thesis. The journey of this doctorate was not as seamless as many would expect. There have been constraints and obstacles throughout the journey. I can still remember the screams of excitement and surprise when I opened the offer letter from Stellenbosch University. Securing admission was only the first step. Although I intended to register for study in 2014, financial challenges held me back. Since I had not applied for any scholarships, I also had no money to pay for the initial registration, which was a requirement before I could proceed with my study. I automatically began the process of applying for any scholarship that might come my way. A few more weeks later, I obtained a scholarship from the National Institute of Humanities and Social Sciences to cover my tuition fees and living expenses.

My PhD research was on: *Democratic citizenship education (DCE) in Zimbabwe's higher education institutions (HEIs)*. I can still remember how I felt starting my PhD at Stellenbosch University. The feeling of having my own timetable was both liberating and a little overwhelming. I felt as if I had little idea of what I was supposed to do from day to day, and I wanted someone to give me a reading list or an assignment just so that I could have a deadline towards which to work. Falling into a routine felt like the hardest part of my first year of PhD study, but once I had started on my introductory chapter and review of related literature, I began to feel more confident in what I was doing and whether I was doing it right. From proposal writing to writing the last chapter, it was a journey of discovery. I learned in this process that the more we learn, the more there is to learn.

The start of the PhD was the most interesting – and the most stressful – part of my academic journey. Academically, my promoter found many mistakes

DOI: 10.4324/9781003530091-8

in my first proposal draft and my proposed topic, which caused me several months to rework the proposal. I was discouraged and nearly threw in the towel. The title of the thesis was changed countless times as new information kept coming. Initially, my proposed topic was on political governance in Zimbabwe, and how this affected university autonomy. This was rightly dismissed and rejected by Prof. Waghid who felt it was too political and too sensitive. He further highlighted that a topic of this nature was likely to be constrained by practical issues, such as bias, access to data, and time. I therefore had a challenge of creating a feasible, interesting, and workable research topic. I felt the promoter was imposing his authority and manipulating the research topic. My voice in the research area was somehow submerged as I lost my own ideas about which I had hoped to write.

Instead of becoming disillusioned or discouraged, I learned that research is an ongoing process with twists and turns that often lead to gaining new knowledge and abandoning previous ideas. I dealt with these issues by examining the titles and research questions and objectives of other dissertations and research articles related to my topic, and this helped me to define the scope of my study. It became clear that one cannot try to focus on a topic or figure out a research question when one has not read the literature on that topic widely. I did not rest working on the topic and the proposal and attending to my promoter's comments and finally, in 2015, I received the approval to proceed with my research. My promoter, a (distinguished professor), firstly oriented me into the expectations of the faculty and the publication requirements. He always responded to emails immediately, and this encouraged me to work harder. The promoter's comments are crucial in research as he or she is an expert in his or her fields. My supportive promoter was distinguished Prof. Yusef Waghid. It is essential to have a supportive promoter who can understand one's situation and circumstances at any given time, and who would guide the student accordingly.

Democratic citizenship education as dialogical encounter

Throughout my academic life, I had never become acquainted with the concept 'democratic citizenship education' (DCE). My promoter introduced me to democratic iterations that are explained in terms of debate, deliberation, dialogue, negotiation, and discussion. These conceptions (iterations) emphasise how learners should engage with one another (Benhabib 2002). Benhabib talks about dialogue as a process where people enact what they have in common, as people might have a real purpose to co-exist. Benhabib adds that, for learning to take place in a democratic encounter, dialogue as a principle of engagement should be promoted so that humanness is cultivated. Dialogue is synonymous with the relationship or pathway of communication between two or more parties. Dialogism opposes the asymmetrical notion of dialogue, which refers to a one-way process in which meaning is transferred in one direction (Adams 2002). According to Adams (2002:76), an asymmetrical relationship opposes the one-way process and emphasises a co-constructive process in which meaning is constructed. Central to that, dialogue is the nurturing of debate and mutual respect between two or more interested parties. The democratic relationship, which my promoter nurtured with his students, was characterised by openness, mutual respect, and trust. As a result, I was able to connect, engage, and grow in confidence with my performance. Through dialogue with my promoter, I could share with him my financial concerns, and I benefited from the 'small' grants that he sought for me to register and finally print my thesis. To elucidate this further, mutual respect and trust are significant tenets of dialogue and can eradicate the traditional oppositional relationships between the lecturer (the knowing expert who imparts knowledge and wisdom) and the learner (the unknowing learner who receives knowledge and wisdom) through dialogue, between the teacher and the learner, there is the establishment of a partnership in which all parties engage with one another (Adams 2002:77). This means that, in a democratic classroom, the listener is not always the student as there is two-way verbal interaction. Moreover, the roles of the teacher and of the student are often interchanged. As the basis of the learning process, dialogue implies the promotion of cooperation, motivation, self-confidence instead of just talking and discussing issues. In democratic citizenship, the encounter does not mean that students and their supervisors do not disagree. My promoter was, for instance, worried about my failure to find my own voice. I struggled initially to find my own voice due to the amount of literature. I had amassed way more data than I needed. Prof. Waghid directed me to seek recent journal articles and seminal works related to DCE. He also encouraged me to follow key scholars in the field and gave me some references to consult. I was not presenting arguments but information and more information. My work was lacking originality. Originality is a prerequisite for doctoral research (Cryer 2000:190). I learned with time that my work was poor because I did not know how to construct convincing arguments. Despite having good ideas, I was often unable to articulate myself in a manner that was expected by my supervisor. This means I needed to work very hard on academic writing skills. I joined the language coaching classes offered by the Language services and further read articles that could improve my academic writing. I also benefited considerably from a series of workshops organised by the language services in terms of personal and professional growth. Attendance of these workshops helped me to improve my academic writing skills.

Justice as a democratic encounter

Without justice, there is no democratic citizenship (Adams 2002). Through my study, I found that educating for citizenship does not only involve cultivating in people a sense of deliberating together freely and equally about their common and collective destiny, but it is also about achieving justice for all, including students at institutions of higher education, such as students and immigrants from Zimbabwe and neighbouring countries who relocated to South Africa for various reasons. I came from Zimbabwe and was doing doctoral research in a foreign country, which sometimes made me feel alienated. Adjusting to a foreign culture, the Stellenbosch culture, which was in many respects different from Harare and different from the University of Zimbabwe where I had done my master's in Curriculum and Arts, unsettled me for some time. Although there were many foreign students at Stellenbosch, not many were from Zimbabwe. I was however helped to settle by my promoter who created an enabling environment for me to feel welcome and accepted. Our democratic encounter was informed by mutual engagement and genuine conversation that made me feel at ease and not alienated. Habermas (1996:88) comments that a student-promoter encounter should be one of openness, where both are permitted to introduce a claim, question a claim, and express themselves without being subjected to any form of coercion.

According to Gutmann (1999:69), democratic citizenship education is anchored in deliberating about the demands of justice. This means that public education ought to cultivate in students the skills and values of DCE. On the other hand, Benhabib (1996) avers that, in order for individuals to become democratic citizens, they need to be exposed to at least three interrelated elements of collective identity: privileges of membership to a community, social rights, and benefits. Through exposure to these three interrelated items, it is hoped that a participatory climate of deliberation will emerge in which the rights of all people are recognised and respected (Waghid 2010:199). Through deliberation with my promoter, educational practices were established based on the construction of reasonable views and arguments by which we made modifications and adjustments. This means deliberation considered argumentation, persuasion, and consensus-making as reasonable endeavours to pursue in search of justifications that enjoy the support of an association of individuals as they embark on educational practices. My supervisor respected my rights as a student, and he had the ability to listen and offer constructive feedback. Our democratic engagement was beneficial to me as a student. Although Prof. Waghid demanded academic rigour and quality work, he worked democratically towards building my confidence. I use 'democratically' according to the explanation by Callan (1997:79) that to be democratic is to allow learners to speak their minds without fear of being silenced. This is based on encouraging learners to participate in a thought-provoking dialogue on the basis that one is not more than the topic of conversation, as well as to care about others as partners and to restrain themselves from violating others' rights. Dewey (1996:115) maintains that a democratic encounter is one that makes provision for participation of all its members on equal terms, and which secures flexible readjustment of its institutions through interaction of different forms of associated life. For Dewey, "belief in equality is an element of the democratic credo" (Waghid 2015 :115). Dewey believes equality means to treat all students equally, without any student receiving preferential treatment in terms of pedagogical support and ignoring the unequal education to which many students from poor backgrounds have been subjected (Waghid 2015:37). I was privileged to be supervised by Prof. Waghid who understood the impoverished economic background of the country I was coming from, and he was compassionate enough to recommend some grants to ensure that I remain part of the university community.

Compiling an abstract

To compile my abstract, I had to search through several other PhD theses to obtain ideas on how to create mine. I noticed from my reading that an abstract of PhD research is different in both content and length from the abstract of a conference research article. Despite having gone through countless abstracts, I still encountered challenges on compiling the abstract content. I had to decide which aspects of my thesis were important enough to be included in the abstract. To my mind, every aspect of my research was valuable; therefore, worth mentioning in the abstract. My first draft abstract comprised three pages. Prof. Waghid refused to read my draft stating that it was too long for an abstract. He insisted that I reduce it by removing 'unnecessary' information and remaining with only a page. I decided to include in the abstract my topic, a brief description of my philosophical and conceptual framework, the research objectives, a short description of the methodology, and a summary of key findings. I was influenced by Trafford and Leshem's (2008:45) seminal thoughts that an abstract is –

> [A]n opportunity to sell the scholarly quality of your thesis to prospective readers... as it presents the merits of your thesis and shows how your contribution to knowledge met the specified gap in knowledge that was your reason for undertaking the research.

Based on this guidance, my goal was to make my abstract short and self-explanatory, provide a synopsis of the entire thesis, and respond to the question of what my thesis is all about in order to whet the appetite of readers. I had a separate notebook where I jotted down main ideas, which I thought were crucial for the abstract. Reserving writing the abstract until I had completed the first full draft of the thesis was helpful to ensure that the text produced for the abstract was factual, clearly written, and free of references, abbreviations or acronyms and jargon, informative but not argumentative, and written in an appealing style that would engage with both lay and expert audiences.

My dilemma in engagement with the body of knowledge

The literature review is an integral part of the doctoral thesis since it allows students to situate their study within the existing literature and to demonstrate the voice of the author (Hofstee, 2006). Undertaking a literature review allows the researcher to define what the field of study is, to establish which research has already been done that relates to one's work, as well as to consider the existing theories, concepts, and models applied in the field of study (Trafford & Leshem 2008; Wellington 2005). This suggests that, at a certain point in the literature review, one's reading informs the kind of research questions posed or the focus of the study, and at another stage, the objectives of the study guide the kind of reading that one does (Trafford & Leshem 2008).

The main challenge I encountered with identification of relevant literature was documentary inundation. I remember my first draft of Chapter 2, which took me a year to compile, was rejected by Prof. Waghid because it covered almost everything on democratic citizenship. There was no direction. I did not know where to start and where to end with my reading until my promoter intervened. He instructed me to read what literature review is all about before writing. Prof. Waghid advised me to "read with your study in mind", and he asked me a seemingly simple question but difficult to answer, "Monica, what do you want to write about?"

This question unsettled me. I abandoned the idea of having a stand-alone chapter on the literature review, although I initially thought this was going to be the case. Instead, my Chapter 2 reflected an investigation of DCE within the liberal framework. Prof. Waghid kept reminding me that this chapter had to serve the needs of my study. It was supposed to be aligned with my research title, and I therefore needed to operate within the confines of the theoretical and conceptual framework. The literature review was therefore narrowed to evaluating the extent to which higher education in Zimbabwe is influenced by the competing theories of individualism (liberalism) and communitarianism (republicanism) that are prevalent in DCE. The conviction is that the values of communitarian liberalism may contribute towards deepening democratic citizenship and democracy in Zimbabwean higher education. Education is a strategic factor for both mental and socio-economic development, but the capacity to do so is enhanced through democratic engagement and dialogical encounter of its citizens. My argument in the chapter was that a plausible conception of DCE could aid in reconceptualising higher education in Zimbabwe. For Zimbabwe to achieve a meaningful democratic citizenship, the country should develop well-thought-out education policies that ensure not only mass literacy but also full utilisation of their graduates, not only for economic achievement but also for citizenship. This can only be achieved if the education system is restructured, redesigned, and implemented in a way that is informed by and promotes democratic principles of justice, participation, equity, tolerance, access, debate, discussion, and dialogue. Throughout my PhD study, my promoter initiated (i.e. acculturated) me into being a democratic citizen, by creating civil spaces where we could share about the political and economic situation at home (Zimbabwe) as well as through engaging me in a conversation underpinned by interdependence and share commonalities. Prof. Waghid's conduct with his students (me included) is greatly influenced by the works of Rorty (1999), such as ideas of socialisation, acculturation, and initiation (see Waghid 2015). For Rorty, socialisation is acquired before the student enters college or university. At college (or university), one's thinking is developed to become critically oriented, and one becomes more autonomous in one's thinking (Rorty 1999:117). The weakness of Rorty's (1999) idea of socialisation is that it associates critical thinking with college (or university) students; yet, self-reflective learning can also happen at school. For Waghid (2015), to be socialised into a discourse is tantamount to being initiated into such discourse, which requires critical engagement with the content of the discourse. In this regard, my doctoral encounter with my promoter was guided by a process of socialisation. I benefited from acculturation by gaining a thorough understanding of democratic citizenship concepts. My promoter extended the process of socialisation by giving me the opportunity to come up with alternatives, to imagine things differently, and to push the boundaries of my doctoral study towards something 'unfamiliar' (Rorty, 1999:118). While it is true that my encounter with my promoter was characterised by me complaining at first that he was expecting too much from me, a year later, the promoter–student relationship developed. My promoter was different from other promoters who dictate what students should research. My task was to convince him – through my proposal – that the topic was researchable.

As I progressed into the third year, I was becoming increasingly independent and enjoyed the control and autonomy to the point where my promoter was almost invisible. I submitted my final thesis for examination in October 2017.

I enjoyed the doctoral journey and had grown as an individual. One of my painful experiences at the time was that my father passed on in January 2018, two months before my graduation. It was devastating. Throughout my educational journey, he had been my hero. He knew every examination I ever wrote, every grade I ever received, and was certainly more concerned about my PhD progress than I was. My dad was my inspiration and the strongest man I knew.

Conclusion

The central theme of a PhD journey is independent scholarship, meaning one has to do all of it by yourself. If I could go back in time, would I go for a PhD again? The answer is a resounding yes! Although it has been difficult, it has also been a fruitful and interesting journey. I was not born intelligent; it was hard work, support from my promoter, Stellenbosch University, Bindura University, and the National Institute of Humanities and Social Sciences that got me where I am now. I am glad to have chosen this path. My promoter initiated me into being a scholar and a philosopher by recommending me to read democratic education: policy and praxis (Waghid 2002), Gutmann's book, *Democratic Education* (1996), and *Pedagogy of the Oppressed* by Paulo Freire (1996). These works stimulated my interest in democratic education.

Lessons learned

Apart from pursuing knowledge for its own sake, a PhD in philosophy (Education Policy) altered the way I see the world concerning multiculturalism, democratic citizenship, and citizenship education. I started to appreciate that every citizen is a global citizen, and in that regard, we all must tolerate people who are different from us. As a scholar, I have contributed to knowledge by publishing five articles from my thesis, two of which are book chapters.

Besides publication and contribution to theoretical knowledge, I have had the opportunity to share my research findings with students at Wits during my placement there while I was on sabbatical attachment. I was attached to Wits School of Education for eight months and was able to share my ideas on DCE. Practically, I used my expertise to mark PhD theses for Unisa as an external examiner. I am still attached to Unisa as an external examiner. This would not have been possible without the democratic encounter I had with my promoter. All of this is an indication that my PhD has contributed considerably to knowledge production not only in Zimbabwe, where I am a university lecturer, but in Africa as well. The thesis has provided me with in-depth knowledge in so far as democratic citizenship is concerned. I remember well when I presented a paper at the University of Botswana in 2018 while I was on contract leave that many academics found the discipline of democratic citizenship fascinating and new. My advice to students who are undertaking PhD research is that the secret to a successful completion is for one to think about one's work always, and to enjoy what one is doing. For one to enjoy one's work, one must understand what one is doing.

References

Adams, M. 2002. Losing one's voice: Dialogical psychology and the unspeakable. *Theory & Psychology*, 20(3):342–361.
Benhabib, S. 1996. Towards a deliberative model of democratic legitimacy. In S. Benhabib (ed.). *Democracy and difference: Contesting the boundaries of the political.* London: Princeton University Press, 63–79.
Benhabib, S. 2002. *The claims of culture: Equality and diversity in the global era.* Princeton, NJ: Princeton University Press.
Cryer, P. 2000. *The research student's guide to success.* Buckingham: Open University Press.
Dewey, J. 1916. *Democracy and education.* New York: Macmillan.
Freire, P. 1996. *Pedagogy of the oppressed.* London: Penguin.
Gutmann, A.1999. *Democratic education.* Princeton, NJ: Princeton University Press.
Habermas, J. 1996. Three normative models of democracy. In S. Benhabib (ed.). *Democracy and difference: Contesting the boundaries of the political.* Princeton, NJ: Princeton University Press, 21–30.
Hofstee, E. 2006.*Constructing a good dissertation: A practical guide to finishing a master's, MBA or PhD on schedule.* Johannesburg: EPE.
Rorty, R. 1999. Education as socialisation and as individuation. In M. Rorty (ed.). *Philosophy and social hope.* New York: Penguin Books, 144–126.
Trafford & Leshem. 2008. *Stepping stones to achieving your doctorate: A practical guide to finishing a PhD.* Maidenhead: McGraw-Hill. Open University Press.
Waghid, Y. (2002). *Democratic education: Policy and praxis.* Stellenbosch: Stellenbosch University.
Waghid, Y. 2010. *Education, democracy and citizenship revisited: Pedagogical encounters.* Stellenbosch: SUN MeDIA.

Waghid, Y. 2015. *Dancing with doctoral encounters: Democratic education in motion.* Stellenbosch: SUN MeDIA.

Wellington, J. & Nixon, J. 2005. Shaping the field: The role of academic journal editors in the construction of education as a field of study. *British Journal of Sociology of Education*, 26(5):643–655.

8 Democratic citizenship pedagogy as recognition of the student's situatedness in doctoral supervision

Chikumbutso Herbert Manthalu

Introduction

This chapter presents the argument that making doctoral supervision encounters democratic should include having the university, through the supervisor as its agent, recognise the student's subjective situatedness as key in the study process. For Education doctoral students, the research problem mostly originates significantly from phenomenon the student experiences in education encounters that are situated in social-cultural contexts. Therefore, the argument this chapter advances is that the student's situatedness should not be divorced from how the supervision encounter conceptualises the research problem. Making doctoral supervision democratic should therefore entail recognising the situationality of the student, and the bearing this situationality has on conceptualisation of the research problem, as well as inquiry tools – such as the theoretical lenses – to be employed in understanding the study problem. A mode of supervision that demands that a student's non-mainstream lived experiences conform to the assumptions of dominant theories and epistemologies is thus undemocratic.

More particularly, it is argued in this chapter that social theories have foundational assumptions that are rooted in the lived experiences of the developers of said social theories (Code, 2012). This being the case, the doctoral student's lived experiences that are considered incompatible with the assumptions of the dominant theories should not be forced to conform to the dominant theories. Rather, where necessary, the supervision should be open-minded in order to accommodate demands for the re-imagination of methods of inquiry and assumptions of the dominant theories. Realisation of such open-mindedness, as is shown in this chapter, demands that the supervisor must necessarily embrace democratic attitudes that are not limited by the surreptitious absolutist authority of social theories that characterise university education. This way, doctoral supervision encounters become a pedagogy that, besides generating knowledge, meaningfully achieve human equality and mutual respect, which are cardinal tenets of democratic citizenship.

DOI: 10.4324/9781003530091-9

In the next section, the nature of the doctoral supervision context in relation to the power imbalances that characterise the context is discussed. In the section, a case is made for the necessity of doctoral supervision to enact democratic citizenship. Referring to the theorisation of global citizenship education (GCE), the subtle essentialist nature of social theories is considered. It is shown that the essentialist nature of social theories ignores that grand social theories, such as those about human nature, standard knowledge, and ultimate goals of education, originated from particularistic experiences (see Code, 2012). The theories should not be inherently dismissive of alternative theoretical assumptions emanating from different lived experiences (ibid). Upon making a case for the indispensability of a doctoral student's lived experiences in the research process, I later draw from my personal doctoral journey to demonstrate the enactment of certain aspects of democratic doctoral supervision. I show how my experiences of globalisation as a citizen from a developing country were incongruent with the assumptions of mainstream GCE. I point out the challenge that the assumptions of the grand theories of GCE posed in my study, threatening to undermine the validity of my lived experiences under globalisation. Finally, I show how the democratic supervision I received supported me in navigating the subtly conformist and essentialist pitfalls of doctoral studies.

The doctoral supervision context

Every human enterprise, including encounters in graduate programmes, is in its own right about governing. In graduate programmes, government entails conducting the policies and affairs of the enterprise, which is the university (Ramdeholl, Giordani, Heaney & Yanow, 2010). The indispensability of the notion of government in doctoral encounters, however, raises questions regarding who actually governs. How is the government formed, and whose interests does the government serve (see Ramdeholl et al., 2010)? These are questions about democracy.

In the context of the modern university, questions of who wields which power, under which conditions, and to what end are pertinent because of the historical evolution of the university. The history of the modern university is steeped in domination, oppression, exclusion, and injustice (Hames, 2009). While the modern university is in stark contrast with its historical past, there remain doctoral study governance elements that are rooted in the structural and cultural orientation of the past. In this regard, it is worth bearing in mind that the academy has inherent systemic barriers to democracy (Ramdeholl et al., 2010).

The doctoral supervision process is characterised by interests, influence, power, and powerlessness, among others (Heaney, 2015). One thing that is central to the occurrence of doctoral studies is decision-making. Very often the supervisor must decide in relation to the study, but there are also decisions the student must make in terms of the study. Such decisions are mostly not easy to make. Making decisions in such contexts involves considering multiple and sometimes conflicting interests of different agents. Acknowledging the complexity of democracy as a decision-making system, Ramdeholl (2010) holds that, at a minimum, educational encounters must respect the fact that people have a right to express their interests in decisions that affect them though this does not necessarily imply that such interests must always prevail. Such responsiveness to democracy is not inconsistent with the authority derived from specialised knowledge or expertise that members of teaching staff have (Ramdeholl et al., 2010).

Why democracy in doctoral supervision?

Universities are characteristically hierarchical and tradition-bound institutions with weak student power (see Heaney, 2015; Ramdeholl et al., 2010). This results into little room for student participation, even in the making of decisions about the student's study. In a sense, the doctoral supervisor embodies the university and performs on its behalf the roles of legitimation of knowledge production and certification of knowledge acquisition (Heaney, 2015). Supervisors, as agents of the university, perform these functions based on certain predetermined values and prevailing belief systems that are institution-specific or underlie higher education in general (Heaney, 2015). Such institutional values and beliefs are however not impartial nor detached from socio-cultural and historical traditions of a particular society. Inevitably, as Heaney (2015) avers, such functions of the university have strong traits specific to a particular race, gender, history, class, and culture influence.

The complexity of democratic decision-making manifests in the multiple roles academic staff have to play depending on the nature of the decision to be made. Should the staff act in an advisory capacity? Do the staff have jurisdiction? Should decision-making be left in the hands of the student, or should others be consulted (Ramdeholl et al., 2010)? It is worth emphasising that demands that doctoral supervision encounters should be democratic are not tantamount to the promotion of a monolithic conception of democracy, which distributes power equally to all those participating in the educational encounter. Rather, the demand for democratisation of the doctoral supervision process is cognisant of the inevitable differences in power and authority owing to possession of expert knowledge and institutional embodiment characterising the supervisor on the one hand and the student's generally relative lack of expert knowledge on the other (Heaney, 2015; Ramdeholl et al., 2010). The demand however is that the exercise of authority and power by the privileged supervisor should occur in a context of mindfulness of the limits of his or her expert knowledge. The awareness implies that, if the expertise is not used in a manner that is considerate of the other, it may serve oppressive tendencies, thus undermining the dignity of the student.

Subtle theoretical and conceptual essentialism

Among the typical decisions made in doctoral supervision encounters are those regarding the theoretical prisms that the student should employ. Supervisors usually have the most influence by way of their recommendations to the student about the ideal theoretical conceptualisation of the study. The theoretical lenses determine the nature of the conceptualisation of the research problem as well as the methodological approaches and tools required to understand the problem (Creswell & Creswell, 2014). Academic theories across disciplines employ concepts and categories to understand and classify things (Ndofirepi & Gwaravanda, 2018). Unlike hard disciplines, such as the natural sciences, which are mostly built on universal laws or theories, have causal propositions, and generalisable findings, social science disciplines, such as education, by contrast, do not have very clear boundaries and have a relatively unspecified structure with loosely defined research problems (Trowler, 2009).

Across different disciplines, different theories dominate as the major prisms through which human experiences should be processed for meaning. Such domination tends to generate and sustain the assumption that the dominant theoretical prisms are the standard for inquiry and knowledge validation (Ladson-Billings, 2014). In due course, the prisms acquire an essentialist status that downgrades and disqualifies anything that does not conform to the fundamental assumptions of the dominant theory (Code, 2012). The assumption that prevails is that such theorisations in the social sciences and humanities are impartial truths that ought to be accepted by all academic inquiry in the discipline (see Ladson-Billings, 2014; Mignolo, 2007; Zeleza, 2009). One would further infer that even the tolerance of competing rival theories is ultimately based on the fact that though in contrast with each other, the theories nevertheless share similar fundamental assumptions, for instance, about human nature and are derived from similar lived experiences. Thus, the differences – no matter how stark – are therefore tolerable insofar as they share fundamental assumptions.

It is also worth recognising that, in a critical sense, knowledge construction is not immune to the social-cultural context of the constructors because "theory does not exist in isolation but is nested within larger philosophical concepts of epistemology, ontology, and axiology" (Thacker & Freeman, 2021:74). One's social, cultural, economic, and geographical conditions have a significant bearing on the nature of knowledge one has about being human and social cooperation among others. This is because knowledge formulation is inextricably conditioned by people's situatedness, i.e. their historical, cultural and linguistic experiences, and ontological frames through which they experience and make meaning of the world (Code, 2012).

It is against this background that, in higher education generally, theoretical assumptions, ontologies, and knowledge – particularly from the Global South – are scarcely accorded validity (Mignolo, 2007; Ndlovu-Gatsheni, 2015). It is largely because the assumptions originate from experiences atypical of those of the dominant standard knowledge (Ladson-Billings, 2014). As a result, the knowledge is scarcely accepted because of it being unfamiliar to modern knowledge gatekeepers in higher education and even to journal editors and publishers as associates in the higher education knowledge production (R'boul, 2022). To gain credibility and acceptance, such other knowledge is required to conform to the lived assumptions of the lived experiences from which the hegemonic standard knowledge derives (see Ladson-Billings, 2014; Mignolo, 2007; Ndlovu-Gatsheni, 2015). More often, the implicit unconditional conformity invalidates the normativity of the unique realities and lived experiences of people from globally marginalised societies (see Manthalu & Waghid, 2019). The demand to conform forces 'subaltern' experiences and outlooks (i.e. the experiences and outlooks that are maligned because of their incompatibility with the dominant) to adapt into a form that is consistent with the assumptions of the ostensible standard universal knowledge (Code, 2012; Mignolo, 2007; Ndlovu-Gatsheni, 2017). The assumptions of the standard universal knowledge and theories are however rooted in the historical, social, cultural, and economic experiences of particular globally dominant societies.

It is in this sense that the African university is far removed from its historical, linguistic, and social-cultural context of existence. This results in the African university being alien to the historical, social, economic, and cultural situated-ness of the African student (Ndlovu-Gatsheni, 2018). This is largely due to the exclusive prioritisation of the dominant epistemologies that were derived from some lived experiences, marginalising knowledge that derives from any other incompatible lived experiences (Code, 2012). Such an inherent marginalising characteristic of the modern university compels the African university to fail to integrate and centre the diverse African experiences, traditions, ontologies, and epistemologies due to their inevitable incompatibility with the foundational assumptions of the ostensibly standard Eurocentric knowledge (Mignolo, 2007; Ndlovu-Gatsheni, 2017; Ndofirepi & Gwaravanda, 2018).

There is an epistemic intolerance and subsequent absence of concepts and categories that could aid a better understanding of African-rooted experiences. The absence of such concepts and categories has resulted in African scholarship seeking to understand situated African lived experiences in the worldviews of other societies (Ndofirepi & Gwaravanda, 2018). In the strictest sense, it is very difficult to talk of an African university, although ideally there ought to be one. Instead, what exists is a university in Africa, detached from African experiences. The knowledge generated upon forcing African lived experiences to conform to the epistemic assumptions derived from Eurocentric lived experiences is ill-positioned to help resolve the problems that are particular to the social, cultural, and economic situatedness of the African continent (see Ndlovu-Gatsheni, 2017).

Such a background of entrenched othering of incompatible experiences and epistemological assumptions different from the dominant standard ones raises an obligation for the re-imagination of the doctoral supervision process. It is now apparent that in a doctoral supervision encounter, decisions about which lived experiences, theoretical assumptions, and epistemological lenses to employ or to exclude are in principle judgements about which lived experiences to validate or invalidate. Whenever theoretical assumptions and epistemological decisions surreptitiously invalidate other human experiences as not worthy of generating or informing an alternative epistemology, such an invalidation by implication denies the being-human of the people who experience life through such prisms (Benhabib, 2011).

In the case of the student in education research – or social science research in general – that which constitutes a problem or problems that a study must answer is inseparable from the student and his or her lived experiences. Human beings are embedded subjective beings with an affective emotional constitution, a particular concrete history, and an individual as well as collective identity or identities (Benhabib, 1992; Freire, 2014). It is therefore worth acknowledging that the student is an embodied being with a particular history, he or she comes from a situated community, and has cultural background that accord him or her with different ontological prisms for meaning making. It is imperative that the student is not only recognised in a generalised sense. Rather the recognition should be expressed in the making of doctoral supervision decisions, such as about the experiences that constitute a problem for a study in educational research. The student's background is therefore worth normative and epistemological consideration in supervision encounters if the doctoral supervision encounter should cultivate democratic citizenship values.

Indispensability of the student's situatedness

In this section, I discuss the necessity of making doctoral supervision democratic by recognising the student's situatedness in the knowledge construction endeavours. The discussion draws much from my doctoral study encounter, particularly the oddness of my doctoral research topic and problem. My research topic on education for global or cosmopolitan citizenship was informed by my lived experiences of the effect of globalisation on education policies in Malawi. In the quest to be accommodative, academic discourses in different disciplines themselves experience the pitfalls of promoting exclusion through the advancement of standard theories and methodologies ostensibly aimed at inclusion. As a result, theories aimed at challenging inequalities sometimes ironically tend to be founded on ontologies that regard any other ontological assumptions as unworthy sources of knowledge. Take, for instance, the question of the place of nationality and the nation-state in global or cosmopolitan citizenship studies, as was the case in my research. A background to my doctoral study problem is necessary to highlight the need for democratic pedagogy in doctoral studies. My research was making a case for the recognition of the role of the nation and localness in configurations of education for global citizenship contrary to prevailing Malawian government educational policies.

Most cosmopolitan citizenship theories are critical and dismissive of nationality and the nation-state, regarding them as inherently inhibitive of cosmopolitan equality (Habermas, 2001; Nili, 2015; Nussbaum, 2002). As already highlighted, a theory is abstracted from assumptions derived from the lived experiences of the one who develops the theory. Different people across the world however experience globalisation in different and contrasting ways.

Global economic, political, legal, social, and educational structures have a systemic design that denies a fair representation of the interests and voices of people in developing countries (Armstrong, 2009; Steger & Roy, 2010; Vázquez-Arroyo, 2008). A total absence of the nation-state from relevant global spaces would exacerbate marginality and take away any possibility of such voices to be considered as voices of equals in the global community. Given the complexity of the global structure and the ambivalent way it irregularly affects the lives and life chances of people across the world, it is presumptuous to advance one way of making sense of global systems and institutions over another. The question regarding the place of the nation-state and its accompanying national solidarity in global citizenship attracts different responses based on the part of the world where people have experienced globalisation. In most cases, those whose societies have been experiencing the systemic subtle displacement of local ontologies, epistemologies, languages, and socio-cultural values regard the role of the nation-state in education for global citizenship differently from those whose societies shape and drive the global order. Unless the supervisor is aware of this reality, summary dismissal of all forms of nation-state solidarity would, as is often the case, be regarded as right-wing thinking and incompatible with equality and cosmopolitan inclusion; yet, they are compatible.

In a critical sense, the student comes into the graduate programme as an other, an outsider of the academic community that is characterised by common standards, perspectives, epistemologies, values, and theoretical assumptions. The student is expected to be initiated into the ways of the academy, to become like the prototype person of the academy. As highlighted earlier, however, the knowledge legitimation standards, values, epistemological assumptions, and ideals of the academy are not insulated from particularistic cultural, historical, and social values that are ostensibly regarded as impartial (Ramdeholl et al., 2010). The above-mentioned standards are products of certain cultures and experiences. This places extra demands on Other students with Other histories, backgrounds, and cultures who want to be part of the academic community. Inevitably, the Other student experiences tensions and contradictions within the academic context that demand him or her to conform. In the doctoral encounter, the student is the most powerless partner. It is, therefore, imperative for academic staff to be cognizant of the reality of the powerlessness that results from the multiple layers of otherness that underlie students with lived experiences that are alien to the assumed experiences of the mainstream theories and methodologies of academic spaces.

As highlighted earlier, theory – particularly in the social sciences – is an abstraction that is largely dependent on one's lived experiences. A detachment of one's lived experiences from theory construction or conceptualisation of the research problem is unattainable because the two are mutually reinforcing (Code, 2012). Democratic pedagogy would demand that, although the student's lived experiences, which inform the research problem, may be inconsistent with the dominant theories, it is the supervision approaches and tools that should reform rather than demand the student's other lived experiences to conform. This does not only ensure epistemic justice but, more importantly, it embodies respect of the experiences of the other as equally valid experiences worth to inform academic reflection just as do those behind the dominant epistemologies and theories (Mignolo, 2007). This way, doctoral study cultivates and promotes democratic citizenship values.

Sometimes – and subtly – PhD students and supervisors alike are under pressure to conform to the values and expectations of their departmental or institutional orientation (Skakni, 2018). Sometimes, the expectation to conform exerts pressure on the student's thesis topic, his or her ontological conceptualisation of the research problem, and the epistemological orientations and methodological choices to be made to understand the research problem (Skakni, 2018). Teaching and doctoral supervision staff should therefore intentionally create space for the expression of student voices that are Other, to hear them, rather than have a prejudiced stance garbed in dominant discipline theories and discourses. Unless this is done, the supervision process implicitly risks denying the being-human and lived experiences of the student and of his or her society.

It is imperative to consider alternative sources of knowledge and theorisation because knowledge production is established on the prevailing structures of global power and global control (Moscovitz & Sabzalieva, 2023). Different people experience globality differently. While one global act is experienced as an opportunity in one part of the world, in another part of the world, it might be seen an existential threat to certain aspects of the citizens' being-human. It is apparent here that knowledge construction is not insulated from global power imbalances. In other words – in social science disciplines, particularly – social theory generation should not be detached from lived social experiences that also have a geo-economic dimension (see Code, 2012; Mignolo, 2007; Ndlovu-Gatsheni, 2017). Alternative models to the hegemonic Eurocentric models of higher education – for instance the *ubuntu* model – pay particular attention to the context for curriculum enactment by considering collective life as central to understanding human nature, values, engagement, and managing difference (Hlatshwayo & Shawa, 2020). A higher education governed by such values is responsive to difference and is mindful that difference is constitutive of the being-human of the other. Ultimately, monopolistic and absolutist claims to what should be valued across global societies to make social and political life practically democratic overlook the complexity of the global condition (Manthalu & Waghid, 2019).

Doctoral supervision should value listening to other perspectives that deviate from the standard and dominant social theories in the academy (Heaney, 2015; Zeleza, 2009). There should be a constant awareness that, under the prevailing global order, different societies are differently positioned relative to the global structures, distribution of opportunities, and burdens. It should further be realised that human equality and democracy across the world demand different forms of social organisation and restructuring of the global order in a manner that is not uniform. Arriving at this conclusion is difficult if not impossible if supervision is restricted to the hegemonic lenses that are not only rooted in the experiences of those in the dominant parts of the world but also simultaneously denies the burdens borne out of the very same structure that gives opportunity to developed countries.

Situatedness-responsive doctoral supervision in my journey

The prevalence of essentialist theories and epistemologies in higher education does not recognise the validity of the situated lived experiences. This denial is based on the mere fact that the student's lived experiences are incongruent with the assumptions and experiences behind dominant theories and epistemologies in higher education (see Ndlovu-Gatsheni, 2015; Zeleza, 2009). In this section, I show that the participants in the supervision encounter should be aware of the subtle pitfalls of exclusive essentialism of dominant theories. Such theories demand conformism rather than an openness to alternative perspectives to human existence (see Ndlovu-Gatsheni, 2015; Zeleza, 2009). Unless there is such awareness, not only are the experiences of 'other' students denied, but then higher education also undermines what makes other people in the world equal human beings (Benhabib, 2011). The required openness in supervision encounters should not be tokenistic. Rather the openness should be driven by the realisation that the world is experienced from different and, at times, contrasting perspectives. Therefore, dismissing a non-mainstream perspective based on its otherness is, in principle, a denial of recognition of the human existence of others, not recognising their being-human.

The argument that I advance is drawn from my research experience and the way dominant scholars have theorised about the topic. Unless one gets the appropriate support, such contexts compel one to conform, thereby denying the reality of one's concrete lived experiences in the societies from which the research problem arose. My doctoral research considered ways to conceptualise and configure education for global citizenship in Malawian schools. The circumstances that led to this study resulted from a series of education policy decisions – apparently in pursuit of globally relevant and competitive education – made by the Malawian government. Firstly, there was the removal of the teaching of Malawian History from Malawian primary and secondary school curricula, replacing it with Social and Environmental Studies. The new subject is essentially about principles, institutions, practices, and processes of democracy, making scanty and uncoordinated reference to Malawian history only when exemplifying a social or democratic concept (Ministry of Education, 2005). Secondly, the government removed mother tongue instruction in the first four years of basic education, replacing it with English, apparently to enable Malawians to participate competitively in the global arena (Malawi Government, 2013). In principle, these policies were modelled on an apparently standard ideal cosmopolitanism whose global citizenship requires detachment from the local in order to embrace impartial universal knowledge and skills for effective global citizenship engagement (see Habermas, 1994, 2003; Nili, 2015; Nussbaum, 2002). My doctoral research interrogated the essentialism of such a cosmopolitanism rooted in impartiality whose normativity demands detachment from sources of local concreteness, such as a shared thin public culture, a shared geographical location, a common history, and a shared language among others (Kymlicka, 2002; Miller, 2002).

Philosophical reflection calls for guarded caution before making absolutist generalisations. There is however widespread consensus about the inherent normative unacceptability of the nation-state in relation to cosmopolitanism as a normative ideal that ensures respect for human dignity and equality across the world. As a normative ideal, cosmopolitanism holds that the individual is the ultimate unit of moral concern. Institutions that affect the human being "should [therefore] be based on an impartial consideration of the claims of each person who would be affected by our choices" (Tan, 2004:94). From this principle arise different versions of cosmopolitan or global citizenship, particularly in relation to the value and role of the nation-state and its attendant patriotic solidarity. The dominant strand of cosmopolitan global citizenship is rooted in the claim that, since the individual is the ultimate unit of moral concern, national boundaries and national solidarity are morally arbitrary (Habermas, 2001; Nili, 2015; Nussbaum, 2002). For this strand, education for global citizenship should therefore promote impartial values and skills, and elements of local solidarity have no normative significance. The practical implication of this conceptualisation of democracy on education for global citizenship is that there is active de-emphasis and subversion of sources of local solidarity in pursuit of an ostensibly impartial and objective understanding of cosmopolitan citizenship (Brighouse, 2003; Nussbaum, 2002). In this case, local sources of being a person are regarded as inherently antagonistic to and incompatible with the detached self of the cosmopolitan citizen. The practical implication of such cosmopolitanism is that, among others, education for global citizenship should not promote the teaching of local history (Brighouse, 2003; Nussbaum, 2002). In pursuit of participation in a global world, governments, such as the Malawian government, scrapped vernacular instruction in the first four years of the basic education level and the teaching of local history, which were construed as nationalist tools and having no normative consequences for the people. Such an impartial cosmopolitanism is modelled on an autonomous self who is necessarily detached from local subjectivities. The elimination of subjectivities, or difference to give room for commonalities of people alone, hides the actual struggles that people face under the global structure because of the relative disadvantagedness of the people.

A question arises regarding the context and probable experiences of those who develop such a strand of cosmopolitanism, which necessarily demands detachment from subjectivity. The conceptualisation of cosmopolitanism is based on the geo-perspective and cultural-economic contexts under which one experiences globalisation. Presently, the framing of the global citizenship scholarship is dominated by ontological perspectives of scholars from the West (Parmenter, 2011). However, theorisation about the prospects of globalisation and its influence on society today cannot be uniform across the global economic divides. This is because generation of globalisation theory is inspired by different – and mostly contrasting – lived experiences of the effects of the global structure. Similarly, no single exclusive position in terms of the question of the place of the nation-state in modern (global) citizenship can justly account for the fairness of the global structure as experienced by those in the Global North and South (Ingram, 2016; Papastephanou, 2015). While the Global North would frown upon initiatives of maintaining local languages as being nationalistic, in developed countries, the threat of underdeveloped languages threatens the voice of the majority, effectively cementing their second place as they unsuccessfully compete in the global order with borrowed second foreign languages (Manthalu & Waghid, 2019; Waghid, Manthalu, Terblanche, Waghid & Waghid, 2020).

The social sciences present a systematic approach to understanding different particularised social phenomena (Gerring, 2012). There are hegemonic social science approaches that understand social theories as being exclusively absolutist and universalistic in nature (Code, 2012). This can be seen in the dominant understanding of the role of the global structure as a foundation for global citizenship. This understanding considers the centring of localness in modern citizenship configuration as being inherently inward-looking rather than outward-looking and therefore inimical to the cultivation of global citizenship (see Habermas, 2001, 2003; Nussbaum, 2002). While the increasing weakening of the nation-state is celebrated as the necessary precursor to the realisation of human equality globally, and that the nation-state is a delimiter of freedoms and equality, the situation is different in developing countries. The argument I posited in my doctoral research is that concern over the weakening of the nation-state is a concern not rooted in nostalgia, as critics would aver. Rather, for most developing countries, it is a concern rooted in the overt forced displacement of local social, linguistic, historical, and cultural outlooks at the hands of globality (Manthalu & Waghid, 2019). Globality is in principle erasing the already marginalised metaphysical and epistemological outlooks from mainstream education for global citizenship (Higgs, 2012; Yosso, 2005). The absence of the nation-state leaves no institution to protect communities in developed countries from their underrepresentation in global economic structures that are driven by market ideologies and skewed advantages favouring a few powerful countries (Giroux, 2010). In developing countries, the weakening of the nation-state implies the banishment and extinction of local languages over the adoption of foreign languages under which local languages cannot be equal competitors.

In modern citizenship studies, citizenship configurations that defend some form of relevance of the nation-state today are maligned and deemed non-cosmopolitan, nationalist, anti-immigration, and promoting narrow-mindedness and covert exclusion of the other (Habermas, 2001; Nili, 2015; Nussbaum, 2002). We cannot deny the historical injustices, inhumane cruelty towards others, and senseless wars waged in the name of defending and advancing the interests of the fatherland. There are several lessons that should be learned from such cruelties of humans upon equal humans. However, it is worth noting that every political ideal can be abused by political leadership to contaminate the minds of the citizenry with hate resulting in the violation of the human dignity of others in the name of defending and advancing the interests of the fatherland (Kymlicka, 2002). It will however be logically and normatively erroneous to conclude that this entails that the political ideal used is bad in and of itself (Miller, 2007). The point being made here is that disregarding the state from the global order will expose the people of the world to more systemic iniquities, which this time around are being institutionalised, thus sanitising the oppression and marginalisation the people in developing countries are already experiencing. One would probably argue that we should endeavour to build a state that has no attachment to any elements of the nation, essentially a state that does not promote any elements of the nation. This looks like an appealing argument, except that it is founded on the wrong assumption that the solidarity foundation of a state can be detached from the historical, linguistic, cultural, and social situationality of the people (Kymlicka, 2002). These are the constitutive elements of nationality. As long as 'the nation' refers to the language of communication and education within the state and to the history and local cultural values and norms that now shape the concrete democratic and public institutions of society, trade deals, and agreements protecting the interests of the people of such geographical area and their historical occupations, it is inaccurate to claim that there can be a puritan state that is detached from the localness of its people (Kymlicka, 2002; Miller, 2007)

Given all this background to the interactions among cosmopolitanism, nationality, and democratic citizenship, the challenge I faced in my doctoral study was to show that the glorified cosmopolitanism informing Malawian education for global citizenship was problematic due to the exclusion of nationality in the configuration of global citizenship. As a Malawian, I have witnessed the implications of the underdevelopment of vernacular languages on education, technology, literature, and the arts in Malawi largely due to the discarding of vernacular language instruction in preference of English so as to have globally relevant and competitive citizens. Furthermore, there is clear evidence that among others, the democracy project is struggling to mature partly due to a lack of learning critical history about Malawi (Kayuni & Tambulasi, 2010). The opportunities that the internet avails to people today cannot be enjoyed by the majority of Malawian citizens since there is scarcely content in the vernacular for a country with a 68% vernacular literacy rate (National

Statistics Office, 2018) and a less than 1% using English as a home language (National Statistics Office of Malawi, 1998).

In contrast, in developed countries, mostly the 'national' language of the people is also the language of the home and the official language of the school, court, bank, and trade. For these countries, investing in and developing the local language means to develop the official language of trade, education, the court, and of the internet simultaneously. However, this is not the case across the globe especially in most African countries. Ultimately, local languages, local art, and local literature are not given public necessary and sufficient support to flourish (Nyamnjoh, 2012).

The key point I advance by this long reference to my doctoral research journey is to instantiate the claim I make in this chapter that social theory, including in education for global or democratic citizenship, has increasingly acquired a surreptitiously founded essentialism. The essentialism, in my given example, is about the worth or lack of worth of the nation-state in configuring cosmopolitan and democratic citizenship in a developing country like Malawi. It is therefore necessary to make doctoral supervision to be democratic pedagogy by being responsive to the experiences derived from the situatedness of the student. As it has been shown, in relation to my doctoral studies topic, as in most developing countries, in the Malawian democratic citizenship education context, the nation-state is the remaining buffer and defence from the ravages of the neoliberal global structure on their education, history, culture, literature, and art (Barrow, 2005; Kymlicka, 2002). Therefore, as a doctoral student researching on education for democratic and global citizenship, I faced the challenge of making a case for the sustenance of a democratic nation-state that is presently the only guaranteed defender of the interests of people situated in the already voiceless developing nations. Making such a case entailed going against standard global citizenship theories. Conforming to the assumptions of impartial cosmopolitan citizenship education, on the other hand, would mean invalidating my experiences and those of people experiencing globalisation from a situatedness like mine. Therefore, it is necessary that doctoral supervision should be responsive to the student's situatedness. In contexts such as these, if doctoral supervision demands the student to assimilate his experiences into those that are the basis for the assumptions of the grand theories of inquiry, such a doctoral encounter would be undemocratic.

The implication for all this in terms of doctoral supervision is that engagement intended at understanding the strange non-mainstream perspective typically experienced by the marginalised others in developing countries needs to be accorded space and a voice. This should not be misconceived as demanding that every strange experience that is inconsistent with dominant theories should be unconditionally taken on board. Instead, it is about developing a reflexive capacity to hear and consider voices and perspectives embodied in the doctoral student's lived experiences that are however marginalised and maligned in doctoral supervision based on their unorthodoxy. It is to realise that social life everywhere is influenced by global interconnectedness. However, this global interconnectedness is itself shaped by globality and unequal power influences (Mignolo, 2007). There are those who experience life from the side of the drivers, makers, and shapers of the global structure (Pogge, 2008). These have their values, culture, epistemologies, and ontologies determining the shape and substance of globalisation. On the other hand, there is most people in developing countries, especially in Africa, who have no presence in the shaping of global economic, political, legal, and educational structures. They are the ones who bear most of the adverse effects of global systems (Pogge, 2008). While the powerful form globalisation, the excluded of the world must conform to the form set by the powerful. This has a significant implication on doctoral supervision. If theorisation during doctoral supervision is in principle rooted only in the particular experiences of those in developed countries, the experiences of those from marginalised countries will be invisible and unheard, effectively invalidating their experiences. Invalidating a person's concrete experiences is in essence denying his or her being-human, as an equal member of humanity. It is worth noting, as Benhabib (2011) argues, that we cannot always project and assume the experiences of the other and what makes or frustrates their being an equal member of the human race. There must be deliberation to establish what makes the other recognised as a person. This prevents us from imposing certain experiences as the only and credible human experiences which is worth forming a theory.

The supervisor for my doctoral study created a space for me to bring my lived experiences to the study process. He enacted democratic pedagogy by practising reflexivity in not summarily dismissing my argument for consideration of certain aspects of nationality in the conceptualisation of education for democratic citizenship, particularly in developing countries. He valued my critical inferring from my situatedness, aware that the situatedness was central to the re-imagination of GCE beyond the textual meaning of existing theories. It is worth emphasising that the study was not about a defence for nationality as an ideal. Rather, it was showing that merely adopting subtly essentialist theories of democratic citizenship that are necessarily dismissive of nationality counter-serves ideal cosmopolitan and democratic citizenship. This is because, in the Malawian context, excluding certain elements that are constitutive of nationality practically results in global citizenship, which undermines human equality.

Conclusion

Given the influence that doctoral degree holders wield generally in societies, it is imperative that the nature and quality of the doctoral supervision they receive be democratic. More importantly, doctoral supervision should be democratic as a moral imperative to respect the humanity of the student as an equal. Recognising the student as an equal human being places an obligation on the supervisor that the experiences of the student – which inevitably shape the conceptualisation of the research problem, particularly in the social sciences and humanities – should not be extinguished based on their incompatibility with the assumptions of standard discipline theories. Enacting doctoral supervision as democratic citizenship pedagogy requires the supervisor's reflexivity and an awareness that the dominant theories of the social sciences and humanities are rooted in particularistic experiences. This being the case, such theories may not account for all phenomena in the world. Conversely, there should be a readiness to accept theoretical assumptions that are different from those that anchor mainstream theories. This is because lived experiences cannot be discounted without denying the being-human of the Other person. Making doctoral supervision democratic guides the supervisor from supressing and denying recognition to the unfamiliar, the strange, the culturally alien, the historically unrelatable as being of no intellectual consequence in the study programme.

References

Armstrong, C. (2009). Global egalitarianism. *Philosophy Compass*, 4(1), 155–171.
Barrow, C. W. (2005). The return of the state: globalization, state theory, and the new imperialism. *New Political Science*, 27(2), 123–145.
Benhabib, S. (1992). *Situating the self: gender, community and postmodernism in contemporary ethics*. Polity.
Benhabib, S. (2011). *Dignity in adversity: human rights in turbulent times*. Polity.
Brighouse, H. (2003). Should we teach patriotic history? In K. Mcdonough & W. Feinberg (Eds.), *Citizenship and education in liberal-democratic societies: teaching for cosmopolitan values and collective identities* (pp. 157–174). Oxford University Press Inc.
Code, L. (2012). Taking subjectivity into account. In C. W. Ruitenberg & D. C. Phillips (Eds.), *Education, culture and epistemological diversity: mapping a disputed terrain* (pp. 85–100). Springer.
Creswell, J. W. & Creswell, J. D. (2014). *Research design: qualitative, quantitative, and mixed methods approaches*. SAGE Publications Limited.
Freire, P. (2014). *Pedagogy of the oppressed* (30th Anniv). Bloomsbury Publishing.
Gerring, J. (2012). *Social science methodology: a unified framework* (Second). Cambridge University Press.
Giroux, H. A. (2010). Bare pedagogy and the scourge of neoliberalism: rethinking higher education as a democratic public sphere. *The Educational Forum*, 74(3), 184–196.
Habermas, J. (1994). Citizenship and national identity. In B. Steenbergen (Ed.), *The condition of citizenship* (pp. 20–35). SAGE Publications Limited.
Habermas, J. (2001). The postnational constellation and the future of democracy. In M. Pensky (Ed.), *The postnational constellation: political essays* (pp. 58–112). MIT Press.
Habermas, J. (2003). Toward a cosmopolitan Europe. *Journal of Democracy*, 14(4), 86–100.
Hames, M. (2009). "Let us burn the house down!" Violence against women in the higher education environment. *Agenda*, 28(40), 42–46.
Heaney, T. (2015). Democracy—unleashing the power of "we". In T. Heaney & D. Ramdeholl (Eds.), *Reimaging doctoral education as adult education*. Wiley, John & Sons, Inc.

Higgs, P. (2012). African philosophy and the decolonisation of education in Africa: some critical reflections. *Educational Philosophy and Theory*, *44*(Sup2), 37–55.
Hlatshwayo, M. N. & Shawa, L. B. (2020). Towards a critical re-conceptualization of the purpose of higher education: the role of Ubuntu-Currere in re-imagining teaching and learning in South African higher education. *Higher Education Research & Development*, *39*(1), 26–38.
Ingram, J. D. (2016). Cosmopolitanism from below: universalism as contestation. *Critical Horizons*, *17*(1), 66–78.
Kayuni, H. M. & Tambulasi, R. I. C. (2010). The Malawi 1964 cabinet crisis and its legacy of 'perpetual regression of trust' amongst contemporary Malawian politicians. *Social Dynamics*, *36*(2), 410–427.
Kymlicka, W. (2002). *Politics in the vernacular: nationalism, multiculturalism and citizenship*. Oxford University Press.
Ladson-Billings, G. (2014). Culturally relevant pedagogy 2.0: a.k.a the remix. *Havard Educational Review*, *84*(1), 74–84.
Malawi Government, *Education Act*, Pub. L. No. 21 of 2013, 42 (2013).
Manthalu, C. H. & Waghid, Y. (2019). Interrogating a cosmopolitanism of African higher education. *South African Journal of Higher Education*, *33*(2), 1–15.
Mignolo, W. E. (2007). Coloniality and modernity/rationality. *Cultural Studies*, *21*(2–3), 155–167.
Miller, D. (2002). Cosmopolitanism: a critique. *Critical Review of International Social and Political Philosophy*, *5*(3), 80–85.
Miller, D. (2007). *National responsibility and global justice*. Oxford University Press.
Ministry of Education. (2005). *Malawi primary school syllabuses, standard 7: Chichewa, English, mathematics, expressive arts, life skills, social and environmental sciences, science and technology, agriculture, bible knowledge, religious education*. Malawi Institute of Education.
Moscovitz, H. & Sabzalieva, E. (2023). Conceptualising the new geopolitics of higher education. *Globalisation, Societies and Education*, *21*(2), 149–165.
National Statistics Office. (2018). *2018 Malawi population and housing census report*. https://malawi.unfpa.org/sites/default/files/resource-pdf/2018 Malawi Population and Housing Census Main Report %281%29.pdf
National Statistics Office of Malawi. (1998). *1998 population and housing census analytical report*. www.nsomalawi.mw/images/stories/data_on_line/demography/census_98/analytical_report.pdf
Ndlovu-Gatsheni, S. J. (2015). Decoloniality as the future of Africa. *History Compass*, *13*(10), 485–496.
Ndlovu-Gatsheni, S. J. (2017). The emergence and trajectories of struggles for an 'African University': the case of unfinished business of African epistemic decolonisation. *Kronos*, *43*(1), 51–77.
Ndlovu-Gatsheni, S. J. (2018). The dynamics of epistemological decolonisation in the 21st century: towards epistemic freedom. *Strategic Review for Southern Africa*, *40*(1), 16–45.
Ndofirepi, A. P. & Gwaravanda, E. T. (2018). Epistemic (in)justice in African universities: a perspective of the politics of knowledge. *Educational Review*, *71*(5), 581–594.
Nili, S. (2015). Who's afraid of a world state? A global sovereign and the statist-cosmopolitan debate. *Critical Review of International Social and Political Philosophy*, *18*(3), 241–263. https://doi.org/10.1080/13698230.2013.850833

Nussbaum, M. (2002). Patritotism and cosmopolitanism. In M. Nussbaum & J. Cohen (Eds.), *For love of country?* (pp. 2–20). Beacon Press.

Nyamnjoh, F. B. (2012). "Potted plants in greenhouses": a critical reflection on the resilience education in Africa. *Journal of Asian and African*, *47*, 129–154.

Papastephanou, M. (2015). *Thinking differently about cosmopolitanism: theory, eccentricity, and the globalized world*. Paradigm Publishers.

Parmenter, L. (2011). Power and place in the discourse of global citizenship education. *Globalisation, Societies and Education*, *9*(3–4), 367–380.

Pogge, T. (2008). *World poverty and human rights: cosmopolitan responsibilities and reforms* (2nd ed.). Polity Press.

Ramdeholl, D., Giordani, T., Heaney, T., & Yanow, W. (2010). Race, power, and democracy in the graduate classroom. *New Directions for Adult and Continuing Education*, *128*, 59–68.

R'boul, H. (2022). Intercultural philosophy and internationalization of higher education: epistemologies of the South, geopolitics of knowledge and epistemological polylogue. *Journal of Further and Higher Education*, *46*(8), 1149–1160.

Skakni, I. (2018). Doctoral studies as an initiatory trial: expected and taken-for-granted practices that impede PhD students' progress. *Teaching in Higher Education*, *23*(8), 927–944.

Steger, M. B. & Roy, R. K. (2010). *Neoliberalism: a very short introduction*. Oxford University Press.

Tan, K.-C. (2004). *Justice without borders*. Cambridge University Press.

Thacker, R. & Freeman, S. J. (2021). Toward a theory of the study of higher education. *Philosophy and Theory in Higher Education*, *3*(1), 67–86.

Trowler, P. (2009). Beyond epistemological essentialism: academic tribes in the twenty-first century. In C. Kreber (Ed.), *The university and its disciplines: teaching and learning within and beyond disciplinary boundaries* (pp. 181–195). Routledge.

Vázquez-Arroyo, A. Y. (2008). Liberal democracy and neoliberalism: a critical juxtaposition. *New Political Science*, *30*(2), 127–159.

Waghid, Y., Manthalu, C. H., Terblanche, J., Waghid, F., & Waghid, Z. (2020). *Cosmopolitan education and inclusion: human engagement and the self*. Palgrave Macmillan.

Yosso, T. J. (2005). Whose culture has capital? A critical race theory discussion of community cultural wealth. *Race Ethnicity and Education*, *8*(1), 69–91.

Zeleza, P. T. (2009). African studies and universities since independence. *Transition*, *101*, 110–135.

9 Reflections on doctoral work in philosophy of education

Narratives in becoming

Judith Terblanche, Elton Pullen and Yusef Waghid

Section 1: Introduction and background

In this chapter, the practice of *currere* is presented as a tool to achieve the citizenship competency aims of the new CA2025 framework, by emphasising the decoloniality of the mind of the chartered accountancy educator. *Currere* is described in literature as a form of self-praxis, which allows individuals to partake in a co-productive process, where they are shaped by the curriculum while they themselves also shape the curriculum. As it relates to the development of the CA2025 objectives, *currere* offers chartered accountancy academics the opportunity to engage with the curriculum rather than just to receive the curriculum, which has shaped their thinking. In other words, chartered accountancy academics can thus resist, rearrange, or respond to the current curriculum. The practice of *currere* is elucidated in this chapter by showing the journey of the first two authors (both chartered accountancy academics) who pursued a doctorate in the Philosophy of Education. Together with their supervisor – a distinguished professor in the Philosophy of Education – they articulate how the practice of *currere* could assist chartered accountancy academics in the development of their own citizenship competence and that of their students.

In this chapter, we explore the views of Judith, Elton, and Yusef. Judith and Elton (who pursued doctorates in the Philosophy of Education) both work as chartered accountancy academics in departments of accounting at South African (SA) higher education institutions (HEIs). Yusef, the supervisor of Judith and Elton, is a distinguished professor in the Philosophy of Education and had obtained three doctorates himself. In Section 1 of this chapter, we provide a short synopsis of the chartered accountancy educational landscape in South Africa. In Section 2 below, we present the following:

- a narrative discussion between Yusef and ourselves, where we respond to eight questions that Yusef had posed;
- Yusef's commentary; and
- a potential outcome from the critical reflection on the PhD journey might assist the chartered accountancy educational landscape to advance the transformation and decoloniality aims.

DOI: 10.4324/9781003530091-10

In the next paragraph, we present a synopsis of the chartered accountancy educational landscape in South Africa. Elsewhere (see Terblanche, 2019; Terblanche & Waghid, 2020a, 2020b; Terblanche & Waghid, 2021) we have extensively reported on the power relations and influence exerted by the South African Institute of Chartered Accountants (SAICA) on the SA chartered accountancy educational landscape. Based on those studies, we firstly present the mechanisms of power, and secondly, the consequences of the disciplinary power mechanisms.

Foucault (1995) describes three mechanisms of disciplinary power in his seminal genealogical work, *Discipline and Punish: The Birth of the Prison*, when he provides details on the development of punishment for offenders: from the outward body to the inward soul. The mechanisms that support the operationality of disciplinary power are hierarchical observation, normalising judgement, and the examination (Foucault, 1995). *Hierarchical observation* is all about creating an environment where the possibility of perpetual surveillance is tangible. Such awareness results in power to be exercised, even independently of the 'person' who exercises it (Foucault, 1995). In the chartered accountancy educational landscape, hierarchical observation is achieved through SAICA, which accredits departments of accounting at certain universities to offer programmes for students who want to become South African chartered accountants (CA(SAs)). Because of the hierarchical observation, power is internalised to the extent that certain behaviour is deemed acceptable; hence, judgement is *normalised*. These accepted actions, norms, and behaviour are created in the chartered accountancy educational landscape through SAICA, which issues a competencies framework listing the abilities that should be developed by a student during his or her time at the accredited HEI. The third disciplinary power mechanism, that of the *examination*, is the differentiating tool by which individuals are measured, using a specific interpretation of what constitutes knowledge. SAICA achieves this through graduates of HEIs who are required to pass an examination, called the initial test of competence (ITC), as the first hurdle to overcome to earn the right to enter the profession. In line with a Foucauldian interpretation of power, we do not deem power or power relations to be inherently negative. To be precise, the consequences of disciplinary power mechanisms – thus how power is used and dispersed – could result in a negative effect on the broader society, particularly so, if an inability is displayed to truly understand the associated effect.

Currently, the disciplinary power mechanisms deployed in the chartered accountancy educational landscape largely stifle the cultivation of the full humanity of students. This is primarily the result of the chartered accountancy academics' identity and skill-set aligned more closely with those of SAICA than with those of the HEI. Firstly, chartered accountancy academics are predominantly teaching on SAICA-accredited programmes. Chartered accountancy academics have significant technical knowledge and expertise; yet, they have limited exposure to or knowledge about Philosophy of Education and diverse pedagogical practices. Secondly, chartered accountancy academics consequently tend to explicate difficult concepts, and students are rarely treated as of equal intelligence but rather as receivers of knowledge imparted by the teacher expert. The style of teaching is therefore seldom participatory in nature. Thirdly, the material used to explicate technical knowledge mostly comprises only those legislations and standards listed in the SAICA competencies framework, and the learning environment is therefore void of the embodied knowledge or lived realities of the students. The ideology influencing the teaching material is that of the neo-liberal capitalist new-market economy, which is mostly concerned with profit-making. In the fourth place, and as a result, learning largely happens within the classroom setting, rather than to include community and business interaction through research projects, community engagements, or work-integrated learning (WIL) (all examples of experiential learning). Lastly, students therefore demonstrate their mastery of the technical knowledge content – as explained by the chartered accountancy academics – mostly through written time-limited examinations that mimic the style of the SAICA ITC examination. 'Passing' becomes the outcome or objective, rather than the development of sound critical and problem-solving thinking abilities or the development of social awareness.

In light of this synopsis of the chartered accountancy educational landscape, we argue that the chartered accountancy academic is significantly influenced and shaped by the neo-liberal infused CA profession – to the extent, we argue, that they are unaware that their minds are held captive by the profession itself. To this day, mainstream education and world views value certain knowledge systems higher than others. This consequence of colonialism, which deemed certain people and certain knowledge systems (non-Western mostly) to be less than others, is still rife in society. This acceptance of a norm, supported by a so-called 'truth', is dangerous. For the chartered accountancy educational landscape, the focus on outcomes, on addressing a certain output-driven knowledge list, and on a narrow measurement of a performance in an examination mostly distorts and limits the true transformational power of this powerful profession. To support this concept, we use an example from the SAICA competencies framework itself.

SAICA is currently in a process of re-imagining the CA of the future, thus ensuring that future CAs remain relevant to lead and dominate the business sector in South Africa. The project is called CA2025 and already resulted in a new competencies framework that was issued in 2021 (SAICA, 2021). Rightly, the new framework includes several new concepts and enabling competencies, such as digital acumen, business acumen, relational acumen, and also notions of citizenship (SAICA, 2021). This is a significant improvement on the old framework, which lacked reference to these important concepts, but we argue that these competencies – especially those related to citizenship – risk becoming mere impotent token ideals. We base this statement on the fact that the old framework only made reference to citizenship in the context of corporate citizenship, with reference to how a business should be governed responsibly. The new framework, however, refers to personal and professional citizenship and uses terminology, such as "the self and others", "societal impact", "rights and responsibilities", "cultural diversity", "impact on local environment", "multiple communities", "valuing and tolerant approach", and "long-term societal impact" – all closely associated with the social sciences (SAICA, 2021:13–16). The primary problem is that the chartered accountancy academic who is responsible for engendering these values and attributes that are associated with the social sciences often has limited experience in the social sciences, Philosophy of Education, diverse pedagogical practices, or research tasks. Secondly, a value such as citizenship is then subsequently at risk of being treated as an outcome that can be achieved, such as a technical competency, rather than recognising that this will require an intentional lifelong process – by the chartered accountancy individual and thus the profession at large – in becoming, always moving along a continuum.

In light of this synopsis of the chartered accountancy educational landscape in South Africa, we consider what moved two chartered accountancy academics to pursue a doctorate in Philosophy of Education and whether there was any perceived value for the chartered accountancy academics as a result of the doctoral studies.

Section 2: Narrative discussion between supervisor and PhD students

Below follows a narrative discussion between Yusef, as the supervisor, who poses questions to his students. The responses are provided firstly, followed by Yusef's commentary at the end.

Part A: Events leading up to pursuing a PhD in Philosophy of Education

1 What were the moments, events, and/or influences that have resulted in you choosing a PhD in Philosophy of Education?

Judith's response

I grew up during the apartheid regime in South Africa and attended school and university with the vast majority of classmates being white and Afrikaans-speaking. Shortly after I had qualified as a CA(SA), I left for the United Kingdom to gain international work experience. Although I always seemed to be standing on the periphery of dominant thought, it was only after my first disruptive encounter that I started to find my voice of dissonance. My first deliberative encounter occurred while working at Mencap, a United Kingdom (UK) charity for people with learning disabilities. The finance team was the most diverse environment I had ever encountered. Every single member of the team was from a different ethnicity. We were diverse in terms of cultural background, gender, and religion. It was a truly humbling, inspiring, and curiosity-provoking time in my life, which resulted in a critical reflection of my ignorant and protected childhood.

I returned to South Africa in 2008 to pursue an academic career at my alma mater with a clear vision of the importance of social redress and my associated individual responsibility through academic endeavours. I found, however, that very little had changed in the SA chartered accountancy educational landscape since I was a student, and I found the environment rather restrictive. In 2013, I moved to the University of the Western Cape (UWC), a HEI, where the majority of students are from marginalised communities. I became acutely aware of the wide inequality gap in South Africa, directly influencing the higher learning project due to the lack of resources at the disposal of historically disadvantaged institutions (HDIs) to assist and support students. In addition, my discomfort with the resistance to research by chartered accountancy academics, the obsession with the examination as an assessment tool, and a teaching style of explication of technical content grew exponentially.

The two deliberative encounters – that of the inclusive and diverse work environment at Mencap and the awareness of the systemic practices that perpetuate inequality in the higher learning space – culminated in my decision to pursue a PhD in Philosophy of Education.

Elton's response

I too grew up during the apartheid regime in South Africa, but I was still very young when apartheid was abolished. Most of my classmates at school and university were coloured and bilingual. It was only during my CA internship years that I worked closely with people from other ethnic backgrounds, particularly white Afrikaans-speaking people. As a young aspiring CA, I believed that the CA-qualification journey more than adequately prepares CAs to lead responsibly, both in commerce and in broader society. This belief stemmed from the fact that the CA designation was often perceived as the leading finance designation in South Africa, and many of the leadership positions within organisations were held by CAs (TerraNova, 2015). It was after my first deliberate encounter that I started to question this belief. As part of the CA-qualification journey, we were required to complete three years of internship after completing a SAICA-accredited undergraduate and post-graduate qualification. The CA internship training enables aspiring CAs to gain practical experience of the audit and accountancy profession. In order to gain this practical experience, aspiring CAs are largely reliant on the coaching and mentoring received from managers and partners who are already fairly experienced CAs. This coaching and mentoring often culminate in feedback and assessment on the performance of trainees in their work, with the aim of continual improvement. On one occasion, a manager reprimanded me because I did not document something the way he wanted it done. When I asked him whether there was anything technically wrong with my work, he answered, "No, I just like things to be documented in a certain way". This was my first real encounter, which made me question whether the narrow technical focus of the CA profession limits the abilities of aspiring CAs to be open to more perspectives. In this specific instance, I was coached into fitting into someone else's preference or perspective, rather than being developed to think rationally.

After qualifying as a CA, I had a short stint as first an audit manager and then as a financial manager, before joining my alma mater, UWC, as an academic. During my time at UWC, I was fortunate to become involved in many SAICA initiatives. I was involved in the marking of the SAICA ITC examinations. SAICA typically invites chartered accountancy academics across all SAICA-accredited universities to assist in the marking of these examinations. In these examinations, every candidate's attempt is marked blindly by two independent markers to ensure that all candidates' work is marked fairly. On one occasion, I became involved in quite a heated debate with another marker who did not agree with the way a candidate answered the question pertaining to an ethical dilemma. In my argument with the marker, I highlighted that ethical dilemmas are not technical accounting issues for which there are accounting standards that we simply apply. When it comes to grey areas, such as responses to ethical dilemmas, we need to be open to view it from diverse perspectives.

These two deliberative encounters highlighted to me that, while the CA profession is recognised globally as a leading finance profession, it falls short of equipping aspiring CAs with the keenness of mind to be open to diverse perspectives, especially as these relate to matters of societal concern. The desire to explore how the accountancy pedagogy could enable the equipping of this 'keenness of mind' largely inspired my pursuit of a PhD in Philosophy of Education.

In addition, I was also motivated to develop critical thinking (CT) skills in my students. I observed this as one of the skills where they were lacking. In my experience, the lack of CT skills in accountancy students often contributed to them not being successful in their studies. I thus also trusted that the PhD in Philosophy of Education would enable me to come up with strategies that could enable the development of CT skills in accountancy students.

Part B: Realisations about the CA profession and education

2 What were the key realisations for you about the CA profession and education in South Africa because of the PhD journey?

Judith's response

Instinctively I felt uneasy in the chartered accountancy educational space, although I lacked the academic vocabulary to explicate it coherently to others. The PhD journey however provided me with the appropriate intellectual theoretical underpinnings for meaning making in terms of my emotions of discomfort. Arguably, to some extent, it is quite easy to notice the inherent problems associated with the over-reliance on a time-measured written examination to measure whether an individual can enter the coveted chartered accountancy profession in South Africa. Not only does the examination reduce education to the accumulation of technical content, but it also results in teaching pedagogy associated with 'teaching-to-the-test', which is counter-intuitive for the development of CT, problem-solving, and deliberation competencies. These competencies are of real importance for an unequal SA society that is desperate for business leaders to make responsible and just decisions to alleviate the dire lived challenges of marginalised citizens. To my mind, one of the most important realisations at that time was how exclusionary the learning and teaching pedagogy was. Exclusionary practices are inherently violent and do not advance or restore human dignity and are therefore intrinsically unjust. In addition, I realised that change will only happen if chartered accountancy academics are willing to be vulnerable, practice reflexivity, and step into unfamiliar practices to accelerate education as a restorative inclusive justice project.

Elton's response

This is an interesting question. I remember at the time of the 'Rhodes Must Fall' movement that much was said about the decolonisation of the curriculum. The response by most accounting departments at universities was that one cannot decolonise 'debits and credits'. While there is some truth to the notion that many of concepts in accountancy do not need decolonisation per se, as they are logical, this should not stop us from questioning the source or context from which the accountancy principles, which we blindly accept, originate. The PhD journey provided me with a philosophical basis to question the principles I so just accepted as aspiring and now qualified CA. For me, one of the biggest learning discoveries during the PhD process was that we expect of students to exhibit CT, but we do not foster environments conducive to CT. Environments are not created where beliefs and assumptions are questioned, and thus information is just accepted. This became particularly surprising to me during my PhD journey because, as academics, we are training aspiring CAs who should have professional scepticism.

Part C: Realisations about the PhD as a project
3 Should a PhD be theoretically strong?

Judith's response

I had so many opinions and beliefs about research – significantly informed by my home discipline of accountancy. Up until I started with the PhD, I had little to no experience of research as such. We could graduate with an honours in Accounting without partaking in any research tasks. My modular master's degree course was on computer auditing, which was technical and governance driven. After my PhD journey in the Philosophy of Education, those initial (unwarranted) thoughts were all turned upside down. I came to understand that, to conceptualise and propose new frameworks for change – hence to expand on existing thought – one needs to interrogate firstly, and secondly, build on a solid theoretical foundation. That translates into endless reading. To evaluate existing theoretical frameworks and thought critically, one needs to understand – in a Foucauldian manner – the power relations that inform the discourse, and equally – in a Derridean manner – which voices are silenced. In my opinion, a strong theoretical base is imperative for a PhD in Philosophy of Education.

Elton's response

At the time I started my PhD, my only exposure to research was my coursework master's in Financial Management, where I had to do an empirical study for my half-thesis. I had a naïve belief at the time that, if research was not based on empirical evidence, it was not valuable at all. Reflecting on my thinking at the time, this belief was mostly influenced by my lack of exposure to research and not having an understanding of the many approaches to research and research paradigms. As I embarked on the PhD journey, I soon realised that the research method or approach depends on the research problem one is looking to explore. In addition, while I just followed the chosen research approach while doing my master's, during my PhD, I learned that I needed to articulate clearly why the specific research method is appropriate for my chosen research problem. I also did not have a full appreciation of how the many theories were developed which I read about in the literature, and which I simply accepted or rejected when I was doing my master's thesis. While my master's was in a sense almost like ticking a box by choosing theories from literature that could fit into my topic, the PhD forced me to aim for an understanding of the theories first. Most importantly, the PhD taught me the importance of developing my own arguments in order to articulate clearly where I agree or disagree with current theories. I thus learned that my own arguments could be seen to have no merit, if I could not show how and why it builds on or disagrees with the arguments of others. The development of sound arguments thus requires a strong theoretical base.

4 Should a PhD be about public responsibility?

Judith's response

I must admit that I was perhaps a bit naïve (or ignorant) as the thought never crossed my mind. Only during my PhD journey did I start to reflect on the responsibility of a university towards society. Today, I cannot comprehend how one can detach education from social and public responsibility. For me, education, which involves the 'in-becoming' of citizens, is now all about solving the dire lived realities of the marginalised. PhD studies should therefore essentially be at the intersection of a technical field and social justice.

Elton's response

This is something that I did not even consider when pursuing my PhD. I knew that education was of national and societal importance. Consequently, I indirectly thought that pursuing a PhD in education would tick that box. During my PhD journey, I was however prompted to consider why universities exist in the first place. It was only then that I realised that the very reason why universities exist is to contribute to society. I now know that, if a PhD is meant to be the highest qualification that a university can bestow on a student, how can a PhD not be about public responsibility?

5 Can reasonableness be avoided in the pursuit of a PhD?

Judith's response

In thinking about the value of a PhD in Philosophy of Education, two things immediately come to mind:

- Firstly, the significant transformation that happened in my being as a result of this particular deliberative encounter, and hence, valuing the importance of creating opportunities for deliberative encounters in the chartered accountancy educational space; and
- Secondly, the importance of deliberation, which happened in conversation with the supervisor initially and then subsequently transpired in the writing of the thesis. The skill of proffering an argument, listening to critical commentary (verbally or in writing), and then attempting to re-articulate one's thinking after some reflection is invaluable. A PhD in Philosophy of Education is premised on justified reasoning after significant interrogation of existing theories in the discipline.

Elton's response

One of the key learning experiences during my PhD journey was discovering the notion of 'governmentality'. Lemke (2001:191) elucidates the notion of governmentality when he states, "to govern means to govern both others and the self, whereas the use of mentality involves exercising rational modes of thought, such as to offer arguments and justifications in intervening in or solving a situation". The PhD in Philosophy of Education offered me a space where the notion of governmentality was continually at play. After submitting a chapter to my supervisor, I received critical commentary, which – after reflecting – invoked rational thought. My supervisor also created a safe space where I could challenge his comments based on my rational reflection. The use of governmentality between myself and my supervisor transcended into reflecting on and analysing the theories applicable to my research. This allowed me to articulate the arguments written in my thesis rationally. I therefore do not believe that reasonableness or rational thought can be avoided in the pursuit of a PhD.

6 Should a PhD be amended or extended to other forms of knowing, besides the actual word count?

Judith's response

I have no recollection that I ever tracked (or cared for) the word count in my thesis. For me, the PhD was always about the potential of triggering a possible transformation in the chartered accountancy educational landscape. To me, it was important that my thesis presented a thoughtful, well-articulated argument, based on solid theoretical underpinnings that could cross the intersection between philosophy, education, and accountancy to provoke chartered accountancy academics and professionals to critical self-reflection. For me, it was all about the quality of the justified claims rather than about the length of the thesis.

Elton's response

The notion of a word count was something that initially scared me before embarking on the PhD journey. After the first meeting with my supervisor, it however became clear that thoughtful articulation of one's research problem, sound theoretical underpinnings, and rationally articulated arguments where much more important than being concerned with word count. Throughout the thesis writing process, I therefore concentrated on the flow and clarity of my arguments, rather than trying to aim for a certain number of words.

Part D: Transformational potential of the PhD in Philosophy of Education

7 Were you transformed by the PhD journey? If so, in which way?

Judith's response

Where does one start? I am grateful for the PhD journey on many levels. The deliberative encounter of the PhD itself – from the diverse material (from the humanities rather than from accountancy), different study fields (philosophy and education, rather than business-oriented), constant critical self-reflection, and the profound relationship with my supervisor – has definitively shaped me. Not only do I increasingly tend to notice exclusionary practices, but I also intentionally look for the marginalised voices that were excluded from the conversation. The stance of critical self-reflection – of considering whether practices and decisions carried over through the years are life-bearing or life-denying – has changed how I function in daily life. I sincerely hope that I would one day be able to guide others in the manner demonstrated by my supervisor, as his manner of rhythmic caring through supervision was inspirational, to say the least. He allowed me to find my voice by delaying judgement at times, just to provoke me at other times to interrogate even deeper to find the truth under the hidden layers – a competency that I hope I can carry forward. Simply put, this was a journey of 'in-becoming'.

Elton's response

Pursuing a PhD in Philosophy of Education has the most intellectually transformational journey of my life. Up until pursuing my PhD, I naively believed that the CA-qualification journey equipped me with all the core skills and competencies required to have a meaningful influence in commerce and in society at large. As has already been pointed out, the accountancy pedagogy is however technically very focused, and thus, it stands to reason that the pedagogy falls short of equipping CAs with the keenness of mind to address matters of societal concern.

The PhD in Philosophy of Education therefore forced me to read broadly across the social sciences and liberal arts literature, rather than just the technically narrowly focused literature on accountancy education. In addition, as mentioned earlier, my pursuit of a PhD in Philosophy of Education was further fuelled by my aim of developing educational strategies, which could enable the development of CT skills in accountancy students. After reading broadly, it soon became apparent that true CT competence is more than just a list of skills to be attained but rather a value to be pursued continually. It also became apparent to me that the ideal critical thinkers are open-minded to divergent world views and fair-minded in appraising reasoning (see Facione, 1990). I then realised that, to develop the dispositions open-mindedness and fair-mindedness, the accountancy pedagogy needs to foster environments that are conducive to the democratic value of *equality*.

I was particularly drawn to the words of Rancière (1991:138), who states, "[e]quality was not an end to attain, but a point of departure, a supposition to maintain in every circumstance". I now find myself continually reflecting on the democratic value of equality, in my teaching as well as in my engagement with others from all walks of life. For me, the most profound matter was that the development of CT and of citizenship competencies is inextricably linked. More important, these competencies are not skills that can simply be ticked off, but skills that should always be ongoing pursuits.

8 How do you see yourself as a CA(SA), with a PhD in Philosophy of Education, contributing to societal good?

Judith's response

I have learned throughout the years that I am comfortable standing on the periphery – being in the room so to speak; yet, seeing and thinking differently from the dominant thought in the room. After the PhD journey, I feel myself in exactly the same position again. I am not leaving the profession or academic life; I will however take up being the voice of dissonance in the room. Therefore, being part of the chartered accountancy educational landscape and from within keep on sharing and writing about the importance of philosophical matters and transformational education that are equally concerned about the ability of graduates to make just decisions and act responsibly in business as with the critical technical competencies. I believe that we only need a few fellow academics to start risking and being vulnerable in the classroom in order to let go of being seen as the expert without whom the student cannot learn. Changed pedagogical actions will result in education that will be concerned with values and justice. In that way, future CAs will perhaps understand that their technical skill-set can and should be used as a tool to alleviate poverty, create jobs, and address inequality through sustainable and sound, yet just, business practices. That is what I hope for!

Elton's response

While I have known from a very young age that I wanted to be a CA, I also inherently knew that I would not fit into the traditional CA role as an auditor or financial manager. I always wanted to be in a role where I would feel I was having a direct societal influence. This is why I joined the academe so soon after qualifying as a CA, and particularly at UWC, which is a historically disadvantaged institution of higher education. I do believe that, up until the time of pursuing my PhD, I was trying my level best to exert a direct societal influence. I argued that, if was able to help students to be successful in their chartered accountancy studies, I would be contributing to poverty alleviation and the redress of societal inequality, as most of the students at UWC come from marginalised backgrounds.

I still see myself as being able to have this influence, but the PhD in Philosophy of Education has also highlighted the need for the chartered accountancy pedagogy to make students more aware of their role in a democratic society, rather than just to be successful in the SAICA examinations. I believe that such an accountancy pedagogy, which makes the ideals of a democratic society more explicit, might allow aspiring and current CAs to reflect on the way their professional actions are not isolated but affect society at large. This is an ideal I hope to champion!

Yusef Waghid's overall commentary

Like any other doctorate, a PhD in Philosophy of Education should be constituted by a strong theoretical premise. To be thin on theory in such a PhD would not only undermine all that Philosophy of Education stands for but also would minimise the doctorate to some opaque piece of writing without any authentic scholarly base. I cannot see how one can write a PhD without building on the ideas of others and even affirming and expanding existing seminal thoughts. There is good reason to undertake what is commonly known in doctoral parlance as a 'literature review'. This implies that one needs grounding in what others have articulated and that one's contributions potentially enhance or take issue with what already exists. To assume that a PhD cannot have a strong theoretical promise is not only to be dismissive of what already exists in the field of inquiry, but it is also actually how one makes sense of that which seems to have influenced the thinking in the field. A PhD in Philosophy of Education therefore ought to be intertwined with a well-grounded theoretical premise. Failing to do so would render one's PhD irrelevant and non-contributory to the corpus of knowledge in the field.

Reasonableness cannot (ever) be disassociated from any form of scholarly work, and a PhD is no exception. What is a doctorate in the first place without any form of justification of arguments? Surely, the claims proffered in any PhD must be substantiated by what can be accepted by others (peers in the field) as reasonable and acceptable, based on sound claims of judgement? For once, a PhD without substantive reasoned justifications would be devoid of legitimate knowledge claims reminiscent of what constitutes scholarly writing. If truth claims cannot be eloquently articulated, and lucidly and coherently substantiated, there is just no point in making sense of what a PhD – especially one in Philosophy of Education – represents.

Should a PhD have some public accountability? For me, pursuing knowledge interests in the world for their own sake is a matter of embarking on such intellectual pursuits for intrinsic reasons. There is a sense of authenticity in making bold claims about this matter or that for their own sake; otherwise, there is no real justification to inquire about knowledge. If one does not love doing research for its own sake, there would never emerge the possibility that one can think differently or even think through the matter at hand or under investigation. Educational research therefore ought to be driven by the intrinsic desire and quest to discover. The pursuit of knowledge can also be linked to some extrinsic purpose. Here, one specifically thinks about rethinking educational paradigms in African universities to ensure that the actual goals and purposes of education truly manifest in universities and/or schools. For many years, SA scholars were deeply engaged in reconceptualising post-apartheid education and, if such initiatives did not have a required purpose in mind, our universities and schools might not have benefitted from the knowledge concerns that constituted the work of theorists and practitioners. In this sense, public accountability of dissertations and theses is an expression of the seriousness and relevance scholars attach to – and ought to do so – dissertations and theses in Philosophy of Education. Together with its knowledge interests – through a PhD with public responsiveness – universities can begin to enact a more relevant and meaningful role in post-colonial (South) Africa. Perhaps, our dissertations and theses in Philosophy of Education ought to become more relevant and responsive to the public good in Africa!

Although the written form of a PhD text seems to have dominated scholarship over many years, there is nothing surreptitious about submitting PhDs for examination in multifarious forms, for instance, through a video or another multimedia platform. The written word coupled with a viva voce however remains the most incisive way to present PhDs, as these forms of knowing invariably expose scholars to levels of deliberative engagement that remain authentic and defensible in the pursuit of excellence in scholarship. For the time being, I will adhere to the written text as seemingly the most tenable way to produce a PhD in Philosophy of Education!

Throughout my professional career – which spans over three decades in higher education – I have promoted and/or supervised 65 MEd and PhD students to completion. Of the 35 PhDs, two of my most recent graduates were CAs. In Judith Terblanche, I have encountered one of the most diligent and thoughtful intellectuals who has a deep-rooted, spiritual conscientiousness in scholarship. For her, completing the doctorate was equally important as producing a text of significance that could possibly affect the responsibility of CAs, especially their sense of citizenship in a democratic South Africa. Elton Pullen's PhD offers an argument in defence of critical theory as complementary to the enhancement of the chartered accountancy profession, and, by implication, his seminal contribution also advocates for a democratic citizenry in this mould. While these two students produced similar dissertations, their work is significant to Philosophy of Education because they showed how emphasis on only quantification could constrain the credibility of scholarship for a socially just, democratic South Africa. In fact, it appears as if their contributions combined could become a major impetus in rethinking chartered accountancy on the African continent. I certainly hope so! What struck me most about these two scholars, however, is their dedication to a Philosophy of Education and their willingness and capabilities to think through arguments in analytically plausible ways. For me, working together with them on their PhDs was inspirational in the sense that mutual respect and dissent seemed to have influenced both our intellectual journeys in the completion of the doctorates! It was however the theoretical strengths of their doctoral work in advancing (post-)critical scholarship that will remain with me for some time. I wish them well with their ensuing endeavours as they make sense of the world of chartered accountancy in relation to the cultivation of a critical democratic citizenry in and beyond the university classroom. They reminded me that less teaching seems more viable in producing genuine critical agents of change in post-apartheid South Africa. I would imagine that their work would invariably influence and reshape the chartered accountancy profession in years to come.

Section 3: Potential value identified through the PhD journey

From Section 1, it was evident that the chartered accountancy educational landscape is in dire need of transformation, inclusive of the decoloniality of the landscape. Following from Section 2, it is evident that the two chartered accountancy academics who have pursued a doctorate in Philosophy of Education were significantly shaped and transformed through the PhD journey. That left us with the following question:

> Is it possible through analysis of the narrative discussion and reflexivity to identify a tangible tool that could assist the CA profession in South Africa with the decoloniality of the teaching space?

From this, three sub-questions were developed:

- How do we invite chartered accountancy educators to be open to other forms of assessment besides the traditional time-limited written test?
- How do we attract chartered accountancy educators to utilise various forms of learning and teaching practices besides the mere explication of technical knowledge? How do we entice chartered accountancy educators to include other teaching material into the curriculum content besides the pure traditional technical knowledge content?

We probed the concept of *currere* in light of the narrative discussion between Yusef, Judith, and Elton.

Currere refers to the highly individual process "wherein the curriculum is experienced, enacted and reconstructed" (Pinar 2011:1). For Pinar (2011:1–2), *currere* "occurs through conversation, not only classroom discourse, but also dialogue among specific students and teachers and within oneself in solitude". Pinar prefers the concept *currere* when referring to curriculum, as *currere* signifies the verb form of the word. Such a perspective emphasises the ongoing, the lived nature, of a curriculum that is about the conversation or journey rather than just about the possible measured outcomes. Of importance is Pinar's (2011) view that such a conversation is firstly intrinsically complex, as participants (students and teachers) are diverse with different lived experiences that shaped their being and thoughts. Secondly, this conversation also happens within the individual, whether the individual student or the individual teacher. Through reflexivity and accessing the embodied knowledge of a diverse group of people, the curriculum could become – in an active ongoing manner (*currere*) – transformational. This is in line with the notion that education ought to be a process of and about a lifelong in-becoming.

This potential, of transformation, of newness, of the individual student or individual teacher makes *currere* inherently decolonial (Le Grange, 2020). Quijano (2007) refers to a colonial matrix of power, which includes the control of subjectivity and knowledge. This implies that colonialism played a role in the formation of the identity and philosophical views (thoughts and mind) of individuals, and that the necessary process of decoloniality should include a component that is focused on the minds and being of individuals, inclusive of the teacher him- or herself. Referring to Pinar's (2011:40) regressive-progressive-analytic-synthetic method of *currere*, Le Grange (2021) explicates the value for individual responsibility:

- the *regressive* step involves a remembrance of past influences;
- the *progressive* step focuses on the not-yet or deferred promises of what could be;
- the *analytical* step requires a moment of reflexivity; and
- in the *synthetic* step, the focus is on finding meaning in the face of current difficulties and complexities.

Le Grange (2021) argues that such continuance of inquiry is required by individuals for collective well-being.

From the narrative discussion between our supervisor and ourselves as doctoral students, it is clear that the PhD in Philosophy of Education acted as an accelerating tool for individual transformation, through the praxis of critical reflexivity. We are now acutely aware of the underlying power relations and the possibility that practices, traditions, and legacies in the chartered accountancy educational landscape might be exclusionary, harmful, and not socially just. Such ability of seeing anew required a letting go of dearly held beliefs in moving towards finding meaning in the chartered accountancy educational landscape – for the sake of the profession and of the broader social context of South Africa. Our doctoral journey and Pinar's (2011) regressive-progressive-analytic-synthetic method of *currere* seem to be aligned and could be a possible tool to assist in the decoloniality of the mind of the chartered accountancy academic. Clearly, we cannot prescribe that a PhD in Philosophy of Education be the only tool or the most suitable tool to accelerate decoloniality in the chartered accountancy educational space. We do propose, however, that the profession, through SAICA, introduce a compulsory continuing professional development (CPD) programme aimed specifically at chartered accountancy academics. We recommend a two-year programme focusing on the reflexivity and meaning-making principles of *currere* by using philosophical reading, deliberation sessions, and individual reflexivity writing exercises.

Conclusion

In closing, we are reminded of the reflections of Baszile (2017:4) when she states, "there was a time when education was more a self-determined act than a compulsory one – a time when we learned by doing, by listening to the testimony of others, and by contemplating self in the world".

It is debatable whether the chartered accountancy education ever lived up to this educational ideal, pointed out by Baszile (2017), but the current chartered accountancy pedagogy is certainly scant, as it relates to democratic iterations of reflective praxis. We would thus contend that a lack of critical self-reflection and critical deliberative encounters within the chartered accountancy pedagogy might be contributing to many of the unresolved issues that the CA profession currently faces. *Currere*, however, provides an opportunity for chartered accountancy academics to reimagine a new way forward.

References

Baszile, D.T. 2017. On the virtues of currere. *Currere Exchange Journal*, 1(1):vi–ix.

Facione, P.A. 1990. *Critical thinking: A statement of expert consensus for purposes of educational assessment and instruction – executive summary of "The Delphi report"*. Oakland, CA: California Academic Press.

Foucault, M. 1995. *Discipline and punish: The birth of the prison*. New York: Vintage Books.

Le Grange, L. 2020. The (post)human condition and decoloniality: Rethinking and doing curriculum. *Alternation*, Special edition, 31:119–142. https://doi.org/10.29086/2519-5476/2020/sp31a7

Le Grange, L. 2021. (Individual) Responsibility in decolonising the university curriculum. *South African Journal of Higher Education*, 35(1):4–20. https://doi.org/10.20853/35-1-4416

Lemke, T. 2001. "The birth of bio-politics": Michel Foucault's lecture at the Collège de France on neo-liberal governmentality. *Economy and Society*, 30(2):190–207.

Pinar, W.F. 2011. *The character of curriculum studies: Bildung, currere, and the recurring question of the subject*. New York: Palgrave Macmillan. https://doi.org/10.1057/9781137015839_9

Quijano, A. 2007. Coloniality and modernity/rationality. *Cultural Studies*, 21(2/3):168–178. https://doi.org/10.1080/09502380601164353

Rancière, J. 1991. *The ignorant schoolmaster*. Volume 1. Stanford, CA: Stanford University Press.

SAICA (South African Institute of Chartered Accountants). 2021. *CA2025*. Retrieved from www.saica.org.za/initiatives/competency-framework/ca-of-the-future-ca2025 [Accessed 8 April 2024].

Terblanche, J. 2019. Cultivating socially just responsible citizens in relation to university accounting education in South Africa. Unpublished PhD dissertation. Stellenbosch: Stellenbosch University.

Terblanche, J. & Waghid, Y. 2020a. A Foucauldian analysis of the CA profession in South Africa: Implications for society. *South African Journal of Higher Education*, 34(1):1–17. https://doi.org/10.20853/34-1-3893

Terblanche, J. & Waghid, Y. 2020b. The CA profession in South Africa: In dire need of decoloniality and ubuntu principles. *Citizenship Teaching and Learning*, 15(2):221–238. https://doi.org/10.1386/ctl_00030_1

Terblanche, J. & Waghid, Y. 2021. Chartered accountancy and resistance in South Africa. *South African Journal of Higher Education*, 35(3):239–253. https://dx.doi.org/10.20853/35-3-3894

TerraNova. 2015. Change is inevitable. Progress is intentional. *SAICA JSE Research 2015*. [Received by e-mail from W. Coates (SAICA), 2 April 2016].

10 Beyond borders

Igniting global citizenship education in doctoral studies in Jordan

*Naima Al-husban and
Hammadallah Ahmad Al-husban*

Introduction

The higher education (HE) landscape is currently undergoing a profound transformation, with universities no longer perceived as mere cultural luxuries but rather as catalysts for societal progress, prosperity, and development. These institutions, characterised by elevated levels of scholarship and education, are primarily tasked with preparing individuals with qualifications for leadership positions across various societal domains. Additionally, they engage in the creation of both theoretical and applied research essential for scientific and technological advancement within the community they serve. Universities fulfil their roles through diverse and varied scientific activities, maintaining continuous connections with the society of which they are part. HE however does not culminate with the attainment of the initial university degree; it extends to encompass continuous learning and growth, commonly known as 'post-graduate studies'. Post-graduate studies are regarded as the pinnacle of HE, embodying conscious intellect and playing a vital role in achieving the objectives of the job market while perpetually driving the cultural system of society towards the future (Teichler, 2011).

Consequently, the development of HE, the enhancement of its quality, the optimisation of its efficiency, and the prudent management of its costs have become pivotal issues in the contemporary world. These concerns are responses to the challenges posed by rapid changes in economic and social aspects of life, coupled with the flow of knowledge resulting from scientific progress and technological applications. In the past two decades, HE, once dominated by traditional research universities, has witnessed a transformation. Several factors have contributed to reshaping colleges and ivory tower universities attended by the elite. Today, HE is diversified and attended by large segments of the population. This expansion has led to the emergence of new modes and roles of governance, including performance, quality, and accountability. Msigwa (2016) explains that over-expansion has extended to most middle-income countries and a significant number of low-income countries. According to data from the United Nations Educational,

Scientific and Cultural Organization (UNESCO) Institute for Statistics, the gross enrolment ratio (GER) in high-income countries moved to the HE in 1993, reaching 75% in 2011. Meanwhile, in most middle-income countries, the GER moved to the mass stage in 2001. Currently, about one third of the college-age population all over the world enrolled in HE (Marginson, 2016). This phenomenon has both positive and negative effects on various HE systems. The situation is no longer different in Jordan. Before the beginning of the twenty-first century, the number of PhD holders was limited. After 2010, the Department of Statistics in Jordan however started listing the number of students pursuing a PhD at Jordanian universities. For example, in 2015, there were 3984 students, with 1080 studying at the Faculty of Education. In 2018, there were 4187 pursuing a PhD, and 1605 of them in the Faculty of Education. In 2021, the number rose to 5525, with 1716 studying in the Faculty of Education. This indicates an over-expansion of students enrolled in doctoral studies, superficially indicating a high level of PhD holders. There is, however, no strategy demonstrating the need of the labour market for this high number of PhD holders, leading to a large number of them being unemployed. Wu, Chang and Hu (2021) note the phenomenon of an oversupply of PhD holders, emphasising the need for strategic policies and regulations for those continuing their doctoral studies.

Hamdan and Battah (2020) highlight admission requirements in doctoral studies as among the crucial causes for the decline in the level of learning outcomes in Jordanian universities. The focus on grade point average (GPA) in previous degrees without considering practical experience, knowledge of the specialisation, as well as skills in research and academic writing contributes to the decline. Admission conditions favour revenue generation for universities without attention to quality, giving rise to a decline in graduates' competitiveness locally, regionally, and globally. The high demand for HE in Jordan has led public universities to focus on quantity over quality, resulting in an increase in the number of unemployed PhD degree holders. The situation in Jordan reflects a global problem of an imbalance between the number of PhD holders and the needs of the labour market. Studies, such as that of Hamdan and Battah (2020), identify the problem and propose solutions. As PhD holders from the Faculty of Education (which produces about 30% of PhD holders) and the Faculty of Business Administration (which produces 10% of the PhD holders), we recognise that the main challenge lies not in the high number of graduates from doctoral studies but in transforming this challenge into opportunities to produce qualified researchers and tutors who could investigate topics in their theses that would make a difference in their society. Mere criticism from professors and waiting for solutions from higher levels of administration or accreditation authorities are insufficient. Reforms from outside take a long time, and the topics investigated in doctoral levels are not their top priority.

In this case, there is a glimmer of light on which students in doctoral studies and supervisors should work to make it their source of enlightenment. Based on our experience and observations of other students in the doctoral studies in the Faculties of Education and Business Administration, several points could develop the traditional trend in preparing doctoral studies. Unfortunately, there is a predetermined model that students should follow. For example, in the field of English as a foreign language, students often select a strategy and investigate its effectiveness on students' performance or motivation, with the dependent variable being one of the English language components. Likewise, in the Faculty of Business Administration, students work on a topic and derive from it the variables they then process in a structured way – without thinking of the humanistic perspective of the variable on the company or the society as a whole. Supervisors are burdened with responsibility for five to six students, leading some to rely on students for topic selection and writing. Limited supervision takes place due to time constraints. Students' skills in writing, research, and literature review and selecting innovative topics require professional supervisors providing constant and continuous feedback.

Hawari, Al-Shboul and Huwari (2022), who interviewed nine Malaysian supervisors overseeing 20 Jordanian students, noted challenges in Jordanian PhD candidates at the Universiti Utara Malaysia (i.e. the Northern University of Malaysia) (UUM). They have difficulty writing their PhD theses in English, displaying low confidence due to a poor educational background and self-efficacy beliefs. Jordanian PhD students are known for arguing with their supervisors, even if they do not fully understand the topic. A generic thesis structure poses problems for some Jordanian PhD candidates, affecting the quality of writing and understanding of various thesis components. The educational background – where most Jordanian students at master's level do not write a thesis but opt for a comprehensive examination – indicates the need for students in doctoral studies to enhance their language skills, research capabilities, and academic writing.

Most importantly, the topics of the theses, demotivating students from developing their skills, make completing a thesis their main concern when pursuing a PhD degree. The rigidity of post-graduate systems and regulations poses challenges to the dynamic nature of HE. Structures and guidelines governing post-graduate studies may exhibit inflexibility, hindering adaptability to the evolving needs of students and the rapidly changing academic landscape. This rigidity could manifest in various aspects, such as fixed programme structures, limited interdisciplinary opportunities, and rigid assessment criteria. While some level of structure is necessary for maintaining academic standards, excessive rigidity may stifle innovation, hinder collaborative research, and limit the responsiveness of post-graduate education to emerging trends. Efforts to address this issue necessitate a comprehensive review and modification of existing curriculum frameworks. Additionally, there is a need to introduce more flexible course structures, foster interdisciplinary collaboration, and incorporate effective feedback mechanisms. By promoting a more adaptable and responsive post-graduate education system, institutions could significantly enhance their ability to prepare students for the complexities of the contemporary world, thus contributing to the advancement of knowledge and society at large. This objective can be achieved by focusing on topics that align meticulously with the intended outcomes of university programmes, playing a pivotal role in the moral and cultural development of society. An exemplary illustration of how doctoral studies could respond effectively to contemporary challenges is through the incorporation of global citizenship education (GCE). This field encompasses components that empower students to heighten their awareness of global issues and, over time, promote values such as peace, tolerance, sustainability, and societal security.

It is crucial to recognise that exposure to these topics at various stages of education – and particularly in-depth exploration at the doctoral level – is paramount. Failure to integrate these elements into HE may result in graduates who are disconnected from societal needs, akin to mere knowledge-dispensing automatons. Fostering awareness of GCE should therefore be among the top priorities for policymakers in the educational sector. Additionally, GCE should serve as a primary focus for future researchers, particularly doctoral students, as they investigate and contribute to the evolving landscape of educational practices.

Global citizenship education as an invaluable topic of investigation at doctoral level

To address this matter, Abdi (2015) posits that educational research should inherently be linked to the social well-being of individuals. According to Abdi (2015), GCE should contribute positively to the contextual enhancement of people's lived reality and their expectations for the future. Despite the controversies surrounding global citizenship, it remains a comprehensive topic that researchers find intriguing due to its incorporation of emotions, humanities, values, skills, and knowledge that mutually complement each other. Moreover, research in GCE plays a pivotal role in broadening the perspectives of doctoral students. For instance, the adoption of a global perspective encourages students to transcend their immediate environment, recognising the world as an interconnected global community. This global outlook is imperative in our increasingly interconnected world, where actions in one part of the globe can have far-reaching reactions elsewhere.

Understanding global challenges is a key facet of GCE research, encompassing issues, such as climate change, conflict, poverty, equity, and sustainability (Piccin & Finardi, 2019). By delving into these challenges, doctoral students can gain a profound understanding of the intricate issues facing the world today, emphasising the necessity for global solutions. Enriching doctoral research through a global perspective fosters a more comprehensive and nuanced understanding of the research topic than focusing on traditional research topics. For example, a doctoral student studying education policy might consider not only the policies of his or her home country but also how these policies compare globally and the overarching trends influencing them.

As clarified by Bosio and Waghid (2023), global citizenship serves as a framework for developing critical consciousness in order to achieve in-depth understanding of the world. This perspective exposes researchers to social practices and rituals that may vary across nations, contributing to the transmission of spiritual values and fostering a powerful spirit of solidarity. Bosio and Waghid (2023) propose that global citizenship is a gateway for doctoral students to think beyond conventional boundaries. Critical consciousness stimulated by global citizenship increases students' commitment to combating widespread injustice, enhancing both academic success and enthusiasm (Bosio & Waghid, 2023). Al-husban and Tawalbeh (2022b) suggest that research projects – whether doctoral or otherwise – should have a mission for humanity, justice, democracy, equity, human rights, diversity, empathy, social responsibility, equality, respect for others' views, tolerance, freedom, acceptance of others, peaceful coexistence, lifelong learning, flexible dialogues, entrepreneurship, innovation, management of strong emotions, ethical thinking, and conflict resolution.

Each of the points could form the basis for a doctoral project that fulfils personal ambitions while contributing to societal solidarity. It is time to move away from producing doctoral dissertations and theses that collect dust on shelves because their topics have no effects on social and personal life. In this context, Yusef Waghid plays a significant role in prompting a reconsideration of research styles, topic selection, and the ultimate aims of research, especially in regions where there is a tendency to conduct research for promotion rather than for contributing positively to society and shaping the minds of future generations (Hamdan & Battah, 2020). Waghid's and his colleague's article "Higher education as a pedagogical site for citizenship Education" serves as a guiding light for intellectual and research journeys. Davids and Waghid (2016) discuss the issue that violence is uneasily seated in the conscience of HE, as educated individuals are as likely as the uneducated to participate in violence.

The concern for conscience is equally present in the notion that the public role of the university is 'the responsibility of a community of thinking' (Thornton & Jaeger, 2007). This implies that HE has both the potentiality and im-potentiality for violence. Davids and Waghid (2016) transcend the superficial presentation of the problem by highlighting that the university – when inclusive and innovative – becomes a place of discovery and knowledge creation, unleashing the potential of students in advancing knowledge for the benefit of all members of society. Engaging in doctoral studies at universities becomes an effective approach to cultivate the next generation, researchers, and tutors. Thorough engagement with the topics of global citizenship, practical application, and competence in the subject can empower individuals to interact with others in society based on humanity, avoiding any form of injustice, discrimination, violence, or disrespect.

Challenges of investigating global citizenship education in doctoral studies

Moul (2017) asserts that GCE is a potent approach capable of empowering individuals to transform their communities into peaceful and sustainable societies. GCE not only nurtures cognitive development but also addresses socio-emotional aspects of learning, influencing behaviours such as tolerance, respect, empathy, and effective communication. UNESCO recognises the significance of GCE by placing it at the core of its priorities, urging nations to integrate it into their education system (Moul, 2017). Despite its importance, GCE however receives limited attention in HE circles; this lack of attention can be attributed to the contested nature of GCE since its inception. Some argue that it is perceived as disconnected from local realities, sparking debates in contexts where the term 'global' is misconstrued, often associated with processes external to their communities, and erroneously linked with Westernisation (Middaugh, 2022).

Moreover, the traditional instructional methods prevalent in primary and secondary education stages often omit GCE concepts, values, and skills (Alhusban & Tawalbeh, 2022a). This omission results in the creation of a generation unaware of the importance of GCE. Consequently, those who proceed to pursue doctoral studies may not consider investigating this crucial topic. Addressing these gaps in understanding is paramount to fostering a comprehensive educational approach that incorporates the principles of GCE across all educational levels.

Difficulty in dealing with these challenges in doctoral studies in Jordan

Jordan is an Islamic country, and several publications have highlighted the alignment of GCE principles with Islamic education. Waghid (2011) elucidates that Islamic education, rooted in the Quran and Sunnah, promotes values, skills, and knowledge synonymous with GCE. This includes fostering respect for others, advocating for peace, embracing racial and colour differences, respecting cultural diversity, and cultivating critical thinking (CT) skills – attributes encouraged by various verses in the Quran Kareem, which prompt individuals to contemplate the world around them. Similarly, Thalgi (2019) affirms that key GCE subjects, such as world peace, global cooperation, moral responsibility, and human rights, find resonance in Islamic religious texts. Saada (2023) further emphasises that Islamic education enhances the understanding and practice of GCE, encouraging the consideration of Islamic ethical codes in addressing global challenges, fostering tolerance, and advocating for justice within Muslim communities.

The current study makes a compelling call for Muslim students at middle and high school level to develop their global and self-reflective identities. This call underscores the observation that, in reality, Muslim students – particularly those busy with doctoral studies – are inattentive to investigating this topic, despite its intrinsic connection to their religion, culture, language, and everyday life.

Scholars and doctoral students should therefore embark on self-exploration of global topics seldom addressed in Islamic religious curricula. These include freedom of belief and expression, personal autonomy, multifaceted identities, gender equality, critical rationalism, moral pluralism, diversity of religious knowing, and democracy (Al-husban & Tawalbeh, 2022b). Notably, these topics intersect with both Islamic education and GCE, emphasising that GCE is not an external concept but an integral part of the Muslim identity and existence.

From an educational perspective, GCE emerges as a comprehensive topic covering all outcomes of the educational system, encompassing values, twenty-first-century skills, and knowledge. This aligns seamlessly with the mission and vision of higher education institutions, as there is no inherent contradiction between GCE and a Muslim background. Investigating GCE at doctoral level is not only possible but also essential.

To raise awareness among university supervisors and doctoral students about the significance of GCE as a doctoral topic, it is crucial to encourage extensive reading, recognising the universal and moral messages of Islamic teachings in the Quran and Hadith. Nurturing Islamic education and establishing links with GCE from the early stages of learning are pivotal to developing students' competencies and awareness. Saada (2023:4) refers to this integration as 'Islamic global citizenship'. As this awareness permeates university settings, the prospect of a large number of students investigating GCE becomes secondary to its enlightening influence on society. Such studies contribute to creating a society devoid of violence, where members respect, tolerate, and collaborate with each other. Students, motivated by a sense of mission, become positive contributors to their religion, society, and future, evolving into enlightened scholars.

Conclusion

The chapter discussed the proliferation of doctoral dissertations in large numbers each semester, highlighting a lack of influence on social life. Paradoxically, an increase in societal violence, crimes, together with a dearth of respect among individuals is observed. This situation suggests a neglect of the essence of GCE, as doctoral dissertations adhere to a predetermined model. Consequently, researchers in HE have not yet influenced societal well-being significantly despite investigating relevant topics. The need for a positive influence on society is therefore emphasised, particularly through topics rooted in GCE emanating from Islamic education.

The solution proposed is straightforward – raising learners' awareness in the early stages of Islamic education and integrating GCE principles into various subjects. This integration aims to dispel misconceptions that GCE is solely derived from Western culture and poses a threat to national identity. The chapter underscored the importance of developing critical awareness of international knowledge to enhance students' knowledge, skills, and values, drawing from diverse resources. Moreover, the narrative advocated for informed decision-makers who integrate these topics into the curriculum, teacher training, and the assessment process from the inception of education. This proactive approach is believed to open HE studies naturally to these critical topics. The chapter concluded by asserting the need to reform doctoral studies in the Middle East and North Africa region, positioning them as a vital source of knowledge for future generations.

Lessons learned

As doctoral candidates, we embark on a scholarly journey that extends beyond academia. Within this context, several important lessons emerge, shaping our approach to research and its broader implications. Drawing from the original passage, we aim to clarify these lessons.

Firstly, our scholarly pursuits should extend beyond theoretical constructs. By promoting societal well-being, we contribute to tangible improvements in people's lives. This requires research topics that address pressing challenges, whether in health, education, or social justice.

Secondly, the pursuit of knowledge demands rigour. Our work must be valuable and beneficial, not only for academic recognition but also for its impact on researchers, students, and society. Rigorous methodologies, insightful findings, and practical applications define quality research.

Thirdly, our research should transcend time. Enduring ideas, infused with values and virtues, outlive trends and fads. When effectively disseminated, these ideas avoid being forgotten.

Fourthly, as custodians of scholarly publications, our primary intention should be to benefit society. We safeguard knowledge, ensuring that it reaches diverse audiences. Generously sharing ideas fosters impact and progress.

Fifthly, our work has a lasting impact. By mentoring students, collaborating across disciplines, and creating resources, we lay the foundation for future scholars. Our legacy extends beyond individual achievements.

Lastly, whether in the context of Islamic principles or universal ethics, our research aligns with global citizenship. Compassion, justice, and ethical ideals guide our endeavours.

In summary, these lessons propel us beyond academic routines. They empower us to contribute meaningfully to society, making a lasting impression on the scholarly landscape. As aspiring scholars, let us embrace these principles and shape a world where knowledge serves humanity's highest ideals.

References

Abdi, A. 2015. Decolonizing global citizenship education: Critical reflections on the epistemic intersections of location, knowledge, and learning. In Abdi, A.A., Shultz, L., & Pillay, T. (eds) *Decolonizing global citizenship education* (pp. 11–26). Rotterdam: SensePublishers. https://doi.org/10.1007/978-94-6300-277-6_2

Al-husban, N. & Tawalbeh, M. 2022a. Investigating global citizenship concepts embedded in primary and secondary textbooks in Jordan. *Citizenship Teaching & Learning*, 17(2):309–326.

Al-husban, N. & Tawalbeh, M. 2022b. Scrutinizing teachers' awareness of global citizenship education (GCED) in Jordan. *Alberta Journal of Educational Research*, 68(4):581–603.

Bosio, E. & Waghid, Y. 2023. *Global citizenship education in the Global South: Educators' perceptions and practices*. Volume 21. Leiden: Brill.

Davids, N. & Waghid, Y. 2016. Higher education as a pedagogical site for citizenship education. *Education, Citizenship and Social Justice*, 11(1):34–43.

Hamdan, M. & Battah, A. 2020. Suggested policies for accepting PhD students at the University of Jordan to align its educational outcomes with the needs of the labor market and to improve its position in the World Universities Rankings according to the experience of Canadian universities. *Journal of Education and Practice*, 11(17):32–45.

Hawari, O.M.D.A., Al-Shboul, Y. & Huwari, I.F. 2022. Supervisors' perspectives on graduate students' problems in academic writing. *European Journal of Educational Research*, 11(1):545–556.

Marginson, S. 2016. The worldwide trend to high participation higher education: Dynamics of social stratification in inclusive systems. *Higher Education*, 72(4):413–434.

Middaugh, E. 2022. Promoting global citizenship education in Arab universities: Proposals for action. UNESCO. Retrieved from https://unesdoc.unesco.org/ark:/48223/pf0000381929 [Accessed 26 December 2023].

Moul, T.R. 2017. Promotion and implementation of global citizenship education in crisis situations. UNESCO. Retrieved from www.edu-links.org/sites/default/files/media/file/252771eng.pdf [Accessed 28 December 2023].

Msigwa, F.M. 2016. Widening participation in higher education: A social justice analysis of student loans in Tanzania. *Higher Education*, 72(4):541–556.

Piccin, G. & Finardi, K. 2019. Questioning global citizenship education in the internationalization agenda. *Educational Review*, 12:73–89. https://doi.org/10.21810/sfuer.v12i3.1015

Saada, N. 2023. Educating for global citizenship in religious education: Islamic perspective. *International Journal of Educational Development*, 103:102894. 2–8

Teichler, U. 2011. International dimensions of higher education and graduate employment. In Allen, J. & van der Velden, R. (eds) *The flexible professional in the knowledge society: New challenges for higher education*. Dordrecht: Springer, 177–197.

Thalgi, M. J. 2019. Global citizenship from an Islamic educational perspective. *Cumhuriyet Ilahiyat Dergisi*, 23(2):1027–1051.

Thornton, C. H. & Jaeger, A.J. 2007. A new context for understanding civic responsibility: Relating culture to action at a research university. *Research in Higher Education*, 48, 993–1020.

Waghid, Y. 2011. *Conceptions of Islamic education: Pedagogical framings. Global studies in education series*, Volume 3. New York: Peter Lang.

Wu, S.J., Chang, D.F. & Hu, H. 2021. Detecting the issue of higher education overexpanded under declining enrollment times. *Higher Education Policy*, 34:747–770.

11 An interpretive analysis of Namibian education policy and its link to citizenship education

A reflection on my doctoral encounters

Tadeus Shikukumwa

Introduction

Pursuing a doctoral qualification requires an intense focus, proper time management, and self-discipline. At one point, the candidate renounces his or her social life, somehow enforces temporary family time abandonment, and instead spends sleepless nights trying to read several sources, doing analyses of academic articles, and paraphrasing and understanding several scholars' views and perspectives. During my studies, I was not exempted from all these aspects. It was an initiation towards achieving the title of 'Doctor'. I had to juggle between a full-time job as a Distance Education Coordinator for Tertiary Programmes at the Namibian College of Open Learning, family, and part-time jobs as a lecturer at some local and regional universities. I was expected to perform exceptionally well in all these circles. During my doctoral journey, I lost my mother and had to take a break to bury my mom and afterwards continue with the doctoral journey and complete what I have started. In fact, there were much turbulence in reaching this qualification. Sadly enough, after my successful doctoral viva voce, I contracted Covid-19 that landed me in the high-care unit of a hospital for ten days. Eventually, I survived to celebrate and enjoy the fruits of my work after going through the hands of my promoter, the seasoned and distinguished professor, Yusef Waghid.

In this chapter, I present democratic citizenship education (DCE). I will also refer to education reform in Namibia. Furthermore, this chapter reflects the reconceptualisation of democratic citizenship in the Namibian basic education system. Lastly, this chapter presents entrenching DCE in the Namibian learner.

Democratic citizenship education

According to Waghid (2018:154), "democratic citizenship invokes people's aspiration to be attentive to their deliberative concerns and co-belonging and rights, interests and aspirations, decolonisation intimates that such change

DOI: 10.4324/9781003530091-12

ought to summon people to act reflectively and openly about their (un)known conditions". It is important to note that the terms 'democracy' and 'citizenship', around which I formed my study, entail participation and belonging of people after being socialised through the education process. In the case of Namibia, in particular, and in other former colonies in general, for the people to participate meaningfully and embrace a sense of belonging, the education system however needs to be decolonised. Decolonisation makes it possible for the citizens of a given country to be actively involved in shaping education through their participation in stakeholder meetings that are convened to garner diverse views on any envisaged education policies (Waghid, 2018:154).

While conducting my study, I aspired for an interpretive analysis of the new curriculum embraced by the Namibian government to illustrate the essential role of transformational and democratic citizenship in achieving a sufficiently democratic form of citizenship education. Interpretive analysis extends beyond mere observation to human explanations of how the new curriculum affects the way teachers and learners interact during the teaching and learning process. For instance, teacher–learner ratios in previously disadvantaged regions are still characterised by higher numbers of learners per teacher, resulting in classrooms being overcrowded, which makes it extremely difficult to provide quality education. The Namibian government has however taken measures to provide quality education, although it is being undermined by factors such as limited resources, inadequate infrastructure, and disparities in access to education.

During my research, I ventured into interpretivism as a vital tool in conceptualising the notion of decolonisation on which transformation of the Namibian education system is built. Using interpretivism has helped me comprehend the new curriculum whose goal is to decolonise the education system in order to bring change. It was by engaging with interpretivism that I found that notions such as 'decolonisation' and 'transformation' as well as 'democratic citizenship' could be made clearer when applied to the Namibian scenario. It is in this light that Waghid (2018:153) argues, "[d]colonisation of the curriculum is not a once-off pedagogic form of engineering [...] decolonisation is an act of taking issue with the debilitating consequences of colonisation [since] for decolonisation to take place, educators and students require deliberation". In addition, Waghid asserts, "whereas citizenship insists that people co-belong unconditionally, decolonisation implies that people already co-belong in their effort to actuate changes in their lives, [hence] ... decolonisation takes further what citizenship initiates" (Waghid, 2018:153).

Against this backdrop, there was a need to undo inherent structural problems in terms of the new Namibian curriculum to achieve its envisaged goals of creating a knowledge-based society. Interpretivism was useful in this context by conceptualising the decolonisation and transformation of the education system as these relate to democratic citizenship. Based on my findings, it can be argued that, in formulating the new curriculum, the Ministry of Education seems to have drawn from two concepts, 'decolonisation of education' and 'an African philosophy of education'. The irony is that the new curriculum seems to entrench the same problems it initially set out to address, such as the lack of properly equipped facilities that disadvantage learners from poor schools in national examinations. In this case, I argue that the new curriculum may be posing another dilemma because decolonising the curriculum seems to be limited to theoretical issues of adoption of a decolonised approach. The practical implementation and extent of decolonisation can be limited or uneven at the expense of the practical issues of implementation of the policy at the level of schools located in different areas. This raises many questions, such as those relating to democracy of the Namibia education policy. My argument for an interpretive analysis of the rationale for my study however was aimed neither at disputing the need for a new curriculum nor at downgrading its envisaged goals. Instead, I intended to establish how the notions of decolonisation and transformation of education are spelled out in the new curriculum to produce a DCE.

In the views above, Waghid (2018:151) further states that DCE cannot be distanced from African educational interests. In other words, Waghid advocates the relevance of an African philosophy in contextualising the educational interests of the people on the continent. Added to that, Waghid and Davids (2018) posit those dimensions such as human co-belonging, in line with African interests and deliberative engagements as some of the defining features of African democratic citizenship. They emphasise the importance of recognising and respecting the dignity and agency of all individuals, as well as promoting active citizenship and meaningful participation in public affairs. By embracing these dimensions, African societies can work towards building more just, equitable, and democratic communities.

I employed interpretivist theory to conceptualise an African philosophy of education as a tool with which to analyse the new Namibian curriculum. I draw in this regard from African philosophies such as *ubuntu* and the Harambee Prosperity Plan (HPP),[1] with the latter serving as a rallying point for the current government's Vision 2030. The Harambee Prosperity Plan (HPP) was indeed launched by the government of Namibia in 2016, under the leadership of President Hage Geingob. The HPP serves as a comprehensive roadmap for socioeconomic development in Namibia, aiming to address key challenges and accelerate progress across various sectors. I, therefore, argue that the interpretivist paradigm is a useful mechanism with which to conceptualise an African philosophy of education as the methodology of inquiry premised on rational justification and argumentation in the hope of transforming African practice and thought. Davids (2018:1–2) notes, "[k]ey to educational reform in post-apartheid South Africa was to undo historical and racial-based inequalities, while simultaneously implementing an education system that would cultivate a citizenship education necessary for a democratic society". In writing about the South African (SA) experience, Davids's views on DCE resonate with the envisaged benefits of the new Namibian curriculum as a tool to engender democratic citizens.

Interpretivism was thus vital in framing my discussion of the new Namibian curriculum and its relation to DCE. HHP attests to the effect of the spirit of communalism, which I equated in my study to the notion of citizenship, which denotes a sense of belonging among a group of people. From an African perspective, the HPP can be applied in terms of educational transformation. Applying these African philosophies, such as communalism, to educational transformation within the context of the HPP suggests a holistic approach that prioritises inclusive and participatory education. It implies fostering a sense of community and shared purpose within educational institutions, promoting collaboration among students, teachers, parents, and other stakeholders. In short, the African philosophies helped to place my research within the context of Namibia.

DCE and the curriculum

The current literature review related to the relationship between the education curriculum and citizenship education identified three major weaknesses in the existing research on this subject, namely lack of longitudinal studies: Many studies in this area tend to be cross-sectional, focusing on a specific point in time rather than tracking the impact of curriculum changes over the long term; limited diversity in samples: A common weakness is the lack of diversity in the samples studied, both in terms of demographics (such as race, ethnicity, socioeconomic status) and geographic location; and insufficient attention to implementation: While research often examines the intended goals of the curriculum, there is often less emphasis on how these curricular initiatives are actually implemented in classrooms.

The central argument in the current study was to explore how Namibians can be nurtured to become democratic citizens through DCE. The discussion of this argument was based on the literature review related to DCE and the curriculum, as mentioned above. An interconnectedness between DCE and the curriculum forms the foundation of creating a democratic citizen. Given the above, the concept 'democratic citizenship' has been expounded as the way humans associate with each other when they voluntarily do things together. There is however a need to link this to the curriculum.

To be educated about democratic citizenship, one needs to be in a position to be an active participant in the political questions of the country and to have a sense of belonging. It should be pointed out, "a theory of democratic citizenship education invokes a form of associational co-belonging and engagement whereby people come into one another's presence" (Waghid, 2018:3). For this reason, a theory of DCE is particularly relevant for a country such as Namibia. A democratic curriculum is associated with democratic education, which refers to an educational practice premised on critical pedagogy but translated more strongly into the organisation of education and participation in society (Apple, 2002:303). Democratic education is geared towards the development of an autonomous, dynamic, and creative personality, rooted in social realities (Audigier, 1999). To attain this, the curriculum must contain developmental aims, which will enable learners to be competently integrated into the society. I therefore contend that a curriculum for democratic citizenship should instil skills of communication and networking, as well as intellectual skills in learners. This will enable them to participate effectively in political, social, and economic activities. DCE should therefore be a requirement for learners to be in a position to perform the role expectations in society.

In this study, I argued that curriculum design should be oriented towards an education that effectively realises a social function premised on a continuous readjustment of the contents, objectives, and action strategies of the curriculum to replace those patterns or principles of traditional static curricula that may not adequately address the current needs and complexities of society considered to be outdated. This is a way for the curriculum to enhance the development of democratic citizenship among learners in line with the needs of a rapidly changing world. It is in this context that social cohesion – which is a comparatively far-flung objective of school education – can be seen as the assimilation and communication of behavioural or action patterns in terms of the conditions of existence of individuals as members of a community (Canivezs, 1990). The curriculum should reflect the changes taking place in education as evidenced by attributes, such as being democratic, participatory, responsible, collaborative, communicative, ethical, and open-minded, among others.

Scholarly discussions around DCE entail delving into the issues that reflect the effect of values, meanings, and principles related to the notion of democratic citizenship and education as the way these affect the school curriculum. Other attendant issues that should appear in curricular documents include educational practice, the content of the curriculum, and pedagogical issues related to DCE. Maximal interpretations lead to a broad mixture of what has been termed as citizenship education. I argue that citizenship education involves a combination of formal and informal approaches in contrast to the narrower focus of civics education.[2] In Kerr's (1999) view, citizenship education comprises the content and knowledge components of minimal interpretations in terms of citizenship education. It further actively spurs an investigation and interpretation of the various ways in which components such as the rights and duties of citizens are established.

In this discussion on the relevance of DCE, I argue that the problems bedevilling most Namibian schools are a result of the lack of DCE in the Namibian education system. As a result, education system is important as it engenders a sense of respect among citizens for others who are different from them while both inhabit the same space (Waghid, 2005). Of significance is that education for democratic citizenship should be premised on education policies that seek to create students who actively contribute to the creation of knowledge since we are residing in societies that are increasingly becoming knowledge based. The point here is that DCE encompasses three concepts, namely 'democracy', 'citizenship', and 'education'. The point here is that one of the terms comprising DCE is 'citizenship'.

The concept 'democratic citizenship education' is defined in various ways. Benhabib (2011:75) states that citizenship education encompasses learning to participate in democratic activities manifested in the way "citizens articulate the specific content of their scheduled rights, as well as making these rights their very own". This implies that citizenship education should enable students to be actively engaged in activities that revolve around the issue of rights. As a result, citizenship education involves inculcating in students communicative ways that would enable them to lay claim to their "right to have rights" (Benhabib, 2011:75).

In analysing the new education policy, I drew from the concepts of diversity, equality, inclusive education, as well as the philosophical underpinnings of the education policies, among others. Translating, assessing, and interpreting an education policy is a multifaceted process (Brown, 2016). This implies that analysis of the policy text is not essentially a straightforward, close-ended or complete process but involves discussions at different stages and is affected by particular ideologies and philosophical standpoints (Naashia, 2006). DCE in Namibia has been conceptualised as a shift from colonial rule to independent Namibia as epitomised by the process of decolonisation (Shanyanana, 2011). DCE in Namibia emanates from the local framework of national education, which resonates with the Namibianisation of education[3] by embracing democracy as an element of education policy in designing national education policies to advance national cohesion and solidarity as well as national identity.

Reconceptualisation of DCE in the Namibian basic education system

In my doctoral encounter, I examined the notion of DCE in the new basic education policy. Of importance is the fact that democratic citizenship denotes a sense of belonging where the learners are educated to accept their respective cultural backgrounds. While colonial education deliberately sought to alienate learners from the cultural milieu, post-colonial education aims to restore a sense of belonging by making learners feel they belong to the environments that produce them. Evidence of DCE in Namibian basic education emerged through the education policies and curricula following independence in 1990. Political independence in Namibia could be argued to have spearheaded the drive towards opening the education space, which had been constrained by apartheid government education. It is apparent in the literature that Namibia incorporated democratic principles in governance when it gained independence and in the years after independence. Furthermore, DCE is based on liberal ideas. It is important to note that DCE is enhanced by local and global developments. Globalisation thus allows for the incorporation of human rights into the education system. Human rights facilitate participation by most groups. Even though the national objectives and principles of Namibia seek to promote equality, it could be argued that Namibia can be considered an unequal society (Shanyanana, 2011).

A question can be posed, namely –

> On which form of democratic citizenry does the Namibian education system operate?

To answer to this question, one must bear in mind that, even though Namibia adopted a form of democracy at independence by opening education, there are striking operational problems and infrastructural features that still make it difficult to implement DCE. Before independence, different educational circuits and regions in Namibia encountered inter alia several infrastructural problems, a lack of access to educational opportunities, as well as a lack of educational development. These problems persist and continue to affect the educational environment. When geographical factors are considered, disparities in Namibian education are continuing. Currently, the education sector in Namibia is hampered by perennial problems, such as a lack of qualified teachers, lopsided enrolment ratios, inadequate schools, and poor infrastructure and facilities at these schools.

The National Curriculum for Basic Education (Ministry of Education, Arts and Culture 2016) champions the values of democracy and democratic engagement. At independence, post-colonial education policies were designed to transform the educational system by shifting from an apartheid repressive system to inclusive education system where every Namibian has access. Like SA education, the Namibian education system "was based on a particular Afrikaner form of Calvinism, known as Christian National Education" (Waghid & Davids, 2017:7). This implies that the Bantu Education curricula and policies of the time were meant to propagate, "[that] an individual's potential and opportunities are defined by race and ethnicity" (Waghid & Davids, 2017:7). This type of education privileged one group of learners compared to others, as manifested in the well-equipped schools with resource centres, science laboratories, modern sporting facilities, small teacher–learner ratios, and experienced and qualified teachers while underprivileged schools did not have those resources, equipment, tools, and qualified teachers. Moreover, teachers were viewed as the only source of knowledge while learners were seen as blank slates that needed to be filled with the knowledge from the teacher. It is in this context that Waghid and Davids (2017:7) observe, "while the teacher was considered the sole authority of knowledge, learners were expected to listen, receive and memorise knowledge, without talking back". This kind of political ideology was infused into the education system, which post-apartheid education policies in Namibia sought to dismantle.

Instead of passive and non-questioning learners, the new basic education policy seeks to produce a type of learner who is inquisitive, explorative, and active in the creation of knowledge. It is my observation that, although the policy propagates on paper DCE among learners, a new form of privileged and non-privileged learnership is present in post-independent Namibia. Although privileges are no longer racially based, they are now class-based and geographically determined. The same education policy is being implemented across the country, irrespective of where the learner is found. There is no discrimination based on ethnicity, race, or religion, but there are inequalities across the classes to which the learners belong. The new policy emphasises information and communication technology (ICT) without due regard to the provision and availability of information infrastructure.

It is clear from that the new policy is silent on the provision of information and communications technology (ICT) infrastructure to schools, especially those in remote parts of the country. The implementation of this aim raises more questions than answers as regards the capacity of and commitment by government to attain this aim. This means that, while the curriculum is designed to address those inequalities that continue to hamper the education system, practical issues of implementation are not fully addressed (National Curriculum for Basic Education [Ministry of Education, Arts and Culture, 2016:49]). It is not clear how this aim should be achieved. The National Curriculum further sets sixteen (16) pre-conditions for the successful curriculum delivery process. Crucially, such conditions should lay the foundation for the implementation of the curriculum. In and around the school, pre-conditions include:

- "that every learner has all the textbooks and materials appropriate to their ability and needs;
- that the school and classroom are conducive to learning by being a well-managed physical, social and material environment;
- that every school is an ICT Level 2 school following the ICT Policy for Education (2005)" (Ministry of Education, Arts and Culture, 2016:387–338).

When applied to the Namibian situation, one notices that the education system is characterised by some conditions that engender structural inequalities that were inherited from apartheid. Based on the abovementioned observations, I argue that the new curriculum is premised on several characteristics that were derived from Namibia Vision 2030 (Government of Namibia, 2004), such as:

- a caring society;
- a healthy society;
- a democratic society;
- a productive society;
- an environmentally sustainable society;
- individual development (National Curriculum for Basic Education, 2016:5–7).

The new curriculum seems to champion the above forms of knowledge in the thrust towards the attainment of DCE. While such a grand scheme is conceivable, it remains questionable whether it can be achieved practically. In Namibia, it is imperative to examine the state of teachers' readiness to be at the forefront of delivering DCE. Although the new policy aims to cultivate DCE among learners, the readiness of teachers to "cultivate the principles of democratic citizenship education" (Davids, 2018:2) remains a considerable obstacle towards efforts in the country to transform the education system. Namibian education has undergone several changes in its attempts to decolonise this sector of structural inequalities, which are the legacy of the apartheid epoch.

The first curriculum revision was initiated in the early 1990s when the country attained independence. The basic education reform sought to achieve four major goals, namely access to education, equity, quality of education, and democracy (Ministry of Education, Arts and Culture, 2020). This reform led to the introduction of the Junior Secondary Certificate (JSC) in 1993, while the International General Certificate of Secondary Education (IGCSE) at National Qualifications Framework (NQF) Level 3 and Higher International General Certificate of Secondary Education (HIGCSE) at NQF Level 4 were introduced in 1994 and 1995, respectively. The second revision of the curriculum was between 2004 and 2006 whose milestone was the respective localisation of IGCSE and HIGCSE to Namibia Senior Secondary Certificate Ordinary Level (NSSCO) and Namibian Senior Secondary Certificate Higher Level (NSSCH) with the first examinations being written in 2006 for NSSCO and in 2007 for NSSCH. The third reform began in 2014 as a mechanism meant to transform the education system in Namibia significantly. The third review is the current curriculum that is being taught in schools.

Despite all these initiatives, the overall aim rested on the transformation of the learner from the passivity and non-questioning style of teacher-centre education to inquiring, knowledge-creating, creative and reflective learner-centred education, as explained below:

> [V]ery limited, if any, attention has been paid to the particular experiences, narratives and identities of [the] teacher [...] although teachers have been expected to adopt and support waves of curriculum reform, very little is known about teachers and teacher professional identity.
>
> (Davids, 2018:2)

Little is known in Namibia about the ICT competency of teachers across the country and their state of readiness to teach a curriculum that seeks to cultivate DCE among a wide-ranging population of learners emanating from diverse backgrounds and geographical locations. The professional identity of the teachers plying their trade in various educational circuits in Namibia remains largely unknown due to the homogenising tendencies of government initiatives. For one, the 2019 pandemic has exposed the often taken-for-granted assumptions about teachers' ICT competencies and their ownership of ICT gadgets.

Entrenching DCE in the Namibian child

In my encounter, I examined the theoretical ideas about DCE practices as contained in the new basic education policy and the new curriculum. I presented an evaluation and offered recommendations for evaluation of the new basic education policy and the new curriculum in the Namibian basic education system to promote access to DCE. I asserted that DCE receives scant attention in the new basic education policy in Namibia, and the attention given to DCE is therefore insufficient for producing democratic citizenry out of the learners receiving basic education. I therefore provided a nuanced view of DCE and a prospect of what it could proffer to basic education in Namibia. This implies that, in my encounter, I explained how the new basic education policy related to the teaching and learning context could be aligned with various strategies and approaches to address the concept of DCE within the Namibian education system.

My study demonstrated that the new basic education policy thinly addresses DCE practices of Namibian learners. The teachers who participated in the study also claimed that the new basic education policy does not fully address historical inequalities or accessibility issues, and it does not encourage critical thinking among the diverse groups of learners scattered across Namibia. Claims about the persistent problems of disparities in the education sector were cited as an impediment to the attainment of DCE among learners in poorly staffed, under-equipped, and under-resourced remote schools in Namibia. Another aspect worth noting in my encounter, which arose from the ones mentioned above, is that the teachers still require intensive training in teaching DCE to learners as well as understanding their professional identities within the new policy here as their roles are limited to facilitation. In my encounter, it became clear that teachers cannot critically engage with the new curriculum to nurture a new group of learners, as they were not properly informed about the new policy. The literature review undertaken for this study showed that DCE does not only consist of inclusive, accessible, and quality education but also includes issues of criticality, reflexivity, and entrepreneurship among learners.

In my doctoral encounter, I discussed the two theories of interpretivism and pragmatism as they relate to education policy. This helped to guide me to understand the formulation and implementation of the education policy. I also explored the notions of DCE, an African philosophy, and decolonisation of education and the influence of these on the new Namibian basic education policy. Essentially, this allowed me to explore the implications that each of the identified notions, which are African philosophy and decolonisation of the education policy, had in creating possibilities of DCE in the Namibian basic education sector. Added to that as part of my encounter, decolonisation was analysed in the education sector to engender a space where the new education policy could thrive in its attempts to provide DCE within the basic schooling system. Crucially, DCE is understood as a situation where learners come together to bring forth their different backgrounds and world views and arrive at meaningful engagement and deliberation to make sense of themselves and others and of themselves with others. Learners as democratic citizens are urged to envision other people's lifeworlds by being empathetic towards other people and how they perceive themselves in order to comprehend human diversities. In other words, I pointed out that DCE embraces concepts such as civic responsibilities, human rights, and interaction, a mutual feeling of belonging and public participation in matters of nation-building.

Of importance is that civic responsibilities and citizenship education have certain behavioural expectations from citizens. These expectations comprise –

- the need to participate in rational political debates to arrive at informed decisions through public debates and consultations;
- the responsibility to tolerate differences and engage in public reasoning as a means to make verdicts; and
- a way of public life (Benhabib, 2011; Davids, 2018; Waghid, 2018).

In this study, DCE is regarded as a contributor to the mutual feeling of belonging manifested in the protection that is extended to citizens who are tied together by collective civic obligations and diversities as encapsulated in the national constitution that binds and safeguards the citizens. Similarly, DCE facilitates the interaction of and mingling among learners from diverse backgrounds. This implies that DCE maintains that basic education is a space where learners from diverse backgrounds are exposed to different ways of interacting and co-existing with others through classroom interactions.

Furthermore, an attempt was made to detail the effect of decolonisation on education within the context of Namibia further. I examined the various meanings of decolonisation, and the way basic education in Namibia has been and still needs to be decolonised to prepare for the successful implementation of the new education policy and the new curriculum. As regards the discussion, I want to state confidently that, at the time the study was carried out, 2021, the education system in Namibia was far from being fully decolonised. There were still vestiges of colonial legacy within the schooling system in Namibia, such as access to quality education. I established that decolonisation extended beyond the political and economic issues in the country to areas that include knowledge systems or epistemologies and pedagogies currently in use in schools which are mainly borrowed from Western traditions. In other words, I want to emphasise that decolonisation remains firmly entrenched in the education systems as evidenced by epistemologies that continue to demote African knowledge systems, preferring those that traditionally originate from the Western world. This would mean that decolonisation extended beyond the removal of colonialism from formerly colonised countries to include undoing even the hold their knowledge systems have on African education systems.

Another aspect that was exposed vividly during this encounter is the contribution of indigenous knowledge systems in education policy formulation in Namibia. For that reason, I examined how an African philosophy could provide a basis on which to situate African knowledge systems within the education sector starting with basic education. This was seen as having significant effects on basic education policy design and application as well as on DCE (Behabib, 2011; Davids, 2019; Waghid, 2018). A closer look at the Namibian education policies revealed the influence that the democratic process had on basic education policies in the country. I also noted that DCE is unlikely to be equally accessed by the learner in Namibia because of the problems that still affect far-flung schools – a situation that has further been exacerbated by the Covid-19 pandemic, which saw a shift from face-to-face classes to online virtual classes. This means that Namibian basic education was largely affected by historical, socioeconomic, and political factors. Moreover, I discovered that the change in education policies did not necessarily lead to educational transformation as shown by several policies that have been formulated and implemented since 1990.

I analysed Namibian education policies with reference to the new Namibian curriculum for basic education that was introduced in 2015. I argue that the new education policy, as well as the new curriculum that guides teaching and learning in Namibian schools, have features that can be reflective of the principles of DCE. My argument is informed by Biesta (2012:1) who argues that citizenship teaching "is always mediated by what children and young people experience in their everyday lives". I evaluated this in the light of the basic education policy documents to establish how learners are guided towards the path of DCE through active participation. I also draw from Davids's (2019:6) argument:

> Students [...] need to learn how to think, how to listen, how to consider different perspectives, and how to critically reconsider their taken-for-granted views [and should] be provided with spaces and opportunities whereby they can step out of who they are, and cross-over into other life-world and perspectives.

The foregoing sharply presents how basic education is being delivered in schools due to the inherent problems that bedevil the way basic curricula in Namibia are implemented in an attempt to teach DCE. My argument is centred on the need for access to quality education and social justice as well as the relevance of the new education policy to the leaders of DCE in the Namibian education sector. The policy documents that inform basic education in Namibia need to enhance access to quality education by promoting the ideals of DCE.

In my encounter on this journey, I explored in detail the subject of DCE, but I observed that the new education policy in Namibia does not provide guidelines of what a basic education that aims to engender democratic citizens should look like. Instead, it offers philosophical perspectives, ideas, and knowledge that could guide basic education in Namibia towards DCE. This encounter proposes a basic education curriculum that acknowledges the role that imagination plays in stimulating the learner to engage in critical thinking and participate in becoming (humane), knowing, and behaving while concurrently recognising other people's humanity (Waghid, 2010:54). This has the potential to achieve the values of DCE.

In this encounter, I agree that Namibian basic education programmes should be framed within the major aims of education. The broader aims of education in Namibia are to create a caring, healthy, democratic, productive, and environmentally sustainable information society that will contribute to individual development. Nevertheless, as has been noted, framing education within democratic citizenship has had no effect on resolving nagging questions around issues of inequalities of access to ICTs, poverty, historical injustices, and the uneven distribution of learning materials and learning facilities, especially as seen by the advent of the Covid-19 pandemic.

I have observed that unresolved historical injustices contradict the ideals of participatory democracy and, in turn, affect one or the other implementation of the Namibian education policy, as some communities still feel aggrieved by persistent historical injustices. The undercurrent of the discussions in my encounter demonstrated that DCE relates to facilitating a process where learners are made to participate actively in learning and teaching processes targeted at achieving social justice and eradicating marginalisation, imbalances, and exclusion of learners from accessing quality education in Namibia.

Conclusion

In this chapter, I presented my doctoral encounter with reference to DCE in the curriculum of the Ministry of Education, Arts, and Culture in Namibia. I also referred to the reconceptualisation of DCE in the Namibian basic education system. Furthermore, I presented entrenching DCE in the Namibian child. I would like to conclude by saying that the current education policy shows that the goals of DCE aim to engender a society of informed citizens who uphold the spirit of humanity and belongingness. There are still uneven distributions of educational resources, which are prerequisite conditions that need to be adhered to for the successful implementation of the education policy.

Key lessons learned

Davids (1984) and Biesta (2012) concur on the need to put the learners at the centre stage of the learning and teaching process. The policy documents that guide the Namibian schooling system seek to place the learner at the centre of the learning and teaching process; hence, I argue that there is an element of DCE in the new educational dispensation in Namibia. My concluding analysis is that the new education policy contains various traits of DCE notions, such as the promotion of indigenous knowledge systems, *ubuntu*, collective social responsibility and national cohesion, freedom, and social justice. I further pointed out that the new policy has several shortcomings in its desire to attain the goals of DCE due to existing challenges.

Notes

1 The **Harambee Prosperity Plan** (HPP) is a national development framework launched by the government of Namibia in 2016 (Author, date:page).
2 **Civics education** refers to the study of the rights and duties of citizenship, especially the duties of voting and participating in government action. – (Saxe, 2014)
3 **Namibianisation of education** refers to the process of tailoring education policies, curriculum, and practices to the specific needs, values, and context of Namibia as a nation (Takako, 2000:55–70).

References

Apple, M. W. (2002). *Educating the 'Right' Way: Markets, Standards, God, and Inequality.* New York: Routledge.
Audigier, F. (1999). Teaching about society, passing on values: Elementary law in civic education. *European Education*, 31(1), 38–63.
Benhabib, S. (2011). *Dignity in Adversity: Human Rights in Troubled Times.*, Cambridge: Polity Press.
Biesta, G. J. J. (2012). Giving teaching back to education: Responding to the disappearance of the teacher. *Phenomenology & Practice*, 6(2), 35–49.
Brown, Z. (2016). *Inclusive Education: Perspectives on Pedagogy, Policy and Practice.* London: Routledge.
Cannivez, L. (1990). *Durkheim et le Socialisme.* Paris: Presses Universitaires de France.
Davids, D. A. (1984). *Experiential Learning: Experience as the Source of Learning and Development.* Englewood Cliffs, NJ: Prentice-Hall.
Davids, N. (2018). Democratic citizenship education: An opportunity for the renegotiation of teacher identity in South African schools. *Education as Change*, 22(1), 1–17.
Davids, N. (2019). Schools as restorative spaces for democratic citizenship education. *Journal of Education*, 77, 79–93.
Government of Namibia. (2004). *Namibia Vision 2030. National Planning Commission.* Windhoek: Government Publishers.
Kerr, D. (1999). *Citizenship Education: An International Comparison.* London: Qualifications and Curriculum Authority.
Ministry of Education, Arts and Culture. (2016). *The National Curriculum for Basic Education.* Windhoek, Namibia: Ministry of Education, Arts and Culture.
Naashia, M. (2006). An exploratory study of the interplay between teachers' beliefs, instructional practices and professional development, Doctoral thesis, University of Auckland, New Zealand. http://researchspace.auckland.ac.nz/docs/rights.htm
Saxe, D. W. (2014). Civics education: Exploring rights and duties of citizenship. *Journal of Civic Education*, 12(3), 45–58.

Shanyanana, R. N. (2011). Education for democratic citizenship and cosmopolitanism: The case of the Republic of Namibia. Unpublished paper. Stellenbosch: Stellenbosch University.

Takako, C. (2000). Education in Namibia before independence with the prospect of "Namibianising" education on independence. *Aomori Perfectual University Health Sciences Bulletin Editorial Committee*, 1, 55–70.

Waghid, Y. (2005). Action as an educational virtue: Toward a different understanding of democratic citizenship education. *Educational Theory*, 55(3), 323–342.

Waghid, Y. (2010). *Education, Democracy and Citizenship Revisited: Pedagogical Encounters*: Stellenbosch: Sun Media Press.

Waghid, Y. (2018). On the educational potential of Ubuntu. In N. Assie-Lumumba & E. Amoako (Eds.) *Re-visioning Education in Africa: Ubuntu-Inspired Education for Humanity*. New York: Palgrave-MacMillan, 55–66.

Waghid, Y. & Davids, N. (Eds.). (2017). *African Democratic Citizenship Education Revisited*. Dordrecht: Springer.

Waghid, Y., & Davids, N. (2018). *Educational Leadership in Becoming: On the Potential of Leadership in Action*. London: Routledge,

Coda The ethical university
From service delivery to development of critical consciousness

Emiliano Bosio

Introduction

Over the past few decades, universities have undergone a significant transformation in their role as neo-liberalism has increasingly exerted its influence on their activities (e.g. teaching, learning, research, community, and access). As Mignolo (2007:450) points out, "under the spell of neo-liberalism and the magic of the media promoting it, modernity and modernisation, together with democracy, are being sold as a package trip to the promised land of happiness". Undeniably, in many cases, the four big Cs of commercialisation, commodification, competition, and classification have led universities to seek deeper engagement with the international market under the guise of *entrepreneurial* or *corporate* universities – institutions that serve existing, mostly economic, needs (Slaughter & Leslie, 1997). As I have advised elsewhere (see Bosio, 2021a; Bosio & Olssen, 2023; Bosio & Waghid, 2022a; Giroux & Bosio, 2021; McLaren & Bosio, 2022; Veugelers & Bosio, 2021), one of the main goals of the university is – or at least should be – however to encourage the development of learners' critical knowledge and values (e.g. human dignity, cultural diversity, democracy, justice, fairness, and equality) in the direction of an orientation that sustains the notion that *knowing without acting is insufficient*. Luckily, alternative forms of universities – such as the human rights university (Barnett & Guzmán-Valenzuela, 2012), the university of wisdom (Maxwell, 2012), the ethically engaged university (Bosio & Gregorutti, 2023), and the ecological university (Barnett, 2013) – have been theorised as capable of connecting and contributing to society in more sustainable ways.

As an extension of the above seminal works on human rights, wisdom, ethically engaged, and ecological universities, in this chapter, I propose the ethical university for the development of critical consciousness (the ethical university) informed and inspired by the idea of a global ethic with its roots in critical pedagogy. Concomitantly, I argue for a notion of ethical leadership that should be associated with the idea of an ethical university of critical praxis. This type of university is more inclusive, permeable, ethically reflective, integrative of diverse experiences, and socially responsible. The ethical university prioritises more than just providing learners with knowledge and transferable

DOI: 10.4324/9781003530091-13

employment skills for international job markets. Such university moves beyond *service delivery* because I conceptualise it here as a means of *conscientisation*, a notion that refers to achieving an in-depth and critical understanding of the world – allowing for the perception and exposure of social and political contradictions – and identity development through the transmission of knowledge, skills, and values across generations (Freire, 2018). The ethical university therefore serves a broader purpose beyond being a mere knowledge factory (Aronowitz, 2000). This purpose, which I and colleagues (see, for instance, Barnett, 2017, 2019) consider feasibly utopian, encompasses the potential conception of new links between universities, humanity, and our planet – because, as Berners-Lee (2021) suggests in his insightful book, there is no "Planet B". From this viewpoint, the purpose of the ethical university is to inspire thoughts around social change, an eco-critical perspective, critical awareness, de-colonialism, empowerment of humanity, democracy, value-pluralism, local and global citizenry, praxis, reflexive dialogue, and caring ethics (Bosio, 2023a; Bosio & Waghid, 2022b; Torres & Bosio, 2020a, 2020b). The ethical university promotes knowledge and values that potentially allow students to contribute to the common good – intended here as a fundamental concept of social and political morality (Bosio & Torres 2019). If discussed in this perspective, the ethical university may advance a *values-based pedagogy* or a *pedagogy of hope* (Freire, 1994), through which educators could engage in political and moral questions.

I therefore contextualise the debate surrounding the ethical university within critical consciousness values and knowledge, as ingrained in Paulo Freire's critical pedagogy and social justice (Freire, 1973, 1983, 2000). This approach focuses on developing an ethical university rooted in critical theories (Bohman, 2010; McLean, 2006; McLaren & Bosio, 2022) that considers the interactions of modernity versus colonialism and pluri/versality (Mignolo, 2000; Mignolo & Walsh, 2018). The ethical university has as its primary objectives, namely, to assist learners in achieving –

- critical self-analysis;
- deep reflection;
- wise action;
- respectful dialogue; and
- carefulness to contribute to building a new society based on sustainability and social justice.

To achieve such objectives, the ethical university requires educators to adopt pedagogical approaches capable of supporting students in developing a sense of solidarity with others, compassion for humanity, and fostering ethical and critical values, such as justice, fairness, equity, respect, and integrity. This is an approach aimed at nurturing the progression of critical consciousness via pedagogical approaches that allow students to analyse their own morals and values in a critical and ethical perspective.

Core principles of an ethical university for the development of critical consciousness

In line with the notions described above, the ethical university is entrenched in six principles: praxis, reflexive dialogue, de-colonialism, caring ethics, empowerment of humanity, and an eco-critical perspective (see Figure 12.1). These principles must be scrutinised in the context of educator–student relationships, where the process of construction of critical consciousness and its implementation can be established and flourish.

Figure 12.1 outlines the key principles of the ethical university, which facilitates self-reflection and action (*praxis*) for students. The ethical university advocates for individual and collective reflective approaches, operating in tandem to promote the growth of critical consciousness (*reflexive dialogue*). This necessitates prioritising diversity over generalisations to enable students to scrutinise and reassess any biases, opinions, and preconceptions that reflect the processes of colonialism (*de-colonialism*). Additionally, it instils values of caution, appreciation of individual worth, respect for human rights, and mindful compassion in students (*caring ethics*). The ethical university also enhances the common humanity in accordance with three crucial empowering aspects, namely interpersonal, personal, and socio-political (*empowerment of humanity*). Moreover, the ethical university encourages environmental

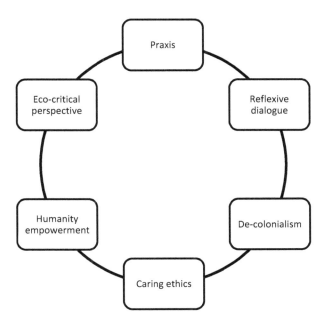

Figure 12.1 Core principles of the ethical university.

consciousness by teaching students about eco-ethical issues (e.g. the loss of biodiversity, destruction of ecosystems, depletion of natural resources, and global climate change) that arise from human beings considering themselves superior to nature (*eco-critical perspective*). In the next section, I discuss each of these dimensions of the ethical university.

Praxis: Critical reflection and action

The development of critical consciousness is a vital aspect of the ethical university, as it encourages a continuous process of praxis, which involves both critical reflection and action. Freire (1993) emphasises the important role critical reflection and action play in attempts to transform the world. An ethical university should therefore foster the development of critical consciousness, with a deep focus on raising student understanding of important societal issues, such as racism, poverty, unemployment, malnutrition, and unequal opportunity, via a praxis-based approach. In this context, an ideal teaching and learning environment requires educators and students to collaborate in order to understand their reality critically, and to discuss how to create a new 'well-being paradigm' based on sustainability and societal happiness. As defined in the World Happiness Report, Helliwell, Layard and Sachs (2013) see societal happiness encompassing personal satisfaction, a sense of purpose, interconnection, self-acceptance, and inner vitality beyond mere material possessions.[1] Such an approach requires an ethical university to:

- respect a wide range of cultural and linguistic traditions;
- embrace change in various contexts, including educational, social, historical, and economic; and
- adopt an effective strategy for community involvement.

To achieve a comprehensive vision of an ethical university, the focus must remain on *critical reflection* and *action*.

Ethical educators employ critical reflection to teach students about injustice and inequality and the way these discriminations have affected people worldwide. Ethical educators help learners to engage in critical reflection, which involves dialogic communication, respectful collaboration, and the creative construction of an ethical self (see Infinito, 2003) to understand better why their communities might have limited resources or potential. To achieve a vision of an ethical university, it is imperative to maintain a focus on critical reflection, which requires a strong sense of purpose. Educators must guide students in understanding inequality and oppression globally, as well as the way it affects individuals. To do this, educators must assess injustices and discriminations that affect the world. By engaging students in critical reflection, educators can help them comprehend why their communities might have limited resources. Critical reflection can be utilised to draw students' attention to social justice, the interconnection between unjust living conditions, and the failure to examine societal issues, which perpetuate the status quo, critically (Giroux & Bosio, 2021). When educators engage students in a process of in-depth critical reflection, the student is less likely to blame the victim for the fact that they are affected by circumstances upheld by institutional oppression,[2] while simultaneously acknowledging how these factors have manifested in the past and continue to play out in the present (Kelly & Varghese, 2018).

Without action, the benefits of critical reflection however remain purely intellectual. The ethical university should therefore encourage:

- sustainable actions, such as political participation, e.g.
  - voting;
  - contacting public officials;
  - petitioning; and
  - working on campaigns; and
- other forms of community activism to address societal inequities, e.g.
  - working for better schools;
  - getting more stop signs or crossing guards in a neighbourhood; and
  - cleaning up a local park

The eventual purpose of the above should be to assist students to shape more sustainable and just societies. According to Freire (2000:73), critical consciousness "results from the intervention in the world as transformers of that world". An ethical university should encourage civic participation, along with other actions that may be social, cultural, or political in nature. Such university should assist students in connecting with relevant social movements (e.g. #MeToo, Green, the Malala Fund for Girls' Right to Education, the Belt Movement, Schools Strike for Climate, and Amnesty International) and sustainable nongovernmental organisations (NGOs) (e.g. Greenpeace, World Wildlife Fund [WWF], and Doctors Without Borders [Médecins Sans Frontières]). In this way, students can learn how to read the word and more importantly the world and their place within it (Bosio & Gregorutti, 2023). Potentially, the ethical university helps students improve their capacities to integrate sustainability agendas, enabling them to become critical global citizens capable of contributing to both local and global issues. They therefore exhibit civic accountability and maintain strong social connections that also benefit from their capacity for helping others (Bosio, 2021b). An ethical university, including its leaders – deans, academic directors or supervisors, and provosts – must develop critical consciousness and continue prioritising student learning about indigenous communities and individual awareness. The university must also address any local oppression fuelled by socio-political causes in a critical way. This should be based on the Freirean notion that "reading the world precedes reading the word, and the subsequent reading of the word cannot dispense with continually reading the world. Language and reality are dynamically intertwined" (Freire, 1983:5). As proposed by Freire (2000:73), critical consciousness "results from the intervention in the world as transformers of that world". An ethical university promotes civic engagement and various social, cultural, or political actions that contribute to students' understanding of our super-complex societies. To achieve this, the ethical university must adopt a Freirean approach (see Freire, 1973, 1994, 2000) constructed on:

- the ethics of virtue or intelligent virtue (Annas, 2011);
- relationship dynamics directed towards benefitting the common good, a pedagogy rooted in dialogic praxis (Bosio, 2023b; Bosio & Olssen, 2023); and
- profound appreciation towards concepts of sustainability (e.g. environmental protection, social equality, and economic viability).

Reflexive dialogue

If integrating critical reflection and action (praxis) in the ethical university is one of the core principles for students' development of critical consciousness, then reflexive dialogue is the path through which that learning journey takes place on a more tangible level. Reflexive dialogue involves a combination of self-reflection, reflective action, and collective reflective action, which combine to ensure that critical consciousness develops in a robust fashion (Freire, 1973). Reflexive dialogue is a collaborative, two-way transformative introspection technique educators use to encourage students to feel comfortable discussing their beliefs and values flexibly and interactively before engaging in subject discussions with other students. This type of instruction is particularly important in challenging and debating the status quo and societal views on issues related to gender, sexuality, and race, emphasising how the exercise of power affects these sensitive topics. Freire (2000) suggests that a dialogical approach is necessary to identify generative themes and increase people's awareness of these topics. The suppression of free expression is a major impediment to achieving social change, particularly with respect to systemic racism and other problems related to structural violence and people's awareness of these topics (Freire & Macedo, 1995). Free speech should therefore be a top priority in the development of critical consciousness at an ethical university, along with emphasis on how language misuse by those in positions of leadership can perpetuate false stereotypes and incite fear of particular minorities or ideologies. To foster critical consciousness, language should be used in a constructive manner – rather than in a destructive and negative manner – enabling students to reconsider their perceptions of themselves and others in reflexive dialogue that facilitates the growth of critical consciousness, respect, and appreciation for diversity. The ethical university thus promotes a type of reflexive dialogue aimed at encouraging democracy, diversity, access to resources, equity, participation, human rights, and de-colonialism. The latter is discussed next.

De-colonialism

Euro-centric or Western-centric hegemony continues to influence modern universities both directly and indirectly (Dussel, 1993; Escobar, 2008). According to implicit and explicit mechanisms, so-called 'Northern standards' affect higher education (HE) both locally and globally. I consequently suggest that the challenge is to approach the ethical university to develop critical consciousness from a *de-colonialised view*. This necessitates that educators understand and re-evaluate pedagogical goals that have been established throughout colonial history and have persisted in how higher education institutions (HEIs) choose to teach their students. More broadly, decolonising the university would involve decolonising –

- research and teaching contents;
- curricula and syllabi;
- teaching and learning methods;
- access to the university (for learners);
- access to a university career (for academics); and
- the institutional structure and university governance as well as relationships between the university, the local community, and society at large.

Effective de-colonising action must involve all stakeholders. Earnest change can however not manifest without students developing a critical consciousness of how privilege continues to dominate society and universities. Our societies are unbalanced as long as there is a clear power imbalance between the Global North and the Global South.

I therefore propose that an ethical university investigate injustice and inequality in addition to poverty and development. Learning objectives are inherently imperfect and susceptible to influences from university leadership, educators, students, and societal and environmental variables. This is inevitable given the fluidity, diversity, and individuality of student and educator perspectives. To fulfil this mandate, an ethical university must foster critical literacy among educators. These educators can then offer these advantages to students, enabling them to evaluate their own values, biases, and orientations, as well as how these relate to the world on a global and local scale. By doing this, educators can put students' conceptions of reality to the test, inspire them to reconsider their roles in their communities and society, and think about how colonial epistemological and ontological ideas might be revisited. For instance, an ethical university needs to encourage educators and students to examine the subtle and less-subtle manifestations of colonisation (e.g. white supremacy, anti-blackness, colourism, ethnicisation, indigenous erasure, elite social distinctions involving class, caste, educational credentialing, de-languaging, and even intellectual pedigree).

As a result, adopting a decolonial perspective on an ethical university necessitates educators investigating:

- how knowledge and values are created and transmitted;
- how hyper-self-reflexivity is developed (Kapoor, 2004; Spivak, 1988);
- how students can approach complex issues through a revolutionary pedagogical focus on dissensus (McLaren & Bosio, 2022); and
- how combining efforts could mean extending ethical engagement, discourse beyond absolute relativism, and ethnocentrism (De Sousa Santos, 2008).

Educators who employ this pedagogical approach could become agents of change who can facilitate the exchange of diverse points of view while assisting students to identify and challenge prejudice and stereotypes.

Empowering humanity

To maintain its core focus on fostering students' development of critical consciousness, the ethical university must promote the empowerment of humanity. To do so, the ethical university and its leadership must provide opportunities for students to genuinely pursue personal development. The concept of empowering humanity is often linked with collective emancipation, as both aim to transform and – potentially – eradicate inequality. While the latter prioritises power dynamics between groups, empowering humanity considers all aspects of human behaviour, not just political ones. Veugelers and Bosio (2021) propose a three-dimensional process for empowering humanity.

The first dimension, the *personal component*, entails an individual striving to lead a virtuous life, which includes having some degree of control over his or her daily activities (Veugelers & Bosio, 2021). The second dimension, the *interpersonal component*, deals with the need to coexist peacefully with others while recognising the mutual obligation to provide assistance when needed and to be open to receiving help. The third dimension, the *socio-political component*, relies on promoting a vision for a type of society that is compassionate and based on ideals of justice, equality, and diversity.

Undoubtedly, these are complex processes. When students are encouraged to examine and re-evaluate their own political and social significance, the relationship between autonomy and social consciousness is challenged. An ethical university that aims to develop critical consciousness should therefore acknowledge and implement both aspects.

Caring ethics

In a similar vein, I argue that an ethical university must direct students towards a clear understanding of how both exclusion and inclusion occur. This requires exploring the complexities of local and global issues (e.g., catalyse public involvement among diverse communities, enable constructive and respectful dialogue among different group of people, develop a sense of inclusion and belonging, and empower marginalised and underrepresented voices) (Bosio & Waghid, 2023a, 2023b). Ideally, this ethical approach aimed at better understanding of how both exclusion and inclusion arise will enable learners to perceive critically the disparities that exist in the distribution of power and wealth throughout the Global North and the Global South. As I suggested in one of my keynotes (Bosio, 2021c) "you cannot solve a problem if you cannot talk about it".[3] Merging these aims into an ethical university therefore means initiating discussions about how to incorporate progressive values (e.g. social responsibility, justice, human rights, global sustainability, and collective involvement) into its deliberative and reflexive pedagogies while encouraging students to take an active role in promoting societal peace, equality, and justice.[4]

An effective ethical university draws attention to the contradictions of globalisation, motivates a reconsideration of the distribution of power between the Global North and the Global South, and raises awareness in terms of the challenges to eradicating global injustices. To achieve future global reforms, particularly in relation to eradicating colonial outlooks that still exist within financial sectors, forging strong links and networks between marginalised communities is imperative. These should be motivated by a strong ethical position on social injustice. From this angle, the ethical university seeks to foster students' critical consciousness based on progressive principles, while also recognising, exploring, and providing solutions to issues pertaining to women's rights. Human rights, especially those pertaining to women, and the core tenets of feminism, as outlined in the publications of bell hooks, are crucial to an ethical university. Hooks' themes of oppression, patriarchy, stereotypes, and sexual objectification continue to shape feminist theory. Examples of hooks's works are *Talking back: Thinking feminist, thinking black* (2015), and *Feminist theory from margin to center* (1984).

Pursuing these goals would place the ethical university in a good position within a social justice model. The ethical university with its ethical leaders must therefore move beyond traditional cognitive education and technocratic approaches that rely solely on numbers to foster students' growth in critical consciousness. According to Jacques Delors (2021) and the United Nations Educational, Scientific and Cultural Organization (UNESCO) commission report, *Learning: The treasure within* (1996), the objective of an ethical university should be to integrate engaging content with aspects of artistic expression, spirituality, aesthetics, and even eco-critical viewpoints into the curriculum. These factors will all help to promote social cohesion.

Eco-critical perspective

An ethical university allows students to engage with issues arising from the belief humanity has in its supremacy on earth. Educators and leadership play a critical role in challenging this presumption by adopting eco-critical educational paradigms to foster students' development of critical consciousness. This approach entails tearing down and rebuilding the industrial values of Western society (e.g. individuality, selfishness, and utility) to deepen students' understanding of the interconnectedness between people and ecosystems. The ethical university encourages students to reflect on how specific actions have shaped human thought, allowed injustices to develop, and discouraged speaking out against issues that cause misery and environmental harm. The ethical university, as I conceptualise it, also emphasises the advantages of diversity and structural eco-social networks in linguistic, cultural, and educational contexts.

To promote eco-centrism, the ethical university moves the focus away from anthropocentric and egocentric views and adopts an eco-ethical consciousness aimed at examining significant social and environmental repercussions caused by human activity (Martusewicz et al., 2015). Eco-centrism, as it should be upheld in the ethical university, entails helping students understand the concept of more-than-human to appreciate the ecological connectivity that exists beyond human-to-human relationships (Abram, 1999). The ethical university should therefore embrace an eco-critical viewpoint to teach human–environment interactions that consider both local and global issues. This approach can also promote social and ecological progress. The work of Lupinacci and Happel-Parkins (2015, 2016a, 2016b) and others, for example Weintraub et al. (2006:55), introduce the term "eco-tistical" in the literature to counterbalance the dearth of an English-language term portraying "humans relating to the nonhuman environment in a harmonious, respectful, and pragmatic manner".

Bosio's (2020) expanding research and literature on eco-critical and eco-ethical philosophies provide further insight into the significance of this discussion. Concrete examples provided by Bosio of eco-critical viewpoints applied ethically in real-world situations could guide this approach, particularly in relation to notions of local and global citizenship in the teaching of core human–environment interactions centred on the concept *el buen vivir*, a notion incorporated into the Ecuadorian Constitution in 2008 and into the Bolivian Constitution in 2009. This concept portrays, as Bosio and Torres (2019) suggest, a way of acting in a society that is community-centric, ecologically balanced, and culturally sensitive, in the ongoing construction of a just and peaceful world.

Ethical university for the development of critical consciousness

Practical implementation

The incorporation of the six key dimensions of praxis (i.e. reflexive dialogue, de-colonialism, caring ethics, empowerment of humanity, and an eco-critical perspective) into the pedagogical strategies of the ethical university will facilitate the development of critical consciousness in learners based on the willingness and reflexive action enacted by its HE leaders. Circular learning, which allows for fluidity in the learning process by not restricting learners to fixed learning pathways, is the most effective pedagogical technique for this material (Bosio & Waghid, 2022c).

From this perspective, cultivating critical consciousness requires educators to assist students in valuing others and placing human rights at the centre of all pathways, which can be accomplished by teaching *caring ethics*. Educators could also encourage students to evaluate their own perspectives, prejudices, and backgrounds in light of regional and global issues, including cyberbullying, hunger, homelessness, and discrimination, and to do so with careful consideration of the environment. Adopting an *eco-critical perspective* is particularly important in recognising an anthropocentric world view, culturally constituted and maintained, and rejecting any notion of human superiority, while promoting ethical and sustainable philosophies that challenge power disparities, oppression, and unfairness. Moreover, students in an ethical university should be made aware of the importance of using the knowledge and insights they gain to contribute to a just and environmentally sustainable society. To achieve this, the ethical university and its educators could assist students in broadening their perspectives in three critical areas: socio-political, interpersonal, and personal. Students should also be encouraged to challenge the notion that neo-liberalism is the only path to successful ethical breakthroughs, and that Western capitalism is the sole source of means for *empowering humanity*.

Lastly, an ethical university should encourage praxis by having students and educators discuss collaboratively how colonial and neo-colonial ideas have led to existing power disparities and poverty – a matter of cultivating human relations based on an exercise of ethical leadership inspired by a notion of critical praxis. To facilitate critical consciousness, reflective questions and group processes should be utilised to examine power dynamics and societal structures based on class, colour, ethnicity, sexual orientation, or disability. *Reflective dialogue* and group processes among leaders, educators, and students should be founded on respect, critique, and humility, and students should be encouraged to consider the causes of persistent oppressive features in daily life. To foster the growth of critical consciousness, an ethical university should prioritise accountability, mutual respect, wisdom, courage, and sensitivity. Debates should be equitable, liberal-minded, and not overly rigid or hierarchical. Educators and leaders should avoid dictating fixed views, morals, and ideals and, instead, provide gentle guidance to ensure positive and constructive conversation while maintaining equality within group dynamics. To achieve this, it is imperative to rethink the role of HE leadership towards ethical HE leadership, as elucidated in the following section.

Implications for rethinking higher education leadership: Towards an ethical approach

In times marked by turbulence and authoritarianism, it is of utmost importance for ethical educational leaders from both the Global South and the Global North to engage in collaborative efforts. This collaboration should aim to challenge the neoliberal approaches (e.g. entrepreneurial or corporate-oriented) that often shape conceptions of HE leadership (Giroux & Bosio,

2021). Instead, the focus should shift towards ethical HE leadership that places value on human rights and ecological considerations, fostering social justice and sustainability. This transition towards an ethical revolution in HE leadership encompasses four principal implications:

- *Emphasising social justice.* Ethical HE leadership acknowledges the importance of addressing systemic inequities and advancing social justice within educational institutions. This entails creating inclusive environments, promoting diversity, and actively challenging discriminatory practices and policies. It also involves embracing inclusive, participatory, and empowering forms of ethical HE leadership that prioritise the well-being and agency of all stakeholders.
- *Integrating sustainability.* Ethical HE leadership recognises the urgent need to incorporate sustainability principles into all aspects of higher education. This includes integrating environmental stewardship, ecological awareness, and sustainable practices into teaching, research, campus operations, and community engagement.
- *Promoting diversity through local and global collaboration.* Ethical HE leadership necessitates promoting diversity while transcending geographical boundaries and fostering collaboration between leaders from different regions in the Global South and Global North. By implementing the expertise and perspectives of diverse cultural and educational contexts, ethical educational leaders develop comprehensive and contextually relevant approaches to addressing global challenges.
- *Prioritising ethical decision-making.* Ethical HE leadership prioritises ethical decision-making processes that consider the social, environmental, and human rights implications of their actions. To achieve this, ethical HE leadership engages in critical reflection, values diverse perspectives, and actively seeks input from all stakeholders to make informed and ethically sound decisions.

By embracing these implications, ethical HE leadership can steer the transformation of HEIs towards just, sustainable, and inclusive models that benefit individuals and societies.

The conceptualisation of ethical HE leadership necessitates active engagement, outspoken advocacy, and decisive action to dismantle systemic forms of domination affecting human beings, ourselves, and the broader ecological community (McLaren & Bosio, 2022). From this perspective, ethical HE leadership becomes a resounding call to action for HE leaders from diverse backgrounds to embrace teaching and leadership roles that support and safeguard our shared planet based on, although not limited to, praxis, reflective dialogue, de-colonialism, caring ethics, empowerment of humanity, and eco-critical perspectives. In closing, as Nixon (2008) aptly articulates, any substantive discussion on the future of the university must also encompass a profound exploration of how we can coexist harmoniously in a world marked by diversity. This debate cannot be reduced merely to technical or economic considerations. It demands a comprehensive, inclusive, and ethical approach that values and nurtures difference in all its forms.

Conclusion

This chapter presented an ethical university paradigm, comprising six essential components, namely praxis, reflective dialogue, de-colonialism, caring ethics, empowerment of humanity, and an eco-critical perspective, to foster students' critical consciousness. The proposed paradigm emphasises the importance of an ongoing process of reflection and action, facilitated by ethical leadership and educators through self-reflection, reflective action, and group reflective action, to guide students' development of critical consciousness. The paradigm also prioritises diversity and de-colonialism over universal subjectivities to re-evaluate students' prejudices, viewpoints, and histories, particularly in the context of local and global institutions. In addition, the paradigm places respect for human rights and consideration for individual well-being at the core of the curriculum and pedagogy, emphasising carefulness. Interpersonal, personal, and socio-political factors are also crucial aspects of the paradigm for fostering respect for humanity. Lastly, the paradigm highlights the significance of environmental concern and encourages students to recognise the peril of anthropocentrism or human-centred thinking.

One of the primary objectives of an ethical university is for leaders and educators to encourage students to re-examine their own viewpoints thoroughly and to motivate them to play an active role in achieving a better world based on social justice and sustainability. Consequently, the mandate of an ethical university should be to reimagine students' perceived obligations towards the outside world, emphasising the idea that knowing without action is insufficient. This discussion of an ethical university however raises issues that go beyond the realm of morals, such as the function of universities and its leadership, the types of people they should aim to produce in modern society, the relevance of globalisation, particularly in addressing the issue of neo-liberal globalisation, and the way universities should define 'ethical values and knowledge'.

Any serious debate about the future of the 'ethical university' and its leadership must also include in-depth conversation about how we may learn to live together in a world of difference and the dissemination of sustainable knowledge and values in ways that advance attuned responsiveness to local and global issues in our super-complex societies.

Chapter summary: Key lessons for leadership in higher education

- It is crucial to redefine the concept of leadership in higher education by moving away from traditional paradigms that are centred on profit-driven and hierarchical models towards the ethical university. Leaders should therefore adopt inclusive, participatory, and empowering forms of leadership that prioritise the well-being and agency of all stakeholders involved in the educational process.

A key focus of leadership in HE should be on social justice. It is essential to recognise and address the systemic inequities that exist within educational institutions and to work actively towards advancing social justice and ethical principles (e.g. praxis, reflective dialogue, de-colonialism, caring ethics, empowerment of the disenfranchised).

Notes

1 The World Happiness Report is fully available from the Columbia Climate School, The Earth Institute. www.earth.columbia.edu/articles/view/2960
2 **Institutional oppression** refers to a complex system of accepted laws, customs, and practices that systematically reflect and produce inequities based on one's membership in targeted social identity groups.
3 Bosio, E. (2021, August 27). *Knowing without acting is insufficient: A call for a sustainable values-based curriculum* [Keynote Speech]. Association for Teacher Education Europe (ATEE), Bruxelles, Belgium. https://atee.education/rd-communities/health-environment-and-sustainability/
4 See, for instance, Bosio (2023), Bosio and Schattle (2021), Bosio (2021), Shaffer, Longo, Manosevitch, and Thomas (2017).

References

Abram, D. 1999. A more than human world. In A. Weston (ed.). *An invitation to environmental philosophy*. New York: Oxford University Press, 17–42.

Annas, J. 2011. *Intelligent virtue*. Oxford: Oxford University Press.

Aronowitz, S. 2000. *The knowledge factory: Dismantling the corporate university and creating true higher learning*. Boston, MA: Beacon Press.

Barnett, R. 2013. Imagining the ecological university. In R. Barnett (ed.). *Imagining the university*. Abingdon: Routledge, 147–157.

Barnett, R. 2017. *The ecological university: A feasible utopia*. London: Routledge. https://doi.org/10.4324/9781315194899

Barnett, R. 2019. The thoughtful university: A feasible utopia. *Beijing International Review of Education*, 1(1):54–72. https://doi.org/10.1163/25902547-00101007

Barnett, R. & Guzmán-Valenzuela, C. 2012. The human rights university: A feasible utopia. In C. Brunner & J. Scherling (eds.). *Bildung, Menschenrechte, Universität. Menschenrechts-Bildung and Hochschulen im Wandel als gesellschaftliche Herausforderung*. Klagenfurt: Drava Verlag, 269–288.

Berners-Lee, T. 2021. A Magna Carta for the web: Fixing the internet's original sin. *Scientific American*, 324(6): 46–51.

Bohman, J. 2010. Critical theory. In E.N. Zalta (ed.). *The Stanford encyclopedia of philosophy*. Retrieved from https://plato.stanford.edu/entries/critical-theory/#pagetopright [Accessed 21 April 2023].

Bosio, E. 2020. Towards an ethical global citizenship education curriculum framework in the modern university. In D. Bourn (ed.). *The Bloomsbury handbook for global education and learning*. London: Bloomsbury, 187–206. https://doi.org/10.5040/9781350108769.0025

Bosio, E. (Ed.). 2021a. *Conversations on global citizenship education: Perspectives on research, teaching, and learning in higher education*. New York: Routledge. https://doi.org/10.4324/9780429346897

Bosio, E. 2021b. Global human resources or critical global citizens? An inquiry into the perspectives of Japanese university educators on global citizenship education. *PROSPECTS Comparative Journal of Curriculum, Learning, and Assessment*. https://doi.org/10.1007/s11125-021-09566-6

Bosio, E. 2021c. *Knowing without acting is insufficient: A call for a sustainable values-based curriculum*. Keynote speech. Association for Teacher Education Europe, Bruxelles, 27 August. Retrieved from https://atee.education/rd-communities/health-environment-and-sustainability/ [Accessed 18 January 2024].

Bosio, E. 2023a. Global citizenship education as a reflexive dialogic pedagogy. *Citizenship Teaching and Learning*, 18(2):177–194. https://doi.org/10.1386/ctl_00119_1

Bosio, E. 2023b. *Decolonizing Education: From Theory to Practice*. Cham, Switzerland: Springer.

Bosio, E. & Gregorutti, G. (Eds.). 2023. *The emergence of the ethically engaged university*. International and Development Education Series. New York: Springer. https://link.springer.com/book/9783031403118

Bosio, E. & Olssen, M. 2023. Critical global citizenship: Foucault as a complexity thinker, social justice and the challenges of higher education in the era of neoliberal globalization – a conversation with Mark Olssen. *Citizenship Teaching & Learning*, 18(2):245–261. https://doi.org/10.1386/ctl_00123_1

Bosio, E. & Schattle, H. 2021. Ethical global citizenship education: From neoliberalism to a values-based pedagogy. *PROSPECTS Comparative Journal of Curriculum, Learning, and Assessment*. https://doi.org/10.1007/s11125-021-09571-9

Bosio, E. & Torres, C.A. 2019. Global citizenship education: An educational theory of the common good? A conversation with Carlos Alberto Torres. *Policy Futures in Education*, 17(6):745–760. https://doi.org/10.1177/1478210319825517

Bosio, E. & Waghid, Y. 2022a. Democratic pluralistic global citizenship education: Embracing educators' voices from the Global South. In E. Bosio & Y. Waghid (eds.). *Global citizenship education in the Global South*. Leiden: Brill, 284–294. https://doi.org/10.1163/9789004521742_015

Bosio, E. & Waghid, Y. 2022b. Global citizenship education for critical consciousness development: The four pillars of de-colonialism, caring ethics, eco-critical views, and humanity empowerment. In E. Bosio & Y. Waghid (eds.). *Global citizenship education in the Global South*. Leiden: Brill, 11–23. https://doi.org/10.1163/9789004521742_002

Bosio, E. & Waghid Y. (Eds.). 2022c. *Global citizenship education in the Global South: Educators' perceptions and practices*. Leiden: Brill. https://brill.com/view/title/63195

Bosio, E. & Waghid, Y. 2023a. Cultivating students' critical consciousness through global citizenship education: Six pedagogical priorities. *PROSPECTS Comparative*

Journal of Curriculum, Learning, and Assessment. https://link.springer.com/article/10.1007/s11125-023-09652-x

Bosio, E. & Waghid, Y. 2023b. Global citizenship education as a living ethical philosophy for social justice. *Citizenship Teaching & Learning*, 18(2):151–158. https://doi.org/10.1386/ctl_00117_2

De Sousa Santos, B. 2008. *Another knowledge is possible: Beyond Northern epistemologies.* London: Verso.

Delors, J. 2021. *UNESCO report: Learning to become.* Paris: United Nations Educational, Scientific and Cultural Organization (UNESCO).

Dussel, E. 1993. Eurocentrism and modernity (Introduction to the Frankfurt Lectures). *Boundary* 2, 20(3):65–76.

Escobar, A. 2008. *Territories of difference: Place, movements, life, redes.* Durham, NC: Duke University Press.

Freire, P. 1973. *Education for critical consciousness.* New York: Seabury.

Freire, P. 1983. The importance of the act of reading. *Journal of Education*, 165(1):5–11. https://doi.org/10.1177/002205748316500103

Freire, P. 1993. *Pedagogy of the oppressed.* New York: Continuum.

Freire, P. 1994. *Pedagogy of hope: Reliving pedagogy of the oppressed.* R.R. Barr (trans.). New York, NY: Continuum.

Freire, P. 2000. *Pedagogy of the oppressed* (30th anniversary edition). New York: Continuum.

Freire, P. 2018. *Pedagogy of the oppressed.* New York: Bloomsbury.

Freire, P. & Macedo, D. 1995. A dialogue: Culture, language, and race. *Harvard Educational Review*, 65(3):377–402.

Giroux, H.A. & Bosio, E. 2021. Critical pedagogy and global citizenship education. In E. Bosio (ed.). *Conversations on global citizenship education: Perspectives on research, teaching, and learning in higher education.* New York: Routledge, 1–10. https://doi.org/10.4324/9780429346897-1

Helliwell, J.F., Layard, R. & Sach, J. 2013. *World happiness report.* New York: Earth Institute, Columbia University.

hooks, b. 1984. *Feminist theory from margin to center.* Boston, MA: South End Press.

Infinito, J. 2003. Ethical self-formation: A look at the later Foucault. *Educational Theory*, 53(2):155–171.

Kapoor, I. 2004. Hyper-self-reflexive development? Spivak on representing the Third World 'other'. *Third World Quarterly*, 25:627–647. https://doi.org/10.1080/01436590410001678898

Kelly, D.C. & Varghese, R. 2018. Four contexts of institutional oppression: Examining the experiences of blacks in education, criminal justice and child welfare. *Journal of Human Behavior in the Social Environment*, 28(7):874–888. https://doi.org/10.1080/10911359.2018.1466751

Lupinacci, J. & Happel-Parkins, A. 2015. Recognize, resist, and reconstitute: An ecocritical framework in teacher education. *The SoJo Journal: Educational Foundations and Social Justice Education*, 1(1):45–61.

Lupinacci, J. & Happel-Parkins, A. 2016a. Ecocritical foundations: Toward social justice and sustainability. In J. Diem (ed.). *The social and cultural foundations of education: A reader.* San Diego, CA: Cognella, 34–56.

Lupinacci, J. & Happel-Parkins, A. 2016b. (Un)learning anthropocentrism: An ecojustice education framework for teaching to resist human-supremacy in schools. In S. Rice & A. Rud (eds.). *The educational significance of human and non-human animal interactions: Blurring the species line.* New York: Palgrave, 13–30.
Martusewicz, R., Edmundson, J. & Lupinacci, J. 2015. *Ecojustice education: Toward diverse, democratic, and sustainable communities* (Second edition). New York: Routledge.
Maxwell, N. 2012. Creating a better world: Towards the university of wisdom. In R. Barnett (ed.), *The future university*. London: Routledge, 135–150.
McLaren, P. & Bosio, E. 2022. Revolutionary critical pedagogy and critical global citizenship education: A conversation with Peter McLaren. *Citizenship Teaching and Learning*, 17(2):165–181. https://doi.org/10.1386/ctl_00089_1
McLean, M. 2006. *Pedagogy and the university: Critical theory and practice.* London: Bloomsbury.
Mignolo, W. 2000. *Local histories/global designs: Coloniality, subaltern knowledges, and border thinking.* Princeton, NJ: Princeton University Press.
Mignolo, W. D. (2007). Delinking: The rhetoric of modernity, the logic of coloniality and the grammar of de-coloniality. *Cultural Studies*, 21(2–3), 449–514.
Mignolo, W.D. & Walsh, C.E. 2018. *On decoloniality: Concepts, analytics, praxis.* Durham: Duke University Press.
Nixon, J. 2008. *Towards the virtuous university: The moral bases of academic practice.* London: Routledge.
Noddings, N. (Ed.). 2004. *Educating citizens for global awareness.* New York: Teachers College Press.
Pashby, K. & Andreotti, V. 2016. Ethical internationalisation in higher education: Interfaces with international development and sustainability. *Environmental Education Research*, 22(6):771–787.
Sachs, J.D. 2015. *The age of sustainable development.* New York: Columbia University Press.
Sachs, J.D. 2016. Happiness and sustainable development: Concepts and evidence. In J. Helliwell, R. Layard & J. Sachs (eds.). *World happiness report 2016, update.* Volume I. New York: Sustainable Development Solutions Network, 56–65.
Shaffer, T.J., Longo, N.V., Manosevitch, I. & Thomas, M.S. 2017. *Deliberative pedagogy: Teaching and learning for democratic engagement.* Lansing, MI: MSU Press.
Slaughter, S. & Leslie, L.L. 1997. *Academic capitalism: Politics, policies, and the entrepreneurial university.* Baltimore, MD: John Hopkins University Press.
Spivak, G. 1988. Can the subaltern speak? In C. Nelson & L. Grossberg (eds.). *Marxism and the interpretation of culture.* Chicago, IL: University of Illinois Press, 271–316. https://doi.org/10.1007/978-1-349-19059-1
Torres, C.A. & Bosio, E. 2020a. Critical reflections on the notion of global citizenship education: A dialogue with Carlos Alberto Torres in relation to higher education in the United States. *Encyclopaideia Journal of Phenomenology and Education*, 24(56):107–117. https://doi.org/10.6092/issn.1825-8670/10742
Torres, C.A. & Bosio, E. 2020b. Global citizenship education at the crossroads: Globalization, global commons, common good, and critical consciousness. *Comparative Journal of Curriculum, Learning, and Assessment*, 48:99–113. https://doi.org/10.1007/s11125-019-09458-w

Veugelers, W. & Bosio, E. 2021. Linking moral and social-political perspectives in global citizenship education: A conversation with Wiel Veugelers. *PROSPECTS Comparative Journal of Curriculum, Learning, and Assessment.* https://doi.org/10.1007/s11125-021-09576-4

Weintraub, P., Clemens, B., & Lewis, M. 2006. *The business environment and concepts of social responsibility.* Mason, OH: South-Western College Publishing.

Additional readings/resources/websites

Giroux, H.A. 2010. Rethinking education as the practice of freedom: Paulo Freire and the promise of critical pedagogy. *Policy Futures in Education*, 8(6):715–721.

Macedo, D. 1994. *Literacies of power.* Boulder, CO: Westview Press.

Index

abstract 18, 19, 21, 22, 74, 99, 110
academic writing 5, 17, 18, 26, 29, 33, 35, 36, 97, 139, 140
Africa 1, 2, 6, 7, 9, 11, 13, 29, 45–7, 54–6, 58, 66, 67, 79–85, 87, 89–91, 97–8, 102, 108, 117, 121–7, 134–6, 145, 150
African Philosophy 1–5, 9–10, 38, 39, 43, 45, 48, 149–50, 157, 159
analysis 2, 7–9, 27, 31, 36, 65–77, 80, 83, 84, 135, 148–61, 164
artificial intelligence (AI) 24–37
assessment 13, 33, 44, 45, 69, 73–6, 82, 87, 125, 135, 140, 145
authenticity 10, 36, 133

bias 7, 29, 36, 69, 70, 96, 165, 169
blended learning 30

citizenship education 1, 3–9, 24, 35–7, 51–9, 65–77, 81, 88–90, 95–102, 116, 138–45, 148–61
collaboration 7, 8, 17–19, 27, 140, 151, 166, 173–4
community engagement 5, 46–7, 123, 174
constructivism 26, 96–8, 168, 170, 173
critical analysis 36, 164
critical consciousness 9, 142, 163–76
critical pedagogy 9, 10, 151, 163, 164
curriculum 5, 7–8, 28, 48, 54, 67, 68, 71, 72, 76, 84, 85, 87, 98, 111, 121, 127, 135, 140, 145, 149–52, 154–61, 171, 175
curriculum design 152

data privacy 36
decolonisation 45–6, 127, 148–50, 153, 156–8, 169

democratic citizenship 1, 3–9, 12, 24, 35–6, 38–9, 43, 45, 48, 51–9, 65–77, 81, 88–90, 95–102, 104–18, 148–53, 156, 160
digital technology 25
doctoral education 1, 5, 8, 12, 46–7, 65, 104
doctoral journey 5–8, 12, 13, 18, 65, 79–91, 101, 105, 136, 148
doctoral supervision 4, 7, 11, 13, 14, 19–23, 88–90, 104–18

educational policy 54
educational practice 68, 86, 90, 98, 141, 151, 152
educational technology 25, 35
emancipatory forces 38–48
employability 5, 51–9
engagement 5, 6, 8, 11, 12, 20, 24, 25, 27, 35–6, 45–7, 59, 71, 85, 87, 91, 96, 98–101, 111, 113, 123, 131, 134, 142–3, 150, 154, 158, 163, 168, 170, 174
English as a Foreign Language (EFL) 140
epistemology 2, 7, 45–7, 104, 107–12, 114, 117, 158, 169
ethical considerations 30, 36–7
ethics 19–23, 27, 45, 71, 164, 165, 168, 170–6
evaluation 9, 45, 68, 69, 72, 73, 157
experiential learning 10–11, 90, 123

faculty development 12, 18, 47
feminist theory 171

global citizenship 8, 105, 109, 110, 112–17, 138–45, 172
global education 8, 105, 138–45
Global South 107, 169, 171, 173, 174

Index

higher education 1–3, 5, 11, 14, 26, 36, 38–49, 51, 52, 56–8, 65–77, 82, 95, 97–8, 100, 106–8, 111, 112, 121, 132, 134, 138, 142, 144, 169, 173–5
human rights 142, 143, 153–4, 158, 163, 165, 168, 171, 173–5

inclusive education 28, 36, 153, 154
indigenous knowledge 84, 159, 161
innovation 140, 142
instructional design 80, 143
interdisciplinary research 66, 140

knowledge dissemination 57, 145, 175
knowledge production 44, 46, 47, 102, 106, 108, 111

language models 26
leadership 6, 43, 44, 90, 115, 125, 138, 150, 163, 168–71, 173–6
learning spaces 84, 125
literature review 7, 14, 68–9, 99–100, 133, 140, 151, 157

methodology 13, 14, 19, 45, 69, 99, 107, 109–11, 145, 150
millennium development goals (MDGs) 56
moral philosophy 14, 20, 70, 113
multicultural education 101–2

narrative inquiry 6, 24, 121

online learning 159

participatory action research 87
pedagogy 1, 4, 6, 7, 9, 10, 13, 46, 48, 67, 69–77, 83–7, 89, 98–9, 101, 104–18, 122, 124, 126, 127, 131, 132, 137, 142, 149, 151, 152, 158, 162, 164, 168–72, 175
policy praxis 164, 165, 172
postcolonial theory 134, 153, 154
professional development 4, 6, 136

qualitative research 7

reflexivity 3, 7, 39, 41, 42, 44, 45, 47, 48, 79, 80, 90, 91, 116–18, 127, 135, 136, 157, 164, 165, 168, 170–2
research design 14
research methodologies 19

scholarly publishing 102, 108
social justice 9, 45, 47, 75, 86, 129, 145, 159–61, 164, 166–167, 171, 174–6
social responsibility 9, 142, 161, 163, 171
student supervision 4, 24–37
sustainable development goals (SDGs) 56

teacher education 55
teacher training 55, 145
theoretical framework 128
transformational potential 79–91, 130–1

Ubuntu 11, 32, 33, 45, 46, 52, 87, 88, 111, 150, 161
university governance 47–8, 169

virtual education 52, 159
virtual learning 28, 52, 159

well-being 12, 32, 33, 136, 141, 144, 145, 166, 174–6

youth education 30–1

Milton Keynes UK
Ingram Content Group UK Ltd.
UKHW031330071224
451979UK00005B/64